Python Data Science

Chaolemen Borjigin

Python Data Science

 Springer

Chaolemen Borjigin
Renmin University of China
Beijing, China

ISBN 978-981-19-7701-5   ISBN 978-981-19-7702-2 (eBook)
https://doi.org/10.1007/978-981-19-7702-2

The print edition is not for sale in China (Mainland). Customers from China (Mainland) please order the print book from: Publishing House of Electronics Industry.
ISBN of the Co-Publisher's edition: 978-7-121-41200-4

This Springer imprint is published by the registered company Springer Nature Singapore Pte Ltd.
The registered company address is: 152 Beach Road, #21-01/04 Gateway East, Singapore 189721, Singapore

Preface

"Writing a textbook" holds immeasurable merit as it allows us to save others' time with our own. In today's impetuous and realistic society, I have dedicated myself to writing textbooks, knowing that they may not be counted among my personal achievements. However, I find immense joy in the process of writing this textbook. As the old saying goes, "If you're afraid, don't do it; if you're doing it, don't be afraid!" It has taken me 18 months of dedicated effort simply because I want to utilize my time to save the valuable time of the readers.

"Writing a textbook" requires an exceptional top-down design and stepwise refinement. Through years of teaching experience, I have come to realize the urgent need for an excellent Python textbook for the education of data science and big data professionals. Existing textbooks face several issues: firstly, they teach (or learn) Python as if it were Java or C, failing to capture the unique characteristics of Python. Secondly, the style of "knowledge first, code later" and the dominance of knowledge over practical implementation seem to invert their proper order of importance. Thirdly, there is no clear distinction between Python textbooks used for data science and computer science, leading to confusion. Lastly, some authors treat the readers (or themselves) as programming novices, neglecting the fact that most readers possess prior knowledge of Java or C and are learning Python as a second programming language. They do not require repetitive explanations of low-level concepts or redundant explanations of the same knowledge in different languages. Overcoming these limitations and exploring new teaching and textbook-writing patterns was my original intention in writing this book. Whether or not I have achieved this goal remains to be seen and depends on your careful reading and fair judgment.

"Writing a textbook" necessitates the knowledge and practice of countless resources. Throughout the writing process, I extensively referred to monographs, textbooks, papers, open-source projects, and original data. The reference list contains detailed citations for the sources I have used. However, I may have inadvertently missed a few. If so, I sincerely apologize to the relevant scholars. This book also incorporates data science research and engineering projects completed by my team since 2012, as well as the questions and discussions raised by my students. The course slides, raw data, source codes, and errata list for this textbook can be found at github.com. For further information, please contact me at chaolemen@ruc.edu.cn.

"Writing a textbook" is impossible without the help of others. The leaders and editors at Springer Press and Publishing House of Electronics Industry, especially editor Zhang Haitao, have made significant contributions to the publication of this book. I would like to express my gratitude to the Ministry of Education-IBM Industry-University Cooperation Collaborative Education Project for their funding and support. Special thanks go to Zhang Chen, Xiao Jiwen, Liu Xuan, Tianyi Zhang, Meng Gang, Sun Zhizhong, Wang Rui, Liu Yan, Yang Canjun, Li Haojing, Wang Yuqing, Qu Hanqing, Zhao Qun, Li Xueming, Ji Jiayu, and other students at Renmin University of China for their invaluable proofreading assistance.

"Writing a textbook" is a lengthy process of iterative refinement. This edition may still have some shortcomings, and I genuinely welcome your feedback and suggestions. This textbook is my third book after Data Science and Data Science Theory and Practice. Someone once said to me, "Prof. Chaolemen, you have already achieved so much, why do you still work so tirelessly? You will become the number one in the field of data science." I replied, "No, that is not my purpose. I have undertaken all these endeavors with the belief that I strive to be the one who works the hardest and is most willing to invest time and energy in this field. As for other matters, I am not concerned. My hope is that my dedication and effort will inspire you to do the same!

In this textbook, I have aimed to provide a comprehensive and cohesive guide to Python programming. I have taken great care in addressing the shortcomings I observed in existing textbooks. Rather than treating Python as a mere translation of Java or C, I have emphasized its unique features and characteristics. The content is structured in a logical and progressive manner, ensuring that knowledge and practical implementation are presented in the right order of importance.

Throughout the writing process, I have drawn from a wide range of resources, including monographs, textbooks, research papers, open-source projects, and my team's own data science endeavors. The reference list provides detailed citations for the sources I have used. While I have made every effort to be thorough, I acknowledge that there may be a few omissions. For any oversights, I sincerely apologize to the respective scholars.

I am immensely grateful to the leaders and editors at Springer Press and Publishing House of Electronics Industry, particularly editor Zhang Haitao, for their invaluable contributions to the publication of this book. Additionally, I would like to express my appreciation to the Ministry of Education-IBM Industry-University Cooperation Collaborative Education Project as well as The Quality Textbook Support Project for Graduate Students at Renmin University of China for their support and funding.

I extend my heartfelt thanks to Zhang Chen, Xiao Jiwen, Liu Xuan, Tianyi Zhang, Meng Gang, Sun Zhizhong, Wang Rui, Liu Yan, Yang Canjun, Li Haojing, Wang Yuqing, Qu Hanqing, Zhao Qun, Li Xueming, Ji Jiayu, and other students at Renmin University of China for their diligent proofreading of the book.

"Writing a textbook" is a laborious process that requires dedication, perseverance, and continuous refinement. While I have strived for excellence in this edition, I acknowledge that there may still be areas for improvement. I genuinely welcome your feedback and advice, as it will contribute to the future enhancement of this textbook.

Once again, I want to emphasize that my purpose in writing this textbook is to share my knowledge and contribute to the field of data science. It is my hope that through your engagement with this book, my efforts will become your efforts, and together we can advance the understanding and application of Python programming in the realm of data science.

Thank you for embarking on this data science journey with me.

Chaolemen Borjigin
May 13, 2023

Contents

1. Python and Data Science

Python has become the most popular data science programming language in recent years. This chapter will introduce:

- How to learn Python for data science
- How to setup my Python IDE for data science
- How to write and run my Python code

1.1 How to learn Python for data science

Q&A

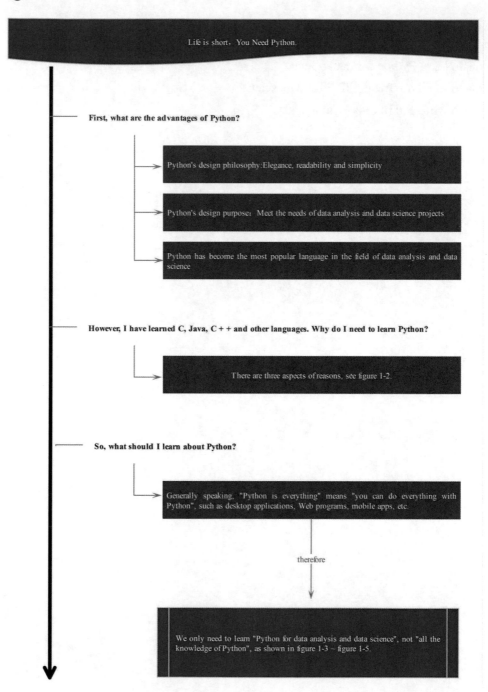

Life is short，You Need Python.

First, what are the advantages of Python?

Python's design philosophy:Elegance, readability and simplicity

Python's design purpose：Meet the needs of data analysis and data science projects

Python has become the most popular language in the field of data analysis and data science

However, I have learned C, Java, C + + and other languages. Why do I need to learn Python?

There are three aspects of reasons, see figure 1-2.

So, what should I learn about Python?

Generally speaking, "Python is everything" means "you can do everything with Python", such as desktop applications, Web programs, mobile apps, etc.

therefore

We only need to learn "Python for data analysis and data science", not "all the knowledge of Python", as shown in figure 1-3 ~ figure 1-5.

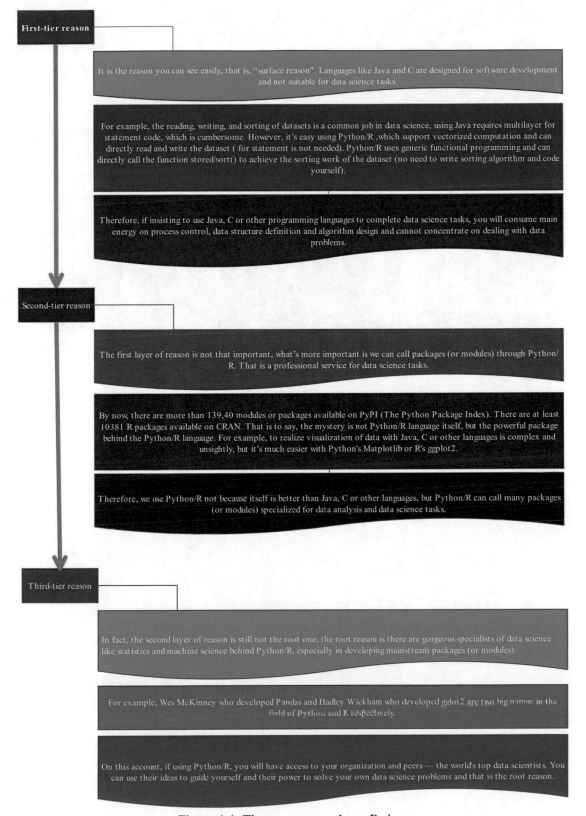

First-tier reason

It is the reason you can see easily, that is, "surface reason". Languages like Java and C are designed for software development and not suitable for data science tasks.

For example, the reading, writing, and sorting of datasets is a common job in data science, using Java requires multilayer for statement code, which is cumbersome. However, it's easy using Python/R ,which support vectorized computation and can directly read and write the dataset (for statement is not needed). Python/R uses generic functional programming and can directly call the function stored/sort() to achieve the sorting work of the dataset (no need to write sorting algorithm and code yourself).

Therefore, if insisting to use Java, C or other programming languages to complete data science tasks, you will consume main energy on process control, data structure definition and algorithm design and cannot concentrate on dealing with data problems.

Second-tier reason

The first layer of reason is not that important, what's more important is we can call packages (or modules) through Python/R. That is a professional service for data science tasks.

By now, there are more than 139,40 modules or packages available on PyPI (The Python Package Index). There are at least 10381 R packages available on CRAN. That is to say, the mystery is not Python/R language itself, but the powerful package behind the Python/R language. For example, to realize visualization of data with Java, C or other languages is complex and unsightly, but it's much easier with Python's Matplotlib or R's ggplot2.

Therefore, we use Python/R not because itself is better than Java, C or other languages, but Python/R can call many packages (or modules) specialized for data analysis and data science tasks.

Third-tier reason

In fact, the second layer of reason is still not the root one, the root reason is there are gorgeous specialists of data science like statistics and machine science behind Python/R, especially in developing mainstream packages (or modules).

For example, Wes McKinney who developed Pandas and Hadley Wickham who developed gglot2 are two big names in the field of Python and R respectively.

On this account, if using Python/R, you will have access to your organization and peers — the world's top data scientists. You can use their ideas to guide yourself and their power to solve your own data science problems and that is the root reason.

Figure 1.1 Three reasons to learn Python

	iPython is an interactive Shell (programming/computing environment) for Python. The IPython Notebook is now known as the Jupyter Notebook, in which you can write Python codes. Jupyter Notebook is widely used in data science/data analysis projects, and it has many features and functions of iPython. See the iPython official website (https://ipython.org) for more details.
Tips	

 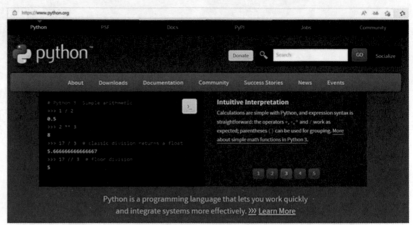

Figure 1.2 Guido van Rossum (the creator of Python Programming language) and the official website of Python

1.2 How to setup my Python IDE for Data Science

Q&A

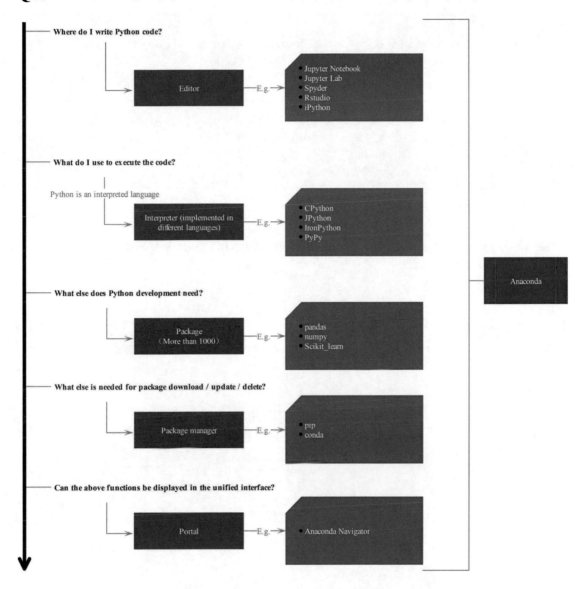

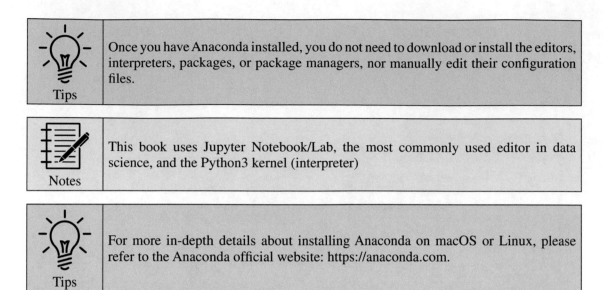	
Tips	Once you have Anaconda installed, you do not need to download or install the editors, interpreters, packages, or package managers, nor manually edit their configuration files.
Notes	This book uses Jupyter Notebook/Lab, the most commonly used editor in data science, and the Python3 kernel (interpreter)
Tips	For more in-depth details about installing Anaconda on macOS or Linux, please refer to the Anaconda official website: https://anaconda.com.

The Anaconda official website and introduction are shown in Figure 1.3. The menu items and their usage are shown in Figure 1.4.

Figure 1.3 The Anaconda official website

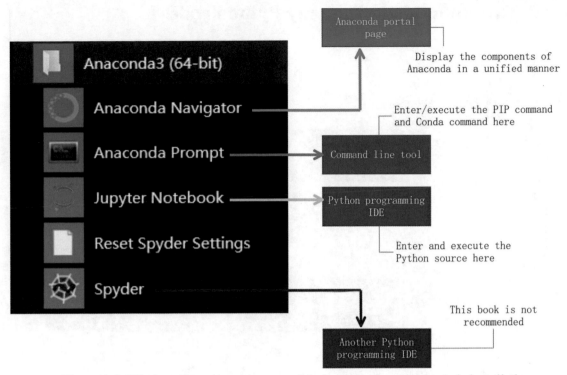

Figure 1.4 Windows Start menu items and their usage after Anaconda is installed

Figure 1.5 shows how to use the Jupter Notebook/Lab editor

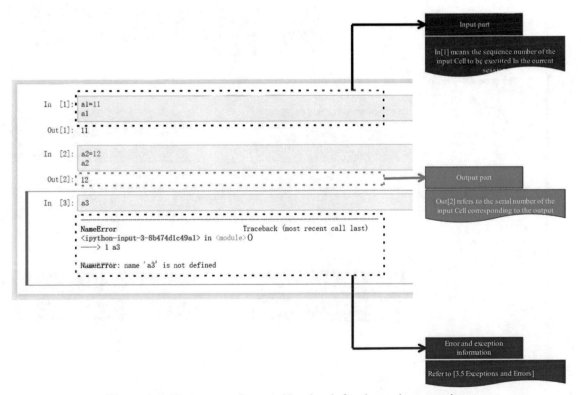

Figure 1.5 How to use Jupyter Notebook for data science projects

1.3 How to write and run my Python codes

Q&A

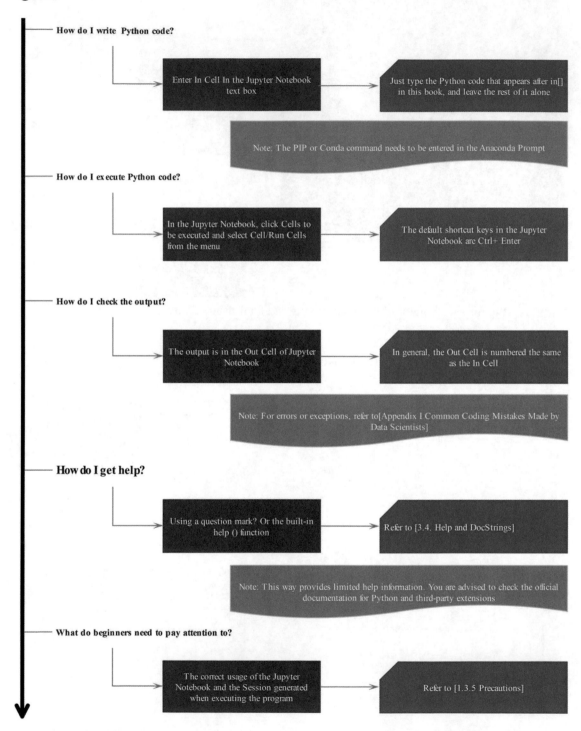

How do I write Python code?

Enter In Cell In the Jupyter Notebook text box

Just type the Python code that appears after in[] in this book, and leave the rest of it alone

Note: The PIP or Conda command needs to be entered in the Anaconda Prompt

How do I execute Python code?

In the Jupyter Notebook, click Cells to be executed and select Cell/Run Cells from the menu

The default shortcut keys in the Jupyter Notebook are Ctrl+ Enter

How do I check the output?

The output is in the Out Cell of Jupyter Notebook

In general, the Out Cell is numbered the same as the In Cell

Note: For errors or exceptions, refer to[Appendix I Common Coding Mistakes Made by Data Scientists]

How do I get help?

Using a question mark? Or the built-in help () function

Refer to [3.4. Help and DocStrings]

Note: This way provides limited help information. You are advised to check the official documentation for Python and third-party extensions

What do beginners need to pay attention to?

The correct usage of the Jupyter Notebook and the Session generated when executing the program

Refer to [1.3.5 Precautions]

1.3.1 Inputs

Tips

Jupyter Notebooks documents consist of "cells": input cells and output cells. We only need to type the codes in the input cell since the output cell is automatically evaluated by Jupyter Notebook. For instance, the Output[1] shows the output of codes in input[1] as the following cell.

In[1]
```
x1=11
x1
```

Out[1]　11

Notes

When writing Python codes, you need to pay attention to their case sensitivity as well as code indentation (the spaces at the beginning of a code line). For more information, please refer to [2.4 Statements].

Tricks

The default shortcut for running a "Cell" in Jupyter Notebook is Ctrl+Enter. For more shortcuts, you can refer to the Help/Keyboard Shortcuts menu item in the "Menu Bar" of Jupyter Notebook.

In[2]
```
#define variable x2
x2=12
x2
```

Out[2]　12

Tips

In an input "Cell" it is not necessary to start a code line with "#" since it denotes a Python comment statement. A comment in Python starts with the hash character(#), and extends to the end of the physical line. Please refer to [2.6 Comments] for more details.

In[3]
```
X3=13
X3
```

Out[3]　13

Tips

The number of In[] is the sequential order in which the input cell was executed in the current session in the Jupyter Notebook Kernel.

Notes

When the same "Cell" is executed multiple times, the number in its In[] will be updated accordingly. This means that the In[] number will reflect the order of execution, indicating the current iteration of the cell. For more details, refer to [1.3.5 Tips for Python programming].

Tricks

To restart or stop the "current session (Session)", we can restart the kernel of Jupyter notebook by clicking Kernel > Restart (or stop) from the Jupyter menu.

In[4]
```
x4=14
```

In[5]
```
x4=x4+1
x4
```
Out[5]   15

Tips

Python is an interpreted programming language, and we can run the cell as many times as we want. As a result, the current values of a variable may be updated simultaneously. For instance, x4=x4+1" is a self-assignment statement, and the value of x4 is incremented each time the cell is executed.

Notes

Checking the current value of a variable is one of good habits for successful programmers of data science projects.

In[6]
```
x5=16
x5
```
Out[6]   16

Notes

In Jupyter Notebook, Python code is executed within "Cell" as the unit, the execution order is different from the C/Java language, and execute items one by one in a non-predetermined order (such as from top to bottom). Therefore, the code cells are executed individually and can be run in a non-sequential order.

Tips

There is no main() function in Python, the execution order of "Cell" is determined by the user and is independent of their location.

1.3.2 Outputs

Tips

The output cell is displayed to the right of the output variable "Out[]:" in Jupyter Notebook "Cell" on the side.

In[7]
```
y1=21
y1
```
Out[7]   21

Notes

The Output in Jupyter Notebook is shown in a "Cell", an "Output Cell" is immediately below the corresponding "Input Cell". This allows for a clear and organized display of the code execution and its corresponding output.

In[8]
```
y2=22
y2
```

Out[8]   22

Tips

The number displayed in the Out[] is the corresponding In[] number of the output result.

In[9]
```
y3=23
print(y3)
```

Out[9]   23

Notes

In Jupyter Notebook, instead of using the print() function, you can directly write the variable name to see the output result. However, in this case, the output result does not have an Out[] number associated with it.

Tips

Both y2 and print(y3) in In[8] and In[9] can produce the same result. Is there any difference between the two?

● The former is not the syntax of Python, but the function provided by Jupyter Notebook to facilitate our programming. In Python, the standard output still needs to use the print() function;

● The former is the syntax of Jupyter Notebook, which output result into the Out queue variable of Jupyter Notebook, and has an Out number put the latter will not be put into Jupyter Notebook In the Out queue variable of, and there is no Out number;

● (3)The former is the display result after "optimization" by Jupyter Notebook, and the output effect is often different from the function of print().

1.3.3 Errors and warnings

In[10]
```
z1=31
z
```

Out[10]   --
NameError   Traceback (most recent call last)
<ipython-input-10-8d66e1a13261> in <module>()
      1 z1=31
----> 2 z
NameError: name 'z' is not defined

The error message indicates that "z is an undefined object" because the name of the defined variable is not "z". but "z1".

Notes

For further details about Python errors or exceptions, please refer to [3.5 Exceptions and Errors].

Tips

1.3.4 External data files

Prior to reading data source files such as Excel, CSV, or JSON, it is necessary to place them in the current working D directory.

Tips

os.getcwd():
  Returns the current working directory of the session.

Tricks

In[11]
```
import os
print(os.getcwd())
```

Out[11]   C:\Users\soloman\clm

For further details about current working directory, please refer to [3.8 Current working directory].

Tips

In[12]
```
from pandas import read_csv
data = read_csv('bc_data.csv')
data.head(2)
```

Out[12]

	id	diagnosis	radius_mean	texture_mean	perimeter_mean
0	842302	M	17.99	10.38	122.8
1	842517	M	20.57	17.77	132.9

2 rows × 32 columns

The data file, named "bc_data.csv", needs to be placed in your current working directory in advance. If the file is not found in the current working directory, it will raise a "FileNotFoundError" error message.

Notes

Tips

The code in the input cell loads the data file "bc_data.csv" from the local disk into memory using the read_csv() method from the Pandas library. This method is specifically designed to read data from CSV files.

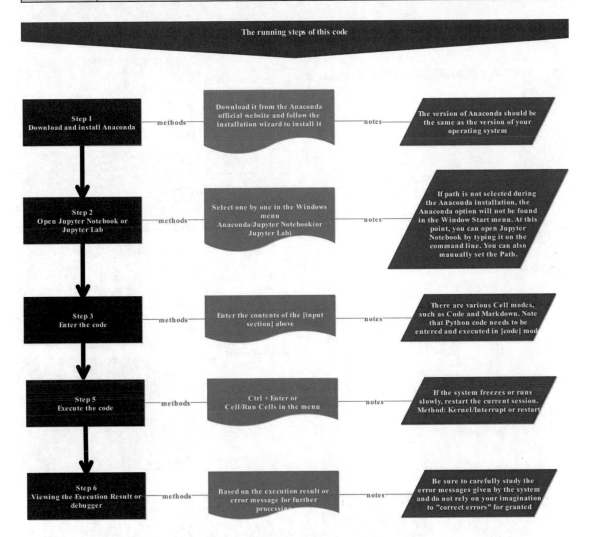

Figure 1.6 The running steps of this code

1.3.5 Tips for Python programming

Tips

Tips for Python programming are shown in Figure 1.7.

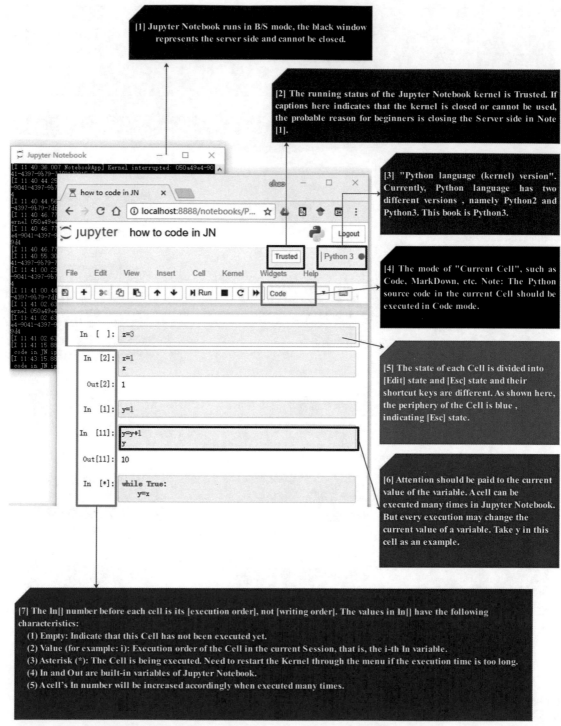

[1] Jupyter Notebook runs in B/S mode, the black window represents the server side and cannot be closed.

[2] The running status of the Jupyter Notebook kernel is Trusted. If captions here indicates that the kernel is closed or cannot be used, the probable reason for beginners is closing the Server side in Note [1].

[3] "Python language (kernel) version". Currently, Python language has two different versions , namely Python2 and Python3. This book is Python3.

[4] The mode of "Current Cell", such as Code, MarkDown, etc. Note: The Python source code in the current Cell should be executed in Code mode.

[5] The state of each Cell is divided into [Edit] state and [Esc] state and their shortcut keys are different. As shown here, the periphery of the Cell is blue , indicating [Esc] state.

[6] Attention should be paid to the current value of the variable. A cell can be executed many times in Jupyter Notebook. But every execution may change the current value of a variable. Take y in this cell as an example.

[7] The In[] number before each cell is its [execution order], not [writing order]. The values in In[] have the following characteristics:
   (1) Empty: Indicate that this Cell has not been executed yet.
   (2) Value (for example: i): Execution order of the Cell in the current Session, that is, the i-th In variable.
   (3) Asterisk (*): The Cell is being executed. Need to restart the Kernel through the menu if the execution time is too long.
   (4) In and Out are built-in variables of Jupyter Notebook.
   (5) A cell's In number will be increased accordingly when executed many times.

Figure 1.7 Seven considerations in Python programming

Tips

Figure 1.8 shows the Edit and Esc state of a cell in Jupyter Notebook.

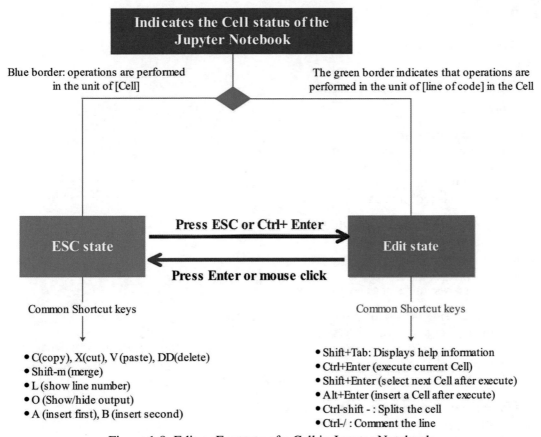

Figure 1.8 Edit or Esc state of a Cell in Jupyter Notebook

 Tricks

Many valuable learning and reference resources are available in the "Help" menu of Jupyter Notebook/Lab. Python beginners are advised to take full advantage of these essential resources, as illustrated in Figure 1.9.

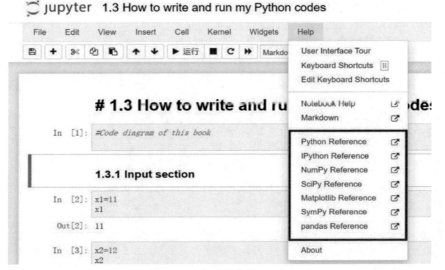

Figure 1.9 "Help" menu

Exercises

[1]   Python is created by ( ).
A. Wes McKinney
B. Guido van Rossum
C. James Gray
D. Hadley Wickham

[2]   Which of the following is true of Python?
A. Python is a programming language that uses compiling.
B. Python is a language that represents simplicity.
C. Python is a scripting language.
D. Python is an advanced language.

[3]   Which of the following is false of Python?
A. Python's syntax is concise.
B. Python is a platform dependent language.
C. Chinese is supported in Python.
D. Python has rich resources of classes and libraries.

[4]   Which of the following is false of programming languages?
A. A programming language is a concrete implementation of programming.
B. Natural languages are simpler, more rigorous and more precise than programming languages.
C. Programming languages are primarily used for interaction between humans and computers.
D. A programming language is an artificial language for interaction.

[5]   What is false about the basic programming strategies?
A. Input is the beginning of a program.
B. Output is the way in which the program displays the results of operations.
C. Processing is the process in which the program calculates the input data and produces the output results.
D. Output is the soul of a program.

[6]   Python is suitable for ()
A. hardware development
B. mobile development
C. data analysis
D. game development

[7]   Which of the following is the Python interpreter?
A. CPython
B. JPython
C. ironpython
D. All of the above

[8]   Which of the following is false of the indentation in Python?
A. Indentation is a part of syntax.
B. Indentation does not affect the running of programs.
C. Indentation is the only way to represent the containing and hierarchical relationship between codes.
D. Indentation is normally represented by 4 spaces or 1 tab.

[9]   Which of the following is false of the Python development environment configuration?
A. The installation of Python may vary depending on the operating system.
B. Python can be integrated into integrated development environment such as Eclipse, PyCharm.
C. Jupyter Notebook editor is widely used in data science and data analysis projects.
D. After installing Anaconda, we need to download the editors and packages required for Python programming one by one.

[10] Which of the following is false of Jupyter Notebook?
    A. *In[1]* indicates that the serial number of the input cell executed in the current session is 1.
    B. *Out[2]* indicates that the serial number of the output cell corresponding to the output is 2.
    C. The line starting with * represents the Python annotation language, which can be entered without input.
    D. The output result in Jupyter notebook is displayed immediately below the corresponding input cell.

2. Basic Python Programming for Data Science

Python is a general-purpose language so that it can be used for a wide range of applications, such as data science, computer science, software engineering, mathematics, life science, linguistics, and journalism. However, learning Python programming for data science requires its unique specific knowledge tailored to its use in that field. This chapter will introduce the basics of python syntax for data science, including:

- Data types (Lists, Tuples, Strings, Sequences, Sets, Dictionaries)
- Variables
- Operators and expressions
- Statements (assignments, comments, if statements, for statements, and while statements)
- Functions (built-in functions, module functions, user-defined functions, and lambda functions)

2.1 Data Types

Q&A

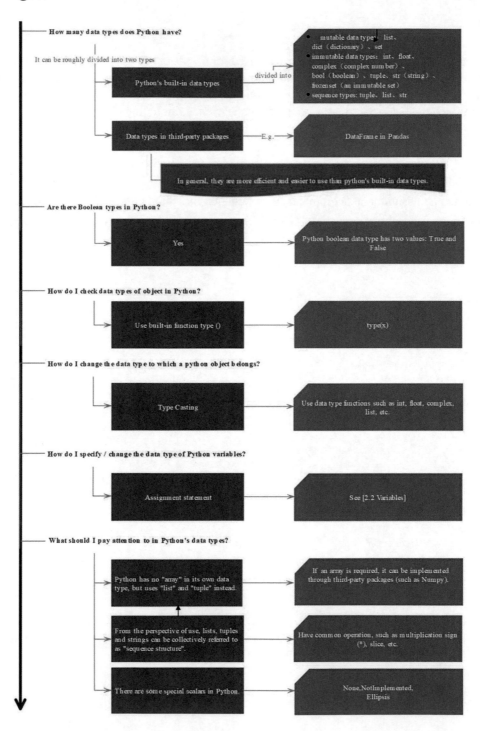

How many data types does Python have?

It can be roughly divided into two types

Python's built-in data types

divided into

- mutable data types: list、 dict（dictionary）、set
- immutable data types: int、float、 complex（complex number）、 bool（boolean）、tuple、str（string）、 frozenset（an immutable set）
- sequence types: tuple、list、str

Data types in third-party packages

E.g.

DataFrame in Pandas

In general, they are more efficient and easier to use than python's built-in data types.

Are there Boolean types in Python?

Yes

Python boolean data type has two values: True and False

How do I check data types of object in Python?

Use built-in function type ()

type(x)

How do I change the data type to which a python object belongs?

Type Casting

Use data type functions such as int, float, complex, list, etc.

How do I specify / change the data type of Python variables?

Assignment statement

See [2.2 Variables]

What should I pay attention to in Python's data types?

Python has no "array" in its own data type, but uses "list" and "tuple" instead.

If an array is required, it can be implemented through third-party packages (such as Numpy).

From the perspective of use, lists, tuples and strings can be collectively referred to as "sequence structure".

Have common operation, such as multiplication sign (*), slice, etc.

There are some special scalars in Python.

None, NotImplemented, Ellipsis

2.1.1 Checking data types

Tricks

The built-in function type():
  returns the type of an object.

In[1]
```
# int
type(1)
```
Out[1] int

Notes

The term "built-in functions" refers to the functions that are inherently available in the Python interpreter and can be used without the need for any additional imports. These functions are part of the core Python language and are commonly used in various programming tasks. The most common used functions, such as type(), ininstance(), dir(), print(), int(), float(), string(). list(), tuple(), and set(), are built-in functions.

In[2]
```
# float
type(1.2)
```
Out[2] float

In[3]
```
# bool
type(True)
```
Out[3] bool

Tips

Python Boolean data type has two values: True and False

In[4]
```
# str (string)
type("DataScience")
```
Out[4] str

Tips

In Python, there is no difference between single and double quoted string. For further details, please refer to [2.13 Strings]

In[5]
```
# list
type([1,2,3,4,5,6,7,8,9])
```
Out[5] list

Tips

In Python, to create a list, the elements are placed inside square brackets ([]), separated by commas. For further details, please refer to [2.10 Lists]

Notes

In contrast to C and Java, Python does not have a built-in data type called "array". Instead, Python uses "list" and "tuple" as its primary data structures for storing collections of elements.

In[6]
```
# tuple
type((1,2,3,4,5,6,7,8,9))
```

Out[6] tuple

Tips

In Python, A tuple is created by placing all the items (elements) inside parentheses (), separated by commas. For further details, please refer to [2.12 Tuples].

In[7]
```
# set
type({1,2,3,4,5,6,7,8,9})
```

Out[7] set

Tips

In Python, a set or a dictionary can be created by placing all the items (elements) inside braces {}, including key-value pairs separated by commas (,). A colon (:) separates each key from its value. For further details, please refer to [2.14 Sets].

In[8]
```
# dict (dictionary)
type({"a":0, "b":1, "c":2})
```

Out[8] dict

Tips

Dictionary holds key-value pair. The nexus between a dictionary and a set: a dictionary is a set containing the keys. For further details, please refer to [2.15 Dictionaries].

2.1.2 Testing data types

Tricks

The built-in function isinstance(object, classinfo)

● If the object argument is an instance of the classinfo argument, or of a (direct, indirect, or virtual) subclass thereof, the function always returns True.

● If object is not an object of the given type, the function always returns False.

● If classinfo is a tuple of type objects (or recursively, other such tuples) or a Union Type of multiple types, return True if object is an instance of any of the types

In[9]
```
# to test whether x is int
x = 10
isinstance(x, int)
```

Out[9] True

In[10]
```
# to test whether y is int
y = 10.0
isinstance(y, int)
```

Out[10] False

In[11]
```
# to test whether True is int
isinstance(True, int)
```

Out[11] True

Notes

Here, the output[11] is True in that the Boolean class is implemented as a subclass of the integer class in Python.

Tips

The difference between type() and isinstances() is as follows:

- type() returns the type of the object we put in as an argument
- isinstance() returns a boolean value(True or False) based on whether the object is of given type

2.1.3 Converting data types

Notes

In explicit type conversion, also known as type casting, we can convert the data type of an object to required data type by calling the predefined functions like int(), float(), str().

In[12] `int(1.6)`

Out[12] 1

Tips

The built-in function int() :
  Convert a number or string to an integer object.

In[13]
```
# Convert an int object to a float object
float(1)
```

Out[13] 1.0

Notes

In general, the name of the type casting function matches the name of the target data type.

In[14]
```
# Convert a int object to a bool object

bool(0)
```

Out[14] False

In[15]
```
# Convert a list object to a tuple object

tuple([1,2,1,1,3])
```

Out[15]   (1, 2, 1, 1, 3)

In[16]
```
# Convert a tuple object to a list object

list((1,2,3,4))
```

Out[16]   [1, 2, 3, 4]

Tips

The difference between a list and a tuple: the former is "a mutable object", while the latter is "an immutable object". In Python, mutable objects are those whose value can be changed after creation, while immutable O objects are those whose value cannot be modified once they are created. For further details, please refer to [2.10 Lists] as well as [2.11 Tuples].

2.1.4 Built-in data types

Tips

Python provides not only basic data types such as int, float, string, list, tuple and set, but also some built-in constants including None, Ellipsis, and NotImplemented.

In[17]
```
# None

x = None
print(x)
```

Out[17]   None

Notes

Notice that the output of None always use the *print()* function, otherwise nothing can be seen in Jupyter Notebook.

Tricks

The None keyword is used to represent a null value or indicate the absence of a value. Consequently, None is distinct from 0, False, or an empty string.

In[18]
```
# NotImplemented

print(NotImplemented)
```

Out[18]   NotImplemented

Tips

In Python, NotImplemented is a special value which should be returned by the binary special methods (e.g. __eq__(), __lt__(), __add__(), __rsub__(), etc.) to indicate that the operation is not implemented with respect to the other type.

In[19]
```
# Ellipsis

print(Ellipsis)
```
Out[19] Ellipsis

Notes

In Python, the Ellipsis keyword, represented by "..." (three dots), is equivalent to the ellipsis literal. It is a special value commonly used in combination with extended slicing syntax, particularly for user-defined container data types.

In[20]
```
# the plural(complex) objects

x = 2+3j
print('x = ', x)
```
Out[20] x = (2+3j)

Tips

The statement 3+4j is equivalent to the statement complex(3,4).

In[21]
```
y=complex(3,4)
print('y = ', y)
```
Out[21] y = (3+4j)

In[22]
```
#to print the plural(complex) objects

print('x+y = ', x+y)
```
Out[22] x+y = (5+7j)

Tricks

To access the documentation for the *print()* function and learn about its arguments and usage in Python, you can use either "print?" or "?print" in most interactive Python environments, such as Jupyter Notebook or IPython.

In[28]
```
# scientific notation
9.8e2
```
Out[28] 980.0

Notes

In this context, the symbol "*e*" represents 10 in scientific notation, not the mathematical constant "*e*" with a value of approximately 2.71828.

2.1.5 Sequences

Notes

In Python, a sequence refers to a collection of items that are ordered by their positions. It is a general term that does not specifically refer to an independent data type but rather encompasses various ordered containers.

In[29]
```python
mySeq1 = "Data Science"
mySeq2 = [1,2,3,4,5]
mySeq3 = (11,12,13,14,15)
```

Tips

There are three basic sequence types: strings, lists, and tuples. The *set* type is not a sequence, because its elements have no order.

In[30]
```python
# to slice a sequence
mySeq1[1:3], mySeq2[1:3], mySeq3[1:3]
```
Out[30]   ('at', [2, 3], (12, 13))

Tips

Sequences have some common properties(variables) and methods(functions), including slicing and extending.

In[31]
```python
# to extend a sequence by multiplication operator

mySeq1*3
```
Out[31]   'Data ScienceData ScienceData Science'

Tips

For further details about Sequences, please refer to [2.13 Sequences].

2.2 Variables

Q&A

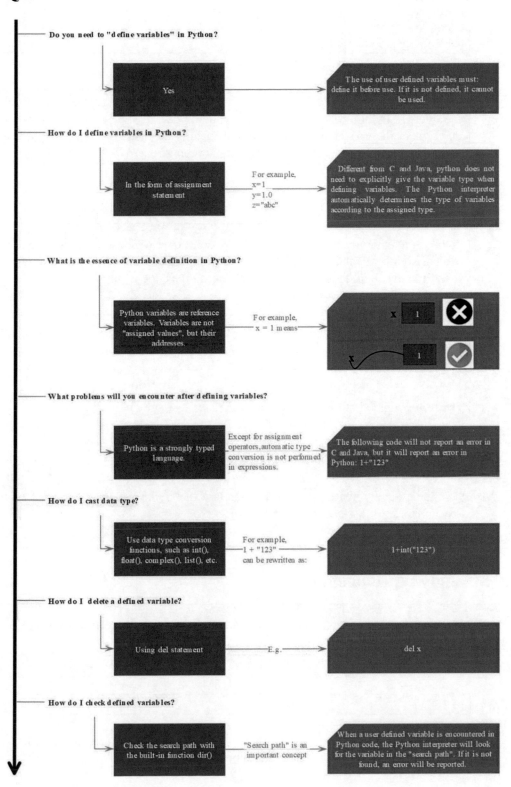

Do you need to "define variables" in Python?

Yes

The use of user defined variables must: define it before use. If it is not defined, it cannot be used.

How do I define variables in Python?

In the form of assignment statement

For example,
x=1
y=1.0
z="abc"

Different from C and Java, python does not need to explicitly give the variable type when defining variables. The Python interpreter automatically determines the type of variables according to the assigned type.

What is the essence of variable definition in Python?

Python variables are reference variables. Variables are not "assigned values", but their addresses.

For example,
x = 1 means

x   1   ✗

x   1   ✓

What problems will you encounter after defining variables?

Python is a strongly typed language.

Except for assignment operators, automatic type conversion is not performed in expressions.

The following code will not report an error in C and Java, but it will report an error in Python: 1+"123"

How do I cast data type?

Use data type conversion functions, such as int(), float(), complex(), list(), etc.

For example,
1 + "123"
can be rewritten as:

1+int("123")

How do I delete a defined variable?

Using del statement

E.g.

del x

How do I check defined variables?

Check the search path with the built-in function dir()

"Search path" is an important concept

When a user defined variable is encountered in Python code, the Python interpreter will look for the variable in the "search path". If it is not found, an error will be reported.

2.2.1 Defining variables

In[1]
```
testBool = True
testlnt = 20
testFloat = 10.6
testStr = "MyStr"
testBool, testlnt, testFloat, testStr
```

Out[1]   (True, 20, 10.6, 'MyStr')

 Notes | Unlike languages such as C or Java, Python uses assignment statements to define variables. In Python, you do not need to explicitly declare the data type of a variable. The type of the variable is determined dynamically based on the value assigned to it at runtime. This feature is known as "dynamic typing."

2.2.2 Dynamically typed language

 Notes | Python is a dynamically typed language. We don't have to declare the type of variable while assigning a value to a variable in Python. In other words, the python interpretor doesn't know about the type of the variable until the code is run.

In[2]
```
x = 10
x = "testMe"
```

 Notes | The following code would raise an error in C or Java, but not in Python.

 Tips | Variables in Python do not need to declare their type in advance, and the same variable can be assigned to different object types.

2.2.3 Strongly typed language

 Notes | Python is considered a strongly typed language because the interpreter keeps track of variable types. Strong typing ensures that the type of a value does not change unexpectedly.

In[3]   `"3" + 2`

Out[3]   --
TypeError   Traceback (most recent call last)
<ipython-input-3-e8240368dace> in <module>
----> 1 "3"+2

TypeError: can only concatenate str (not "int") to str

Notes In Python, automatic data type conversion during runtime is not performed by default, except for conversions between int, float, bool, and complex types.

In[4]	3+True # Here, no error was raised.

Out[4] 4

In[5]	3+3.3 # Here, no error was raised.

Out[5] 6.3

In[6]	3+(1+3j) # Here, no error was raised.

Out[6] (4+3j)

2.2.4 Variable naming rules

Notes In Python, variables are simply names that refer to objects. In other words, a Python variable is a symbolic name that is a reference or pointer to an object.

In[7]	i = 20 i = "myStr" i = 30.1 i

Out[7] 30.1

Tips The variable name represents (or is essentially) "a reference to a value", rather than "the value of the variable".

2.2.5 Case-sensitivity

In[8]	i = 20 I

```
Out[8]  ---------------------------------------------------------------------------
        NameError                                Traceback (most recent call last)
        <ipython-input-8-447541a63ca9> in <module>
                1 i=20
        ----> 2 I

        NameError: name 'I' is not defined
```

Tips Defined variables are named lowercase "i", while output variables are named uppercase "I".

Tricks

In Python, a NameError is raised when the identifier being accessed is neither defined in advance nor imported from other modules/packages. Hence, we can correct NameErrors by:

- declaring it in advance or quoting it to be a string constant
- importing the modules/packages that declared it

2.2.6 Variable naming rules

Notes

In Python, variable naming rules are:

- A variable name must start with a letter or the underscore character.
- A variable name cannot start with a number.
- A variable name can only contain alpha-numeric characters and underscores (A-z, 0-9, and _)
- Variable names are case-sensitive (age, Age and AGE are three different variables)

In[10]
```
myvariable_2 = 0
```

In[11]
```
2_ myvariable = 0
```
Out[11]
```
  File "<ipython-input-10-6006d03e9e23>", line 1
    2_myvariable=0
     ^
SyntaxError: invalid decimal literal
```

Tips

The reason for the error is that the variable name starts with a number.

In[12]
```
print = 0 # no error
x = 0
print(x) #error
```
Out[12]
```
---------------------------------------------------------------------------
TypeError                                 Traceback (most recent call last)
<ipython-input-11-c2a031c18500> in <module>
      1 print=0
      2 x=0
----> 3 print(x)

TypeError: 'int' object is not callable
```

Notes | If a keyword is used as a variable name, it will cause the meaning of the keyword to change, and the original function of the keyword will be invalidated.

Workaround: Restart the session. To do this: Select Kernel→Restart in the menu bar of Jupyter Notebook.

Tips | Here, the meaning of print is redefined as a reference to the value 0. Hence, within the scope of the current session of Jupyter Notebook Kernel, the variable "print" refers to 0, not to the original print(output) function.

2.2.7 Checking IPython variables

Notes | IPython is an enhanced interactive Python shell. The IPython Notebook is now known as the Jupyter Notebook. It is an interactive computational environment, in which you can combine code execution, rich text, mathematics, plots and rich media. For more details on the Jupyter Notebook.

Notes | IPython offers numbered prompts (In/Out) with input and output caching, also referred to as 'input history'. All input is saved and can be retrieved as variables.

In[13] | `x = 12+13`

Out[13] x

In[14] | `# to retrieve the In[] variables`
`In[13]`

Out[14] 'x = 12+13\nx'

Notes | Here, the In[] and Out[] are not Python variables, but a special variable offered by IPython for editing code conveniently and tracing execution process.

In[15] | `# to retrieve the Out[] variables`
`Out[13]`

Out[15] 25

In[16] | `# to retrieve the temporary variables:_`
`-`
`# The symbol "_" represents "the most recent Out variable".`

Out[16] 25

2.2.8 Checking Python keywords

Notes

The Python built-in module keyword enables us to test for Python keywords.

● keyword.kwlist: Return a sequence containing all the keywords defined for the interpreter.

● keyword.iskeyword(s): Return True if s is a Python keyword.

In[17]
```
import keyword
print(keyword.kwlist)
```

Out[17] ['False', 'None', 'True', 'and', 'as', 'assert', 'async', 'await', 'break', 'class', 'continue', 'def', 'del', 'elif', 'else', 'except', 'finally', 'for', 'from', 'global', 'if', 'import', 'in', 'is', 'lambda', 'nonlocal', 'not', 'or', 'pass', 'raise', 'return', 'try', 'while', 'with', 'yield']

2.2.9 Checking all defined variables

Notes

The built-in function dir([object]):

● Without arguments, return the list of names in the current local scope.

● With an argument, return a list of valid attributes for that object.

In[18]
```
print(dir())
```
Out[18] ['In', 'Out', '_', '__', '___', '__builtin__', '__builtins__', '__doc__', '__loader__', '__name__', '__package__', '__spec__', '_dh', '_i', '_i1', '_i2', '_i3', '_ih', '_ii', '_iii', '_oh', 'exit', 'get_ipython', 'keyword', 'quit', 'x']

2.2.10 Deleting variables

In[19]
```
i = 20
print(i)
del i
```

Notes

Here you need to restart Jupyter Notebook Kernel, otherwise an error will be raised, because "print=0" in In[12], that is, print is redefined as a variable name.

In earlier versions of Python, del was a statement, not a function.
Hence, an error will be raised when written as del(i).

Tricks

To restart Kernel: Select Kernel→Restart in the menu of Jupyter Notebook/Lab.

In[20]
```
i
```
Out[20] ---

NameError   Traceback (most recent call last)
<ipython-input-2-397d543883c5> in <module>
----> 1 i
NameError: name 'i' is not defined

Tips

The naming convention recommended by Guido, the father of Python, includes the following points.

1. Module or package names use lowercase letters and underscore-separated words, e.g. regex_syntax, py_compile, winreg

2. Class or exception names should capitalize the first letter of each word, e.g. BaseServer, ForkingMixIn, KeyboardInterrupt

3. Global constants or class constants use uppercase letters and underscore-separated words, e.g.
MAX_LOAD

4. The names of other objects, including method names, function names, and common variable names, use lowercase letters with underscore-separated words, e.g. my_thread

5. If the above objects are private types, name them start with an underscore, e.g. __init__, _new__

Notes

Considering the specificity of data analysis/data science projects, the naming convention of this book has fine-tuned for the naming convention recommended by Guido.

Notes

To write better code in Python, you can follow the guidelines provided by PEP (Python Enhancement Proposal). PEP8 is specifically focused on the *Python Code Writing Specification*, which serves as a style guide for Python code. PEP20, known as *"The Zen of Python,"* also provides valuable principles to guide Python programmers.

To access the official PEP documents and read more about them, you can visit the official website at https://www.python.org/dev/peps/. It is a valuable resource for understanding the recommended practices and conventions in Python programming.

In addition to PEP, the Google Style Guide is another commonly used coding specification, particularly in data science practices. It provides guidelines and best practices for writing code in a consistent and readable manner.

By following these coding specifications, you can enhance the quality, readability, and maintainability of your Python code.

2.3 Operators and Expressions

Q&A

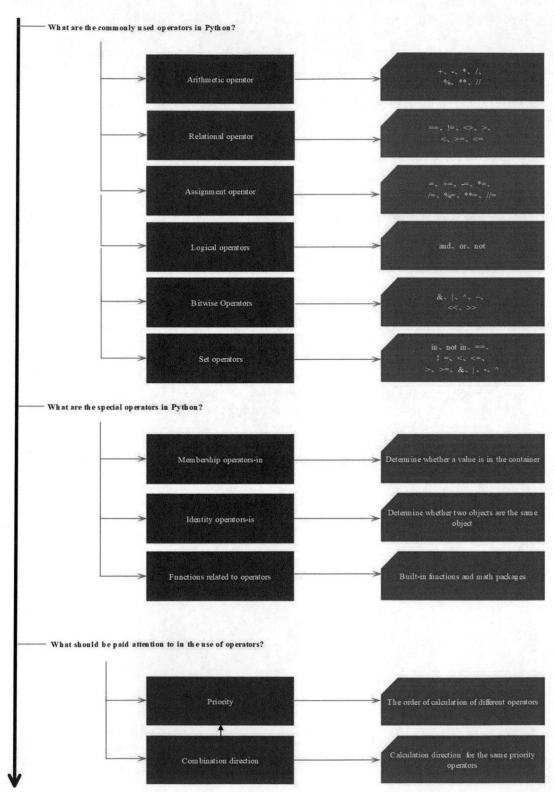

Table 3-1 Arithmetic operators (x=2, y=5)

Operators	Meanings	Instances	Results
+	Addition	x + y	7
-	Subtraction	x - y	-3
*	Multiplication	x * y	10
/	Division	y / x	2.5
%	Remainder	y % x	1
//	Floor division	y//2	2
**	Exponentiation	x**y	32

Table 3-2 Relational operators (x=2, y=5)

Operators	Meanings	Instances	Results
==	equal to	x == y	False
!=	not equal to	x != y	True
>	greater than	x > y	False
<	less than	x < y	True
>=	greater than or equal to	x >= y	False
<=	less than or equal to	x <= y	True

Table 3-3 Assignment operators

Operators	Instances	Equivalence
=	y=x	y=x
+=	y+=x	y=y+x
-=	y-=x	y=y-x
*=	y*=x	y=y*x
/=	y/=x	y=y/x
%=	y%=x	y=y%x
**=	y**=x	y=y**x
//=	y//=x	y=y//x

Table 3-4 Logical operators (x=2, y=5)

Operators	Meanings	Instances	Results
and	Logical AND	x and y	5
or	Logical OR	x or y	2
not	Logical NOT	not (x and y)	False

Table 3-5 Bitwise operators(x=2, y=5; Note: You can use the built-in function bin() to get the corresponding binary.)

Operators	Meanings	Instances	Results
&	Bitwise AND	x & y	0
I	Bitwise OR	x I y	7
^	Bitwise XOR	x ^ y	7
~	Bitwise NOT	~x	-3
<<	Bitwise left shift	x << y	64
>>	Bitwise right shift	x >> y	0

Table 3-6 Set operations

Mathematical symbols	Python operators	Description
$\in \not\subset$	in	be a member of …
$\notin$	not in	not be a member of …
$=$	==	equal to
$\neq$	!=	not equal to
$\subset$	<	be a (strict) subset of …
$\subseteq$	<=	be a subset of …
$\supset$	>	be a (strict) superset of …
$\supseteq$	>=	be a superset of …
$\cap$	&	intersection
$\cup$	I	union
$-\text{or}\backslash$	-	difference or relative complement
$\triangle$	^	symmetric difference

The operator precedence in Python is shown in Figure 3.1.

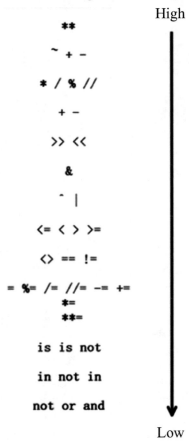

Figure 3.1 Precedence of Python operators

2.3.1 Common used operators

In[1]
```
# division(Arithmetic Operators)
x = 2
y = 5
y / x
```

Out[1] 2.5

Tips

According to PEP8, the Python style guide, it is recommended to use a single whitespace on each side of assignment operators, comparisons, and boolean operators. This improves readability and helps make the code more consistent.

In[2]
```
# modules (Arithmetic Operators)
x = 2
y = 5
y % x
```

Out[2] 1

In[3]
```
# floor division (Arithmetic Operators)

x = 2
y = 5
y // x
```
Out[3] 2

In[4]
```
# Exponentiation

x = 2
y = 5
x ** y
```
Out[4] 32

In[5]
```
# Equal (Comparison Operators)

x = 2
y = 5
x == y
```
Out[5] False

In[6]
```
# Not equal (Comparison Operators)

x = 2
y = 5
x != y
```
Out[6] True

Notes

Types	Operators	Descriptions
identity operators	is is not	Check if the variables on either side of the operator point to the same object
membership operator	in not in	Check if a value exists in a sequence or not.

In[7]
```
#is (identity operators)

x = 2
y = 5
x is y
```
Out[7] False

In[8]
```
# s not (identity operators)

x=2
y=5
x is not y
```
Out[8] True

In[9]
```
#in (membership operators)

x in [1,2,3,4]
```
Out[9] True

In[10]
```
# not in (membership operators)
y in [1,2,3,4]
```
Out[10] False

In[11]
```
x not in [1,2,3,4]
```
Out[11] False

In[12]
```
#//=(augmented assignment operators)
x=2
y=5
y//=x
print(x,y)
```
Out[12] 2.2

> 💡 **Tips**
> An augmented assignment is generally used to replace a statement where an operator takes a variable as one of its arguments and then assigns the result back to the same variable. Hence, y//=x is equivalent to y = y // x.

In[13]
```
x=2
y=5
y//=x+8
print(y)
```
Out[13] 0

> 📝 **Notes**
> The Ouput[13] y is 0, not 10. For more details, please refer to [2.5 Assignment statement].

In[14]
```
# Logical Operators
x=True
y=False
x and y
```
Out[14] False

In[15]
```
x=True
y=False
x or y
```
Out[15] True

In[16]
```
x=True
not x
```
Out[16] False

In[17]
```
# Bitwise operators
x=2
y=3
print(x,y)
print(bin(x),bin(y))
```
Out[17]
```
2 3
0b10 0b11
```

Notes

Bitwise operators and logical operators are two different concepts.

Tips

Decimal data can be converted to binary data with built-in function bin().

In[18]
```
x=2
y=3
x&y
```
Out[18]   2

Tips

& is a bitwise operator which means "bitwise and".

In[19]
```
x=2
y=3
bin(x&y)
```
Out[19]   '0b10'

In[20]
```
x=2
y=3
bin(x | y)
```
Out[20]   '0b11'

In[21]
```
bin(x^y)
```
Out[21]   '0b1'

In[22]
```
bin(~x)
```
Out[22]   '-0b11'

In[23]
```
x=2
y=3
bin(x<<y)
```
Out[23]   '0b10000'

In[24]	x=2 y=3 bin(x>>y)

Out[24] '0b0'

2.3.2 Built-in functions

In[25]	pow(2,10)

Out[25] 1024

Tips Built-in functions (BIFs) are functions that are built into the Python interpreter and can be called directly by their function name.

Notes pow() is a built-in function, but sin() is not.

Tricks To get built-in functions: dir(__builtins__)

In[26]	round(2.991)

Out[26] 3

Tips Rounding function: round(number, ndigits). Its function is to round its first argument *number*, and retain *ndigits* significant figures after the decimal point. The *ndigits* argument defaults to 0.

In[27]	round(2.991,2)

Out[27] 2.99

Tips The meaning of argument "2" is "retain 2 significant figures after the decimal point".

Notes We can get the help information of round() function through "?round" or "round?". The help information given by the system is as follows:

$$round(number[,ndigits])$$

The arguments placed in [] are optional such as ndigits.

2.3.3 Math modules

In[28]
```
import math
math.sin(5/2)
```
Out[28]   0.5984721441039564

Tips   In Python, many commonly used mathematical functions (such as sin(), cos()), and others, are not built-in functions, but are placed in the *math* module. The math module provides a wide range of mathematical operations and functions.

In[29]
```
import math
math.pi
```
Out[29]   3.141592653589793

Tips   The way to get the value of pi.

In[30]
```
import math
math.sqrt(2.0)
```
Out[30]   1.4142135623730951

In[31]
```
import math
math.sqrt(-1)
```
Out[31]   ---
ValueError   Traceback (most recent call last)
<ipython-input-31-101bb87dcaf5> in <module>
      1 import math
----> 2 math.sqrt(-1)

ValueError: math domain error

Tips   An error will be raised when attempting to take the square root of a negative number using the *math* module.

In[32]
```
import cmath
cmath.sqrt(-2)
```
Out[32]   1.4142135623730951j

The functions for complex numbers are in another module called cmath.

2.3.4 Precedence and associativity

In[33]   `2**2**3`

Out[33]   256

Tips

Operator precedence determines the order in which operators are evaluated in an expression that contains multiple operators with different precedences. Operators with higher precedence are evaluated first.

Operator associativity is relevant when two or more operators have the same precedence in an expression. It determines the order in which operators are evaluated when they have the same precedence. Associativity can be either left to right (left-associative) or right to left (right-associative).

Notes

In Python, "2**2**3" is different from "(2**2)**3"

In[34]   `(2**2)**3`

Out[34]   64

In[35]   `x=2+3`
         `x`

Out[35]   5

Notes

The precedence and associativity assignment operators.

In[36]   `1+2 and 3+4`

Out[36]   7

Tips

Please analyze the reason why the result of the expression "1+2 and 3+4" is "7".

2.4 Statements

Q&A

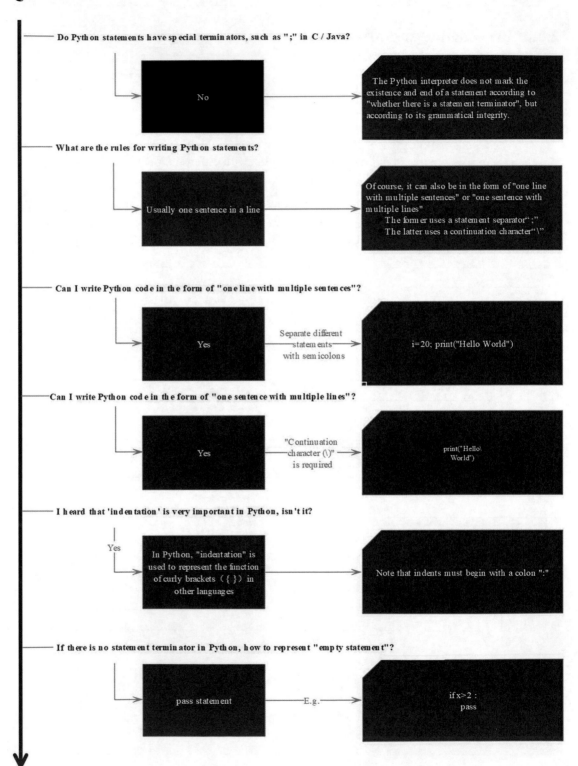

Do Python statements have special terminators, such as ";" in C / Java?

No

The Python interpreter does not mark the existence and end of a statement according to "whether there is a statement terminator", but according to its grammatical integrity.

What are the rules for writing Python statements?

Usually one sentence in a line

Of course, it can also be in the form of "one line with multiple sentences" or "one sentence with multiple lines"
  The former uses a statement separator";"
  The latter uses a continuation character"\"

Can I write Python code in the form of "one line with multiple sentences"?

Yes

Separate different statements with semicolons

i=20; print("Hello World")

Can I write Python code in the form of "one sentence with multiple lines"?

Yes

"Continuation character (\)" is required

print("Hello\ World")

I heard that 'indentation' is very important in Python, isn't it?

Yes

In Python, "indentation" is used to represent the function of curly brackets（ { }）in other languages

Note that indents must begin with a colon ":"

If there is no statement terminator in Python, how to represent "empty statement"?

pass statement

E.g.

if x>2 :
  pass

2.4.1 Writing a statement in a line

Notes

Python statements are usually written in a single line. The newline character marks the end of the statement.

In[1]
```
i=20
j=30
k=40
```

Notes

Unlike C and Java, Python does not have statement terminators such as ";".

Tips

Please refer to *PEP8-Style Guide for Python Code* and *Google Python Style Guide* for the writing specifications of Python code.

2.4.2 Writing multiple statements in a single line

In[2]
```
i=20; j=30; k=40
```

Tips

Though not typically recommended, you can separate different statements on the same line with a semicolon ";" in Python.

In[3]
```
i;j;k
```
Out[3]   40

Tips

In Python, "i, j, k" differs from "i; j; k". The former creates a tuple, while the latter represents multiple statements.

In[4]
```
i,j,k
```
Out[4]   (20, 30, 40)

Notes

In Python, there is a distinct difference between ";" and ",". The former is used for representing multiple statements in a single line, while the latter is used for creating tuples. Detailed information about tuples is described in Section [2.11 Tuples].

In[5] `print(i;j;k)`

Out[5]   File "<ipython-input-5-efd9c261ba8d>", line 1
         print(i;j;k) #Exception, SyntaxError: invalid syntax
               ^
         SyntaxError: invalid syntax

Notes

It is easy for beginners to confuse the use of semicolons and commas. For example, the above code will raise an error.

Tips

Attempting to print a statement like "print(i; j; k)" will result in a SyntaxError ("invalid syntax") exception. This is because semicolons represent statement separators in Python and cannot be used in this context.

2.4.3 Splitting a statement into multiple lines

In[6]
```
print("nin \
hao")
```

Out[6]   nin hao

Notes

Here, "\" refers to the line continuation character. PEP8 recommends that a line of Python code should be limited to a maximum of 79 characters. If a line needs to extend beyond this limit, it should generally be split into multiple lines. You can use the line continuation character "\" to indicate that a line should be continued, although in many cases, Python allows line continuation inside parentheses, brackets, and braces without the need for this character.

2.4.4 Compound statements

Tips

Compound statements contain (groups of) other statements. there are three main kinds of compound statements:

● control flow constructs: for(or while)statements and if statements

● exception handlers: try statements and with statements

● function and class definitions: def statements and class statements

In[7]
```
sum=0
for i in range(1,10):
    sum=sum+i
    print(i)
print(sum)
```

Out[7]   1
          2
          3
          4
          5
          6
          7
          8
          9
          45

Notes

In Python, indentation is used to represent the block structure of code, similar to the way braces "{ }" are used in Java and C. However, there are some unique aspects of Python's indentation rules:

- A colon (":") is required at the end of the line before the start of an indented block. This is usually at the end of control flow statements like if, for, while, def, and class.

- The consistency of indentation is very important. All lines within the same block of code must be indented at the same level. This alignment is required to correctly represent the structure of the code.

Tips

PEP8 recommends to use 4 spaces per indentation level.

In[8]
```
a = 10
if a > 5:
        print("a+1=",a+1)
print("a=",a)
```

Out[8]   a+1= 11
          a= 10

Tips

Please note that incorrect indentation can cause SyntaxError exceptions or lead to unexpected behavior due to the code's logic being interpreted differently than intended.

Tricks

Python doesn't require a specific number of spaces for indentation, but by convention and according to PEP 8 (the official Python style guide), four spaces are typically used to denote one level of indentation.

Notes

In Python, a colon (:) must be added at the end of the line before starting an indented block.

2.4.5 Empty statements

Notes

An empty statement is a statement that does nothing. In Python, the pass statement serves this purpose, essentially acting as a placeholder for future code and having no effect when executed.

In[9]
```
x=1
y=2
if x>y:
    pass
else:
    print(y)
```

Out[9]   2

Tips

Python is often described as being like "executable pseudocode" due to its readability. In Python, if you need to create an empty block (for instance, a function or a loop that you have not yet implemented), you would use the pass statement as a placeholder. If you don't include a pass statement or some other statement in such a block, Python will raise a syntax error.

Notes

Unlike C and Java, an empty statement in Python is represented by a pass statement, not by a semicolon(;).

Notes

Two important versions of Python:
Currently, there are two important versions of Python: Python 2 and Python 3. There are many differences in syntax between the two. This book observes Python 3 syntax. The main difference between the two and the ways of porting Python 2 code to Python 3 can be found at https://docs.python.org/3/howto/pyporting.html or https://www.python.org/.

2.5 Assignment statements

Q&A

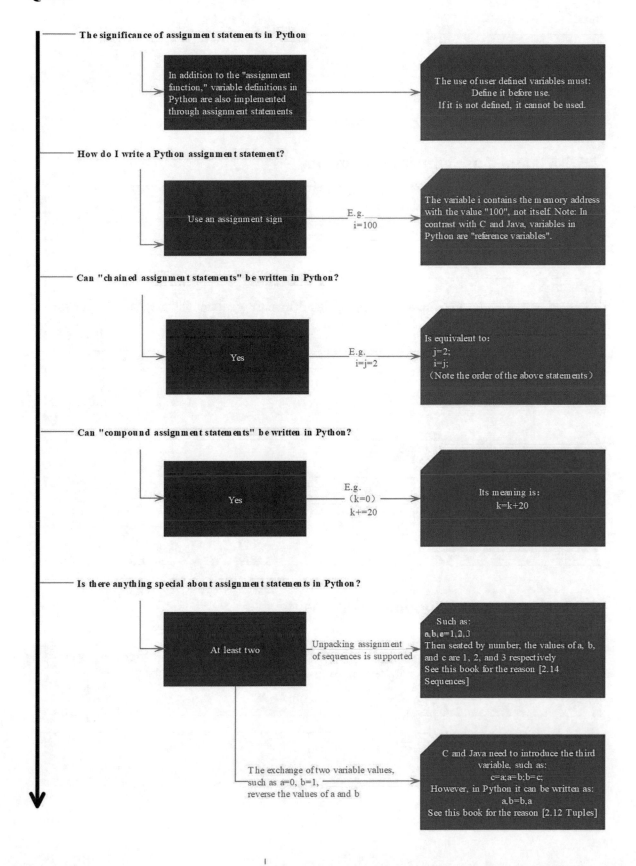

The significance of assignment statements in Python

In addition to the "assignment function," variable definitions in Python are also implemented through assignment statements

The use of user defined variables must:
Define it before use.
If it is not defined, it cannot be used.

How do I write a Python assignment statement?

Use an assignment sign

E.g.
i=100

The variable i contains the memory address with the value "100", not itself. Note: In contrast with C and Java, variables in Python are "reference variables".

Can "chained assignment statements" be written in Python?

Yes

E.g.
i=j=2

Is equivalent to:
j=2;
i=j;
（Note the order of the above statements）

Can "compound assignment statements" be written in Python?

Yes

E.g.
(k=0)
k+=20

Its meaning is:
k=k+20

Is there anything special about assignment statements in Python?

At least two

Unpacking assignment of sequences is supported

Such as:
a,b,c=1,2,3
Then seated by number, the values of a, b, and c are 1, 2, and 3 respectively
See this book for the reason [2.14 Sequences]

The exchange of two variable values, such as a=0, b=1, reverse the values of a and b

C and Java need to introduce the third variable, such as:
c=a;a=b;b=c;
However, in Python it can be written as:
a,b=b,a
See this book for the reason [2.12 Tuples]

2.5.1 Assigning objects

In[1]
```
i=1
i
```

Out[1]   1

In Python, assignment statements are also used to define new variables.

Tips

2.5.2 Chained assignment statements

In[2]
```
i=j=2
i
j
```

Out[2]   2

The associativity of assignment operators in most programming languages, including Python, follows a 'right-to-left' rule.

Notes

In[3]
```
j=2
i=j
i
j
```

Out[3]   2

The chained assignment 'i = j = 2' is functionally equivalent to the sequence of statements 'j = 2; i = j;'.

Tips

2.5.3 Augmented assignment statements

Augmented assignment, also known as compound assignment, refers to specific assignment operators in certain programming languages, particularly those derived from C.

Tips

In[4]
```
i=1
i+=20
i
```

Out[4]   21

Operator	Description
+=	Addition
-=	Subtraction
*=	Multiplication
/=	Division
%=	Modulus
<<=	Left bit shift
>>=	Right bit shift

Notes

In[6]
```
a=2
a*=1+3
a
```
Out[5]   8

Tips

Here, the Out[5] is 8 (not 5) because the right hand side is always evaluated completely before the assignment when running an augmented assignment.

2.5.4 Sequence unpacking

In[6]
```
a,b,c=1,2,3
a,b,c
```
Out[6]   (1, 2, 3)

Notes

The assignment rule for sequence unpacking follows a 'position-based' approach. In other words, the values on the right side of the assignment operator are assigned to the variables on the left, according to their respective positions.

Tips

For further details about sequences and their unpacked assignments, please refer to [2.13 Sequences].

Notes

The output here is a tuple, in other words, numbers with parentheses. Please refer to [2.11 Tuples].

2.5.5 Swapping two variables

In[7]
```
a=1
b=2
a,b=b,a
a,b
```

Out[7]   (2, 1)

Tips

Here, a,b is equivalent to the tuple (a,b). Therefore, a,b=b,a is equivalent to (a,b)=(b,a) which is an example of is a sequence unpacking described in [2.5.4 Sequence unpacking].

Notes

In C and Java, swapping two variables (a, b) requires the introduction of a third variable (c), as shown in the sequence 'c = a; a = b; b = c;'. Python, on the other hand, allows the same operation to be performed more succinctly with the line 'a, b = b, a'. However, this does not necessarily mean that Python consumes less memory than C or Java. It's worth noting that in Python, the 'a, b = b, a' operation creates temporary tuples under the hood for the swap, which can consume additional memory beyond just the variables a and b.

2.6 Comments

Q&A

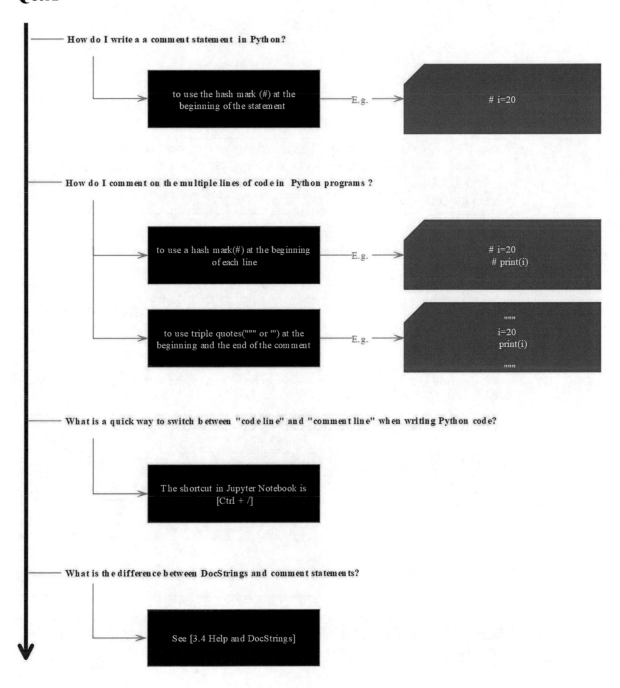

How do I write a a comment statement in Python?

to use the hash mark (#) at the beginning of the statement

E.g. → # i=20

How do I comment on the multiple lines of code in Python programs ?

to use a hash mark(#) at the beginning of each line

E.g. → # i=20
print(i)

to use triple quotes(""" or ''') at the beginning and the end of the comment

E.g. → """
i=20
print(i)
"""

What is a quick way to switch between "code line" and "comment line" when writing Python code?

The shortcut in Jupyter Notebook is [Ctrl + /]

What is the difference between DocStrings and comment statements?

See [3.4 Help and DocStrings]

2.6.1 Line comments

Notes

Unlike Java and C, comments in Python start with a hash mark(#) and extend to the end of the physical line.

In[1]
```
x=1
# y=2
print(x)
```
Out[1] 1

Tricks

The Python interpreter always ignores comments. Therefore, we can prevent a section of code from executing by commenting it out during the debugging of Python programs. Additionally, it's important to prioritize keeping comments up-to-date when the code changes.

In[2]
```
x=1
# y=2
print(y)
```
Out[2] ---
```
NameError                                    Traceback (most recent call last)
<ipython-input-4-f9b039d12571> in <module>
      1 x=1
      2 # y=2
----> 3 print(y) # why that exception: the defined part of the variable is the comment
line.

NameError: name 'y' is not defined
```

Tips

A NameError exception was raised when the Python Interpreter executed In[2] in that y=2 was commented out.

2.6.2 Block comments

Notes

Python does not have a specific syntax for multiline comments. However, we can implement multi-line comments in Python either by using single-line comments consecutively or by using triple-quoted Python strings.

In[3]
```
x=1
y=2
print(y)
"""
    This is
    a
    multiline comment
    in python
"""
```
2

Tips

In Jupyter Notebook, we can switch between "code line" and "comment line" by keyboard shortcut 【Ctrl + /】.

Tricks

In Jupyter Notebook, we can conveniently switch between Comment Lines and Code Lines using the shortcut Ctrl+/. Please note that these shortcut keys in Jupyter Notebook cannot be used when a non-English input method is active.

Notes

By convention, the triple quotes that appear right after the function, method or class definition are docstrings (documentation strings). For more details, please refer to "3.4 Help documetation".

2.7 If statements

Q&A

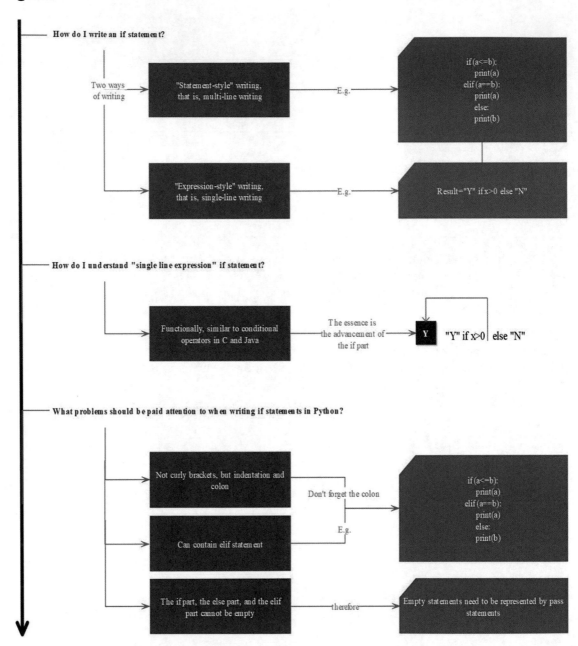

2.7.1 Basic syntax

```
In[1]  a=2
       b=3
       if(a<b):
            print("a is less than b")
       else:
            print("a is not less than b")
Out[1]  a is less than b
```

In Python, indentation serves the same function as braces ({ }) in C and Java; that is, it signifies the scope of compound statements.

Notes

In Python, a colon (:) is required at the end of the line that introduces a new indentation level, such as the start of a control structure or a function definition. Thus, a colon often precedes an indentation.

Notes

In[2]
```python
if(a<=b):
    if(a<b):
        print(a)
    else:
        print(a)
else:
    print(b)
```

Out[2] 2

Similar to C and Java, Python supports the nesting of *'if'* statements.

Tips

2.7.2 Elif statement

In Python, the keyword 'clif' is shorthand for 'clsc if'. It's useful in avoiding excessive indentation and keeping the code concise.

Notes

In[3]
```python
if(a<=b):
    print(a)
elif(a==b):
    print(a)
else:
    print(b)
```

Out[3] 2

Unlike C and Java, the *'if'* statement in Python can include an *'elif'* clause. Additionally, Python's 'try-catch', 'while', 'for', and other control statements can all include an *'else'* clause. In Python, the *'else'* statement signifies that the preceding code block was exited normally, meaning without a 'break', 'continue', or an exception being thrown.

Tips

2.7.3 Ternary operators

| Notes | Ternary operators allow us to quickly test a condition, providing a more compact alternative to a multiline 'if' statement. |

In[4]
```
x=0
Result="Y" if x>0 else "N"
Result
```
Out[4]   'N'

| Notes | The 'if' statement in Python can be written as a single-line expression, similar to the ternary conditional operator (?:) in C and Java. |

| Tips | In Python's ternary operators, the 'true' expression (Y) precedes the 'if' statement. |

| Notes | In Python, the if statements, the for statements, and functions can all be written on a single line, using ternary operators, list comprehensions, and lambda functions, respectively. |

In[5]
```
x=1
Result="Y" if x>0 else "N"
Result
```
Out[5]   'Y'

2.7.4 Advanced syntax

In[6]
```
if(a<=b):
else:
    print(b)
```
Out[6]   File "<ipython-input-6-12262625dfcc>", line 2
              else:
              ^
          IndentationError: expected an indented block

| Notes | In Python, each part of an if statement must have some code or statement. If any part is empty, the Python interpreter will raise an error because Python is executable pseudocode. You can refer to [2.10 The pass statements (In[1])] for more information. |

Can I write an empty statement? No.
IndentationError: expected an indented block

Tips

The pass statement is equivalent to the empty statement in other languages.

Tips

In[7]
```
if(a<=b):
    pass  # no error
else:
    print(b)
```

In this case, the *pass* statement serves as a placeholder to indicate that no action is taken when a is less than or equal to b. If a is greater than b, the code will execute the print(b) statement in the else block.

Tips

To check whether a year is a leap year in Python, you can use the following suggestion:

Tips

In[8]
```
import calendar
calendar.isleap(2019)
```
Out[8]   False

Software development projects and data analysis projects are fundamentally different from each other. Therefore, Python should not be approached in the same way as C or Java when it comes to data science projects. Let's take the example of checking whether a year is a leap year. Instead of attempting to translate Java or C code directly into Python, it is better to embrace Python's unique features and idiomatic style for a more effective solution.

Tricks

2.8 For statements

Q&A

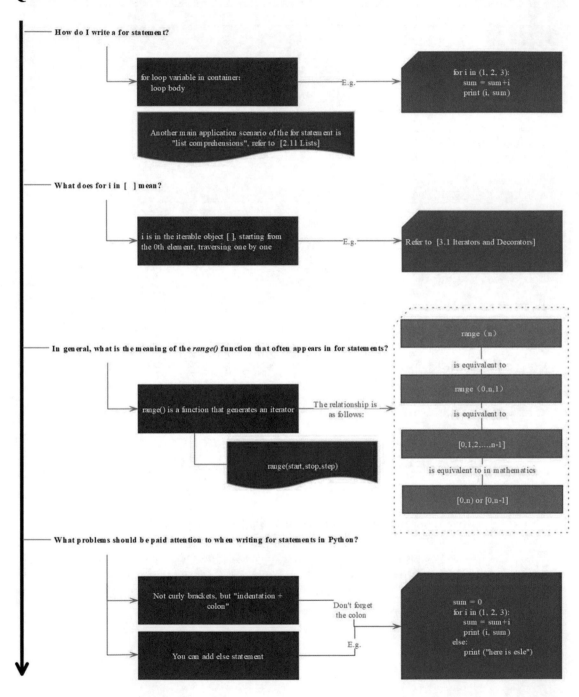

How do I write a for statement?

for loop variable in container:
    loop body

E.g.

for i in (1, 2, 3):
    sum = sum+i
    print (i, sum)

Another main application scenario of the for statement is "list comprehensions", refer to [2.11 Lists]

What does for i in [ ] mean?

i is in the iterable object [ ], starting from the 0th element, traversing one by one

E.g.

Refer to [3.1 Iterators and Decorators]

In general, what is the meaning of the *range()* function that often appears in for statements?

range() is a function that generates an iterator

The relationship is as follows:

range(start, stop, step)

range（n）

is equivalent to

range（0,n,1）

is equivalent to

[0,1,2,...,n-1]

is equivalent to in mathematics

[0,n) or [0,n-1]

What problems should be paid attention to when writing for statements in Python?

Not curly brackets, but "indentation + colon"

You can add else statement

Don't forget the colon

E.g.

sum = 0
for i in (1, 2, 3):
    sum = sum+i
    print (i, sum)
else:
    print ("here is esle")

2.8.1 Basic syntax

```
In[1]   sum=0
        for i in (1,2,3):
            sum=sum+i
            print(i,sum)
```

```
Out[1]  1 1
        2 3
        3 6
```

Notes

Unlike C and Java, there is only one way to write the *for* statement in Python: [for ... in ...]. Make sure to include the colon at the end of the line and pay attention to the indentation. You can refer to [2.4 Statements] for more information.

Tips

The *in* keyword in Python is used to iterate over iterables or iterators. In the given context, the parentheses *( )* represent a tuple, which is an iterable. For more information on iterators and decorators, you can refer to [3.1 Iterators and Decorators].

Notes

Before the *for* statement, it is necessary to assign a value to the *sum* variable; otherwise, an error will be raised due to the variable being undefined.

2.8.2 The range( ) function

```
In[2]   range(1,10)
```

```
Out[2]  range(1, 10)
```

Notes

The *range()* function is commonly used after the *in* keyword in the *for* statement, such as range(1, 10). The range() function returns a "range iterator" that generates a sequence of numbers from the start value (1 in this case) to the end value (10 in this case).

Tips

Please refer to [3.1 Iterators and Decorators] for more information on iterators.

```
In[3]   myList=list(range(1,10))
        myList
```

```
Out[3]  [1, 2, 3, 4, 5, 6, 7, 8, 9]
```

| Tricks | To examine the contents of an iterator, you can use the *list()* function to convert the "range iterator" into a *list type*. This allows you to view all the elements generated by the iterator. |

| Notes | In the return value of the *range(1, 10)* function, the generated sequence includes the number 1 but excludes the number 10. This is a characteristic of the *range()* function in Python, where the end value is exclusive. For more details on working with lists, you can refer to [2.10 Lists]. |

2.8.3 Advanced syntax

In[4]
```python
sum=0
for i in (1,2,3):
    sum=sum+i
    print(i,sum)
else:
    print("here is esle")
```

Out[4]
```
1 1
2 3
3 6
here is esle
```

| Tips | Unlike C and Java, the *for* statement in Python can be used together with the *else* statement. |

In[5]
```python
myList=list(range(1,10))
for j in [1,3,4,5]:
    print(myList[j])
```

Out[5]
```
2
4
5
6
```

| Tips | Similar to C, Java, etc., the *for* statement in Python supports the *break* and *continue* statements. |

```
In[6]    for k in range(0,16,2):
             if(k==8):
                 break
             print(k)
```

Out[6]   0
          2
          4
          6

Notes   The difference between the *break* and *continue* statements is as follows: The break statement "exits the loop entirely," while the continue statement "skips the remaining code inside the loop for the current iteration and moves to the next iteration."

```
In[7]    for k in range(0,16,2):
             if(k==8):
                 continue
             print(k)
```

Out[7]   0
          2
          4
          6
          10
          12
          14

Tips   In contrast to the *break* statement, the *continue* statement in Python means "jump inside the loop body." It allows you to skip the remaining statements in the current iteration of the loop and move on to the next iteration. This means that any code following the continue statement within the loop for the current iteration will be bypassed.

2.9 While statements

Q&A

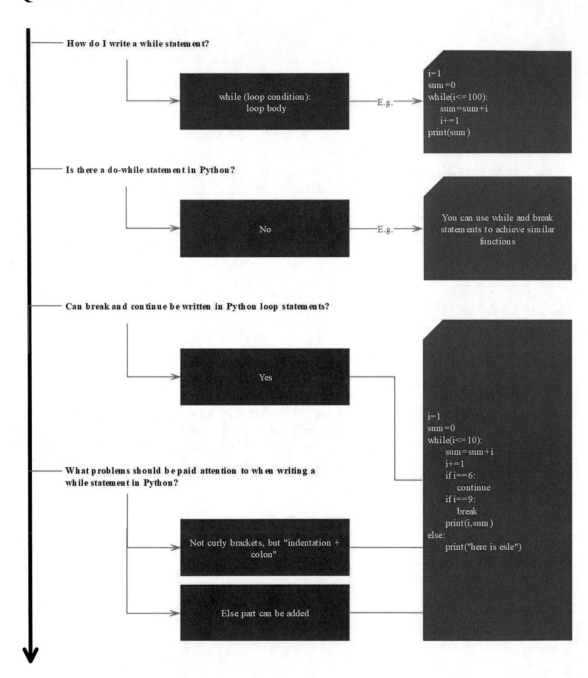

How do I write a while statement?

while (loop condition):
    loop body

E.g.

```
i=1
sum=0
while(i<=100):
    sum=sum+i
    i+=1
print(sum)
```

Is there a do-while statement in Python?

No

E.g.

You can use while and break statements to achieve similar functions

Can break and continue be written in Python loop statements?

Yes

What problems should be paid attention to when writing a while statement in Python?

Not curly brackets, but "indentation + colon"

Else part can be added

```
i=1
sum=0
while(i<=10):
    sum=sum+i
    i+=1
    if i==6:
        continue
    if i==9:
        break
    print(i,sum)
else:
    print("here is esle")
```

2.9.1 Basic syntax

In[1]
```
i=1
sum=0
while(i<=100):
        sum=sum+i
        i+=1
print(sum)
```

Out[1]   5050

Notes

In Python, the *while* statement is written in a single way, and there is no equivalent *do-while* statement as found in some other programming languages. The while loop in Python allows you to repeatedly execute a block of code as long as a specified condition is true. The condition is checked before each iteration, and if it evaluates to False initially, the loop will not be executed.

2.9.2 Advanced syntax

In[2]
```
i=1
sum=0
while(i<=10):
        sum=sum+i
        i+=1
        if i==6:
            continue
        if i==9:
            break
        print(i,sum)
else:
    print("here is esle")
```

Out[2]   2 1
         3 3
         4 6
         5 10
         7 21
         8 28

Notes

To summarize, break exits the loop entirely, while continue skips the remaining statements within the loop for the current iteration and proceeds to the next iteration.

In[3]
```
i=1
sum=0
while(i<=10):
    sum=sum+i
    i+=1
    print(i,sum)
else:
    print("here is esle")
```

Out[3]   2 1
         3 3
         4 6
         5 10
         6 15
         7 21
         8 28
         9 36
         10 45
         11 55
         here is esle

Tips

Unlike C and Java, the *while* statement in Python can indeed include an *else* clause. The *else* clause in a *while* loop will be executed only when the condition of the loop becomes False and the loop completes its iterations normally, without encountering a break or return statement.

Notes

How to distinguish the types of Python code:

(1) Code that starts with "#" is a comment statement. You can refer to [2.6 Comments] for more information.
(2) Code that starts with "%" is a magic command, which is not part of Python syntax but belongs to iPython/Jupyter Notebook syntax.
(3) Code that starts with "@" is a decorator. You can refer to [3.1 Iterators and Decorators] for more details.
(4) Code that starts with "!" is a Python pip/conda command.

2.10 Lists

Q&A

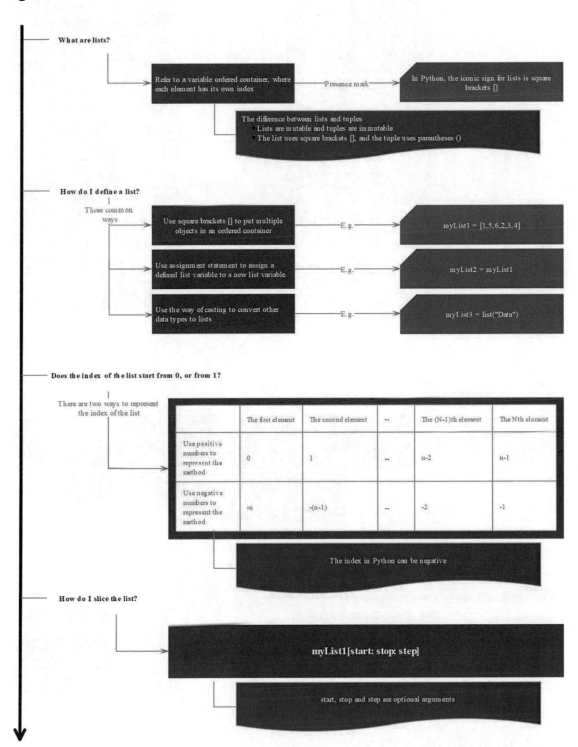

What are lists?

Refer to a variable ordered container, where each element has its own index

— Presence mark →

In Python, the iconic sign for lists is square brackets []

The difference between lists and tuples
- Lists are mutable and tuples are immutable
- The list uses square brackets [], and the tuple uses parentheses ()

How do I define a list?

Three common ways

Use square brackets [] to put multiple objects in an ordered container

— E.g. →

myList1 = [1,5,6,2,3,4]

Use assignment statement to assign a defined list variable to a new list variable

— E.g. →

myList2 = myList1

Use the way of casting to convert other data types to lists

— E.g. →

myList3 = list("Data")

Does the index of the list start from 0, or from 1?

There are two ways to represent the index of the list

	The first element	The second element	...	The (N-1)th element	The Nth element
Use positive numbers to represent the method	0	1	...	n-2	n-1
Use negative numbers to represent the method	-n	-(n-1)	...	-2	-1

The index in Python can be negative

How do I slice the list?

myList1[start: stop: step]

start, stop and step are optional arguments

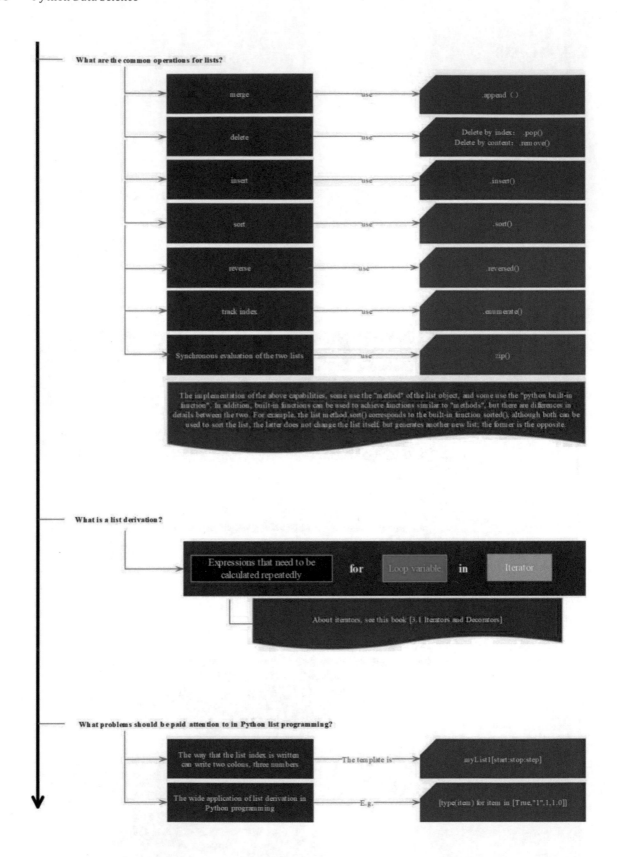

What are the common operations for lists?

merge	use → .append（）
delete	use → Delete by index： .pop() Delete by content： .remove()
insert	use → .insert()
sort	use → .sort()
reverse	use → .reversed()
track index	use → .enumerate()
Synchronous evaluation of the two lists	use → zip()

The implementation of the above capabilities, some use the "method" of the list object, and some use the "python built-in function". In addition, built-in functions can be used to achieve functions similar to "methods", but there are differences in details between the two. For example, the list method .sort() corresponds to the built-in function sorted(), although both can be used to sort the list, the latter does not change the list itself, but generates another new list; the former is the opposite.

What is a list derivation?

Expressions that need to be calculated repeatedly **for** Loop variable **in** Iterator

About iterators, see this book [3.1 Iterators and Decorators]

What problems should be paid attention to in Python list programming?

The way that the list index is written can write two colons, three numbers	The template is →	myList1[start:stop:step]
The wide application of list derivation in Python programming	E.g. →	[type(item) for item in [True,"1",1,1.0]]

2.10.1 Defining lists

In[1] myList1 = [21,22,23,24,25,26,27,28,29]
       myList1

Out[1]   [21, 22, 23, 24, 25, 26, 27, 28, 29]

To define a list in Python, you can use the following methods:

Method 1: Using brackets []

Tips

In the basic Python syntax, parentheses (), brackets [], and braces { } represent tuples, lists, and sets/dictionaries, respectively.

Notes

In[2]
```
myList2=myList1
myList2
```

Out[2] [21, 22, 23, 24, 25, 26, 27, 28, 29]

Method 2: Using an assignment statement, where you assign a defined list variable to a new list variable.

Tips

In[3]
```
myList3=list("Data")
myList3
```

Out[3] ['D', 'a', 't', 'a']

Method 3: Using type casting to convert other types of objects to the *list* type.

Tips

Negative subscripts or negative indexes can be used in Python to access elements from the end of a sequence, such as a string or a list.
The positive indexes start from 0, where 0 represents the first element.
The negative indexes start from –1, where –1 represents the last element.

Notes

In[4]
```
myList1[-1]
```
Out[4] 29

In[5]
```
myList1[-9]
```
Out[5] 21

In[6]
```
myList1[9]
```
Out[6] ---
IndexError   Traceback (most recent call last)
<ipython-input-6-8724c27fc4be> in <module>
----> 1 myList1[9]

IndexError: list index out of range

Notes | Here, the reason for the error is that the index is out of range.

Tips | The difference between positive indexes and negative indexes in Python is as follows: Positive indexes start with 0 and are numbered from left to right, while negative indexes start with −1 and are numbered from right to left.

2.10.2 Slicing

In[7] | `myList1`

Out[7] | [21, 22, 23, 24, 25, 26, 27, 28, 29]

Tips | By printing the variable, you can view its current value in your data science project. It's indeed important to pay attention to the current values of variables throughout your project to ensure accurate results and proper data analysis.

In[8] | `myList1[1:8]`

Out[8] | [22, 23, 24, 25, 26, 27, 28]

Tips | In Python, we can slice a list using indexes, and the notation for slicing is Start:Stop:Step.

Notes | When a colon (:) appears in the index of a Python sequence, it typically indicates slicing the sequence. This slicing notation allows you to specify the start, stop, and step values to extract a portion of the sequence.

In[9] | `myList1[1:8:2]`

Out[9] | [22, 24, 26, 28]

Tips | It's important to note that the start, stop, and *step* values can be omitted when writing a slice. When any of these values are omitted, they take on default values:

In[10] | `myList1[:5]`

Out[10] | [21, 22, 23, 24, 25]

If the start value is omitted, it defaults to the beginning of the sequence. If the stop value is omitted, it defaults to the end of the sequence.If the step value is omitted, it defaults to 1, indicating consecutive elements.For more details on working with sequences and slicing, you can refer to [2.13 Sequences].

Tips

The element with the index of "stop" is not included in the slicing. For example, in the case of an element with an index of 5, which corresponds to a value of 26 in this example, it is not included in the slice.

Notes

In[11] `myList1[:]`
Out[11] [21, 22, 23, 24, 25, 26, 27, 28, 29]

The start, stop and step arguments are omitted.

Tips

In[12] `myList1[2:]`
Out[12] [23, 24, 25, 26, 27, 28, 29]

The stop and step arguments are omitted.

Tips

In[13] `myList1[:-1]`
Out[13] [21, 22, 23, 24, 25, 26, 27, 28]

The slicing operation supports negative indexes.

Tips

2.10.3 Reversing

In[14] `myList1`
Out[14] [21, 22, 23, 24, 25, 26, 27, 28, 29]

In[15] `myList1[::-1]`
Out[15] [29, 28, 27, 26, 25, 24, 23, 22, 21]

Tricks

Reversing lists can be achieved using the index [::-1], which means setting step to -1.

Notes

Note that there are two colons in myList1[::-1].

In[16] `myList1`

Out[16] [21, 22, 23, 24, 25, 26, 27, 28, 29]

Notes

In Python, slicing a list does not change the list itself; instead, it creates a new list with the selected elements.

In[17] `myList1[:-1]`

Out[17] [21, 22, 23, 24, 25, 26, 27, 28]

Tips

Here, *[:-1]* has the same meaning as *[:n-1]*. In data science projects, there is always a case where the index is -1, which indicates the maximum value of the index.

In[18] `reversed(myList1)`

Out[18] <list_reverseiterator at 0x18ef35863d0>

Tricks

In Python, to reverse lists, we can also use the built-in function reversed() or the list method reverse().

Notes

The return value of the *reversed( )* function is an iterator, and its values can be displayed by passing it to the list() function.

Tips

For information about iterators, you can refer to the section titled "Iterators and Decorators" in the Python documentation or resource you mentioned, specifically section 3.1.

In[19] `list(reversed(myList1))`

Out[19] [29, 28, 27, 26, 25, 24, 23, 22, 21]

In[20] | myList1

Out[20]   [21, 22, 23, 24, 25, 26, 27, 28, 29]

Tips

To check the current value of the *myList1* list, you can use the reverse() method as follows: myList1.reverse().

In[21] | myList1.reverse()
          | myList1

Out[21]   [29, 28, 27, 26, 25, 24, 23, 22, 21]

Notes

When you use reversed(), it returns an iterator that allows you to iterate over the list in reverse order without modifying the original list. However, if you use the reverse() method directly on a list, it will reverse the elements of the list itself.

2.10.4 Type conversion

In[22] | list("chaolemen")

Out[22]   ['c', 'h', 'a', 'o', 'l', 'e', 'm', 'e', 'n']

Tips

We can use the *list()* function to convert an object of a different type into a list.

2.10.5 the extend and append operator

In[23] | # The *addition* (+) operator of the list
          | myList1 = [21,22,23,24,25,26,27,28,29]
          | myList2=myList1
          | myList1 + myList2

Out[23]   [21, 22, 23, 24, 25, 26, 27, 28, 29, 21, 22, 23, 24, 25, 26, 27, 28, 29]

In[24] | myList1 = [21,22,23,24,25,26,27,28,29]
          | myList2=myList1
          | myList1.extend(myList2)
          | myList1

Out[24]   [21, 22, 23, 24, 25, 26, 27, 28, 29, 21, 22, 23, 24, 25, 26, 27, 28, 29]

Notes

In Python, the "+" operation for lists and the *extend()* method of a list have similar functionality. Both operations are used to concatenate or combine lists.

In[25]
```
# The append() method of the list
myList1 = [21,22,23,24,25,26,27,28,29]
myList2 = myList1
myList1.append(myList2)
myList1
```

Out[25]   [21, 22, 23, 24, 25, 26, 27, 28, 29, [21, 22, 23, 24, 25, 26, 27, 28, 29]]

Notes

The difference between the *append()* and *extend()* methods of a list is that append() is used to add a single element to the list, while extend() is used to add multiple individual elements.

In[26]
```
myList1 = [1,2,3,4,5,6,7,8,9]
myList3 = [11,12,13,14,15,16,17,18,19]
[i + j for i, j in zip(myList1, myList3)]
```

Out[26]   [12, 14, 16, 18, 20, 22, 24, 26, 28]

Notes

The *zip()* function in Python is used to iterate in parallel over two or more iterables. It takes multiple iterables as input and returns an iterator that generates tuples containing elements from each iterable, paired together based on their respective positions.

Tips

In Python, list comprehension (or list derivation) is a concise way to create lists based on existing lists or other iterables. List comprehension is typically written within square brackets ([]).
You can refer to section 2.10.6 titled "Lists Derivation" for more detailed information on this topic.

2.10.6 List derivation

In[27]
```
[2 for i in range(20)]
   # Excute the range() function firstly, then the value of i, and finally the value of 2.
```

Out[27]   [2, 2, 2, 2, 2, 2, 2, 2, 2, 2, 2, 2, 2, 2, 2, 2, 2, 2, 2, 2]

Tips

List comprehension (or list derivation) must be enclosed within square brackets ([]).
You can refer to section 2.10 titled "Lists" for more information on this topic.

Notes

Since Python provides mechanisms such as list comprehensions, *ufunc* functions, vectorized calculations, and more, complex *for* statements are generally not commonly found in Python-based data science projects. These mechanisms offer more efficient and concise ways to perform computations on data structures, allowing for faster and more readable code. Consequently, Python developers often leverage these techniques instead of writing complex for loops when working on data science projects.

List comprehension is typically written within square brackets ([]), and it allows you to generate new lists by applying an expression to each item in an iterable, optionally including conditions for filtering the elements.

Tips

In[28] `[i for i in range(1, 21)]`

Out[28] [1, 2, 3, 4, 5, 6, 7, 8, 9, 10, 11, 12, 13, 14, 15, 16, 17, 18, 19, 20]

In[29] `[i for i in range(1, 21, 2)]`

Out[29] [1, 3, 5, 7, 9, 11, 13, 15, 17, 19]

In[30] `range(10)`

Out[30] range(0, 10)

range(10) is equivalent to range(0,10).

Tips

In[31] `list(range(0,10,2))`

Out[31] [0, 2, 4, 6, 8]

In the code snippet (range(0,10,2)), the numbers 0, 10, and 2 represent the start, stop, and step arguments of the iterator, respectively.

Tips

In[32] `[type(item) for item in [True,"1",1,1.0]]`

Out[32] [bool, str, int, float]

In[33] `print([ord(i) for i in ['朝', '乐', '门']])`

Out[33] [26397, 20048, 38376]

In[34] `["input/%d.txt" % i + "dd%d" % i for i in range(5)]`

Out[34] ['input/0.txtdd0',
    'input/1.txtdd1',
    'input/2.txtdd2',
    'input/3.txtdd3',
    'input/4.txtdd4']

String placeholders, such as %d, can be used in Python list comprehensions, which are similar to the placeholders used in the *printf( )* and *scanf( )* functions in C.

Tricks

In[35]   ["input/%d.txt"%i + "_%d" %i for i in range(5)]

Out[35]   ['input/0.txt_0',
         'input/1.txt_1',
         'input/2.txt_2',
         'input/3.txt_3',
         'input/4.txt_4']

Notes

Here, %d is a placeholder that represents an integer value, and %i is another placeholder that is used to display the corresponding value in the resulting string.

2.10.7 Insertion and deletion

In[36]
```
lst_1 = [10,10,11,12,13,14,15]
lst_1.insert(1, 8)
lst_1
```

Out[36]   [10, 8, 10, 11, 12, 13, 14, 15]

Tips

We can add or insert elements to a list using the *insert()* method of the list.

Notes

Here, the number "8" represents the element to be inserted, and the number "1" represents the position at which the element will be inserted into the lst_1 list.

In[37]
```
lst_1 = [10,10,11,12,13,14,15]
lst_1.pop(2)
lst_1
```

Out[37]   [10, 10, 12, 13, 14, 15]

Tips

We can use the *pop()* method of a list to delete a specific element based on its index. To remove the element at index 2, you can use the above code.

In[38]
```
lst_1 = [10,10,11,12,13,14,15]
del lst_1[2]
lst_1
```

Out[38]   [10, 10, 12, 13, 14, 15]

Tips

Python supports deleting an element from a list based on its index.

In[39]
```
lst_1 = [10,10,11,12,13,14,15]
lst_1.remove(10)
lst_1
```

Out[39]   [10, 11, 12, 13, 14, 15]

In addition to deleting an element based on its index, Python also supports removing an element from a list based on its value. You can use the remove() method for this purpose.

Tips

Here, only the first occurrence of 10 is removed, not the second occurrence.

Notes

If you want to remove all occurrences of a particular value from the list, you can use other techniques such as a list comprehension or a loop.

Tips

2.10.8 Basic functions

In[40]
```
len(lst_1)
```
Out[40]   8

To calculate the length of a list in Python, you can use the built-in function len().

Tips

This function is named len(), not length().

Notes

In[41]
```
lst_1 = [10,10,11,12,11,13,14,15]
sorted(lst_1)
```
Out[41]   [10, 10, 11, 11, 12, 13, 14, 15]

To sort lists in Python, you can use the built-in function sorted().

Tips

In[42]
```
lst_1
```
Out[42]   [10, 10, 11, 12, 11, 13, 14, 15]

Notes

In Python, the built-in function sorted() does not change the order of the elements in a list.

In[43]
```
lst_1 = [10,10,11,12,11,13,14,15]
lst_1.sort()
lst_1
```

Out[43]   [10, 10, 11, 11, 12, 13, 14, 15]

Tips

In addition to the built-in function sorted(), the list method sort() can also be used to sort lists.

Notes

The difference between the built-in function *sorted()* and the list method *sort()* is that the *sort()* method directly modifies the order of elements within the list itself, while the *sorted()* function returns a new sorted list without modifying the original list.

In[44]
```
lst_1 = [10,10,11,12,11,13,14,15]
lst_2=[11,12,13,14]
lst_1.append(lst_2)
print(lst_1)
```

Out[44]   [10, 10, 11, 12, 11, 13, 14, 15, [11, 12, 13, 14]]

Notes

Note the difference between the list methods extend() and append().

Tips

lst_2 is appended as an element of lst_1.

In[45]
```
lst_1 = [10,10,11,12,11,13,14,15]
lst_2=[11,12,13,14]
lst_1.extend(lst_2)
print(lst_1)
```

Out[45]   [10, 10, 11, 12, 11, 13, 14, 15, 11, 12, 13, 14]

Tips

Appending lst_1 directly after lst_2, that is, directly merging the elements in the two lists.

In[46]
```
lst_1 = [1,2,3,'Python',True,4.3,None]
lst_2 = [1,2,[2,3]]
print(lst_1, lst_2)
```
Out[46]   [1, 2, 3, 'Python', True, 4.3, None] [1, 2, [2, 3]]

To print lists in Python, you can use the built-in function print().

Tips

In[47]
```
lst_1 = [1,2,3,'Python',True,4.3,None]
list(reversed(lst_1))
```
Out[47]   [None, 4.3, True, 'Python', 3, 2, 1]

The difference between the built-in function *reversed()* and the list method *reverse()* is that the former does not modify the list itself, while the latter directly modifies the list itself.

Tips

'reversed(lst_1)' returns an iterator that needs to be converted using the *list()* function before printing.

Notes

In[48]
```
reversed(lst_1)
```
Out[48]   <list_reverseiterator at 0x18ef367bf10>

In data science projects, it is important to pay attention to whether a "function" or "method" modifies the value of the object being operated upon.

Notes

In[49]
```
lst_1
```
Out[49]   [1, 2, 3, 'Python', True, 4.3, None]

The reversed() function is a built-in function in Python that does not change the list itself. Instead, it temporarily returns the list in reverse order as an iterator.

Tips

In[50]
```
lst_1 = [1,2,3,'Python',True,4.3,None]
lst_1.reverse()
lst_1
```
Out[50]   [None, 4.3, True, 'Python', 3, 2, 1]

In[51]
```
str1=[1,2,3,4,5]
str2=[20,21,23,24,25]
print(zip(str1,str2))
```

Out[51] <zip object at 0x0000018EF368C280>

Tips

To aggregate elements from two lists simultaneously in Python, you can use the *zip()* function.

In[52]
```
print(list(zip(str1,str2)))
```

Out[52] [(1, 20), (2, 21), (3, 23), (4, 24), (5, 25)]

Tips

The return value of the *zip()* function is an iterator, which needs to be cast by list() to get its value. Please refer to [3.1 Iterators and Decorators] for details.

In[53]
```
str1=["a","about","c","china","b","beijing"]
[x.upper() for x in str1 if len(x)>1]
```

Out[53] ['ABOUT', 'CHINA', 'BEIJING']

Tips

Unlike C and Java, Python introduces the concept of list comprehension, which can be used to simplify complex *for* statements.

Notes

For a list comprehension, there are three main components:

1. Before the *"for"* keyword is the expression or formula that will be executed repeatedly to generate elements for the new list.

2. Between the *"for"* and *"in"* keywords is the loop variable that is extracted from the iterator and represents each element from the iterable.

3. After the *"in"* keyword is the iterable or iterator from which the loop variable is extracted, which can also include conditional statements *if* needed.

In[54]
```
[x**2 for x in range(10)]
```

Out[54] [0, 1, 4, 9, 16, 25, 36, 49, 64, 81]

Tips

The list derivation above is executed in the following order:
#First execute range(10)
#Then execute x
#Finally execute x**2

In[55]
```
str1=["a","about","c","china","b","beijing"]
[str2.upper() for str2 in str1 if len(str2)>1]
```

Out[55]   ['ABOUT', 'CHINA', 'BEIJING']

Tips

The code above contains the ternary operators of the *if* statement, please refer to [2.7 The if statement] for details.

In[56]
```
myList=[2,3,5,6,7,3,2]
list(enumerate(myList))
```

Out[56]   [(0, 2), (1, 3), (2, 5), (3, 6), (4, 7), (5, 3), (6, 2)]

Tips

In Python, to track the index of a list, you can use the built-in function *enumerate()*.

Notes

In data science projects, it is important to pay attention to the difference between writing code for software development and code for data analysis/data science. For instance, in data science, we often prefer using list comprehension instead of complex for statements.

List comprehension provides a concise and efficient way to create lists based on existing lists or other iterables. It simplifies code by condensing multiple lines of code into a single line, making it more readable and expressive. This approach is particularly valuable in data analysis and data science tasks that involve working with large datasets.

By utilizing list comprehension, data scientists can express complex operations more succinctly and intuitively, resulting in more manageable and error-resistant code.

Therefore, in data science projects, it is important to recognize the advantages of using list comprehension as a preferable alternative to complex for statements, enhancing code clarity and efficiency.

2.11 Tuples

Q&A

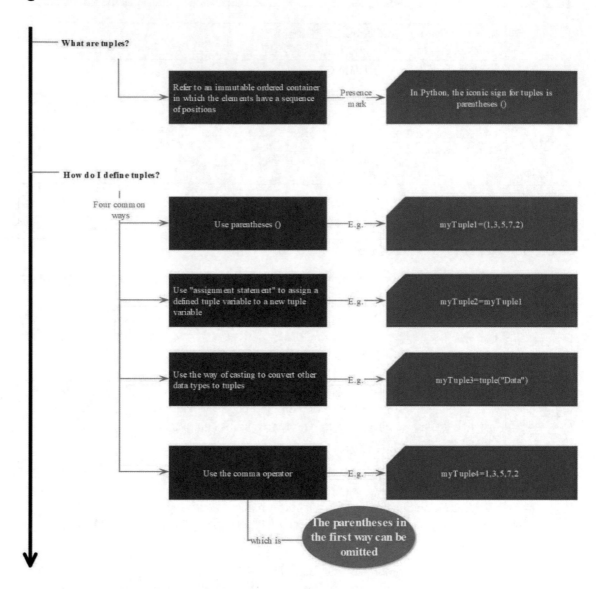

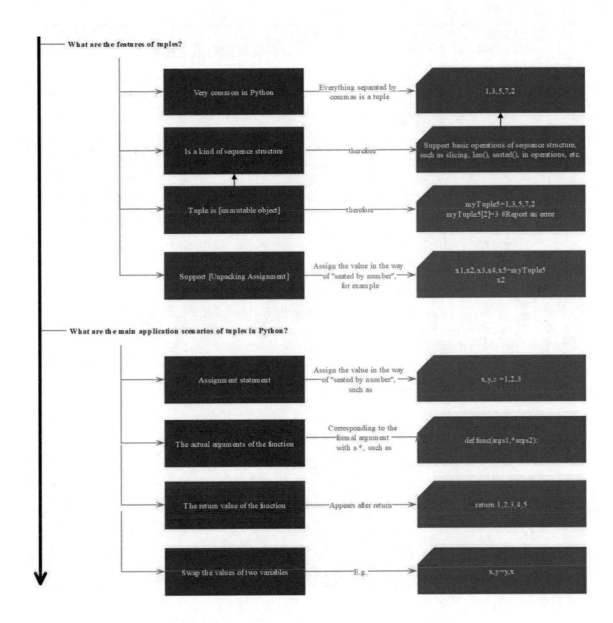

What are the features of tuples?

Very common in Python	Everything separated by commas is a tuple → 1,3,5,7,2
Is a kind of sequence structure	therefore → Support basic operations of sequence structure, such as slicing, len(), sorted(), in operations, etc.
Tuple is [immutable object]	therefore → myTuple5=1,3,5,7,2 myTuple5[2]=3 #Report an error
Support [Unpacking Assignment]	Assign the value in the way of "seated by number", for example → x1,x2,x3,x4,x5=myTuple5 x2

What are the main application scenarios of tuples in Python?

Assignment statement	Assign the value in the way of "seated by number", such as → x,y,z =1,2,3
The actual arguments of the function	Corresponding to the formal argument with a *, such as → def func(args1,*args2):
The return value of the function	Appears after return → return 1,2,3,4,5
Swap the values of two variables	E.g. → x,y=y,x

2.11.1 Define tuples

In[1]
```
myTuple1=(1,3,5,7,2)
print(myTuple1)
```
Out[1] (1, 3, 5, 7, 2)

Notes

To define a tuple in Python, you can use the following methods:

1. Using parentheses and commas:

In[2]
```
1,3,5,7,2
```
Out[2] (1, 3, 5, 7, 2)

Notes

In Python, parentheses can be omitted when defining tuples; however, commas cannot be omitted

Tips

In Python, when a tuple is output or printed, parentheses are automatically added to encapsulate the comma-separated values. This helps in differentiating a tuple from other data types.

In[3]
```
myTuple2=myTuple1
print(myTuple2)
```
Out[3] (1, 3, 5, 7, 2)

Notes

The second method to create a tuple in Python is through tuple unpacking. This involves using an 'assignment statement' to assign the values of an existing tuple to the variables of a new tuple.

In[4]
```
myTuple3=tuple("Data")
myTuple3
```
Out[4] ('D', 'a', 't', 'a')

Notes

The third method involves using type casting to convert other data types into tuples.

In[5]
```
myTuple4=1,3,5,7,2
print(myTuple4)
```
Out[5] (1, 3, 5, 7, 2)

Notes

The fourth method involves using the 'comma operator'. This means that the parentheses which are typically used in the first method can be omitted. In Python, a comma operator signifies a tuple, even without parentheses.

2.11.2 Main features

In[6] `1,3,5,7,2`

Out[6] (1, 3, 5, 7, 2)

Tips

Tuples are widely used in Python.

Notes

In Python, when a list is output in the Jupyter Notebook, it is automatically encapsulated in square brackets.

In[7]
```
myTuple=1,3,5,7,2
myTuple[2]=100
```

Out[7]
```
---------------------------------------------------------------------------
TypeError                                 Traceback (most recent call last)
<ipython-input-7-bab615dd7a09> in <module>
      1 myTuple=1,3,5,7,2
----> 2 myTuple[2]=100  # Why that exception: Tuples are immutable objects.

TypeError: 'tuple' object does not support item assignment
```

Tips

One of the key differences between tuples and lists in Python is that tuples are 'immutable objects', which means they cannot be changed after they are created. Lists, on the other hand, are 'mutable objects' and can be modified even after their creation.

In[8]
```
myList=[1,3,5,7,2]
myList[2]=100
myList
```

Out[8]   [1, 3, 100, 7, 2]

Tips

In this case, no exception is raised when performing certain operations because a 'list' is a mutable object in Python, allowing modifications without causing errors.

In[9]
```
myTuple=1,3,5,7,2
myTuple[2:5]
```

Out[9]   (5, 7, 2)

Notes

Similar to lists, tuples support slicing operations because both are *sequence* types in Python.

In[10]
```
myTuple=1,3,5,7,2
len(myTuple)
```

Out[10]   5

Tips

To calculate the length of a tuple in Python, you can use the built-in function, *len( )*.

In[11]
```
myTuple=1,3,5,7,2
print(sorted(myTuple))
```

Out[11]   [1, 2, 3, 5, 7]

Notes

To sort tuples in Python, you can use the built-in function *sorted()*.

Tips

The *sorted()* function in Python returns a new result that is of type 'list', not 'tuple'.

In[12]
```
myTuple=1,3,5,7,2
myTuple.sort()
```

Out[12]
```
---------------------------------------------------------------------------
AttributeError                            Traceback (most recent call last)
<ipython-input-12-d7b571f24488> in <module>
      1 myTuple=1,3,5,7,2
----> 2 myTuple.sort()
      3  #   Why that exception: Tuples do not have the method.
AttributeError: 'tuple' object has no attribute 'sort'
```

Notes

Unlike lists, tuples in Python do not have a *sort()* method. This is because tuples are immutable objects and the *sort()* method would require changing the original object itself, which is not possible with tuples.

Tips

The code myTuple.sort() causes an error because tuples in Python do not have a sort() method, given their immutability.

In[13]
```
myTuple=1,3,5,7,2
5 in myTuple
```

Out[13]   True

Tips

The in operator can be used with tuples in Python to check if a specific value exists within the tuple. For example, 5 in myTuple checks if the number 5 is an element of the myTuple tuple.

In[14]
```
myTuple=1,3,5,7,2
myTuple.count(11)
```

Out[14]   0

To count the frequency of an element in a tuple, you can use the *count( )* method. For instance, myTuple.count(11) counts the occurrences of the value 11 in the *myTuple* tuple.

Tips

In[15]
```
myTuple=1,3,5,7,2
x1,x2,x3,x4,x5=myTuple
x2
```

Out[15]   3

In Python, the rule for unpacking tuples is 'assignment by position'. This means that variables are assigned to the corresponding values in the tuple based on their positions.

Tips

2.11.3 Basic usage

In[16]
```
x,y,z =1,2,3
print(x,y,z)
```

Out[16]   1 2 3

Unpacking assignment is a special method in Python where variables are assigned values from a collection (like a list or tuple) directly in a single line of code.

Tips

In[17]
```
myTuple=(1,5,6,3,4)
print(myTuple)
print(len(myTuple))
print(max(myTuple))
```

Out[17]   (1, 5, 6, 3, 4)
         5
         6

In Python, a tuple is typically represented by 'parentheses and commas'. However, the parentheses can be omitted, and the presence of the comma is what primarily defines a tuple.

Tips

In[18]
```
myTuple=(11,12,13,12,11,11)
a1,a2,a3,a4,a5,a6=myTuple
a3
```

Out[18]   13

In Python, tuples support the feature of unpacking assignment, which allows for the assignment of tuple values to a corresponding set of variables in a single line of code.

Tips

In[19]
```
myTuple=(11,12,13,12,11,11)
myTuple.count(11)
```

Out[19]   3

Counting the frequency of value 11 in the *myTuple* tuple.

Tips

2.11.4 Tuples in data science

In[20]
```
def func(args1,*args2):
    print(args1)
    print(args2)
func("a","b","c","d","e","f")
```

Out[20]   a
('b', 'c', 'd', 'e', 'f')

In Python, a tuple used as a formal parameter with a '*' prefix in function definition means that the function can receive a variable number of actual arguments. These arguments are collected into a tuple.

Tips

In[21]
```
def func(args1,**args2):
    print(args1)
    print(args2)
func("a",x1="b",x2="c",x3="d",x4="e",x5="f")
```

Out[21]   a
{'x1': 'b', 'x2': 'c', 'x3': 'd', 'x4': 'e', 'x5': 'f'}

In Python, the '' operator is used to represent a tuple, while the '**' operator is used to represent a dictionary. The '' operator unpacks elements into a tuple, and the '**' operator unpacks key-value pairs into a dictionary.

Tips

In a dictionary, the keys must be explicitly present in the actual parameters, such as x1, x2.

Notes

In[22]
```
def func():
  return 1,2,3,4,5
func()
```
Out[22]   (1, 2, 3, 4, 5)

In Python, the return value of many functions is often a tuple because the syntax 'return 1, 2, 3' is equivalent to 'return (1, 2, 3)'. This shorthand allows multiple values to be returned as a tuple without explicitly using parentheses.

Tips

In[23]
```
1,2
```
Out[23]   (1, 2)

For example, (1, 2, 3) represents a *tuple* of three elements, while 1, 2, 3 without parentheses would be treated as separate values rather than a *tuple*.

Notes

It's important to note that the parentheses are not part of the tuple itself; they are added for clarity and readability.

Tips

In[24]
```
x=1
y=2
x,y=y,x
print(x,y)
```
Out[24]   2 1

In Python, swapping the values of two variables can be achieved using tuples. This is commonly known as "tuple unpacking".

Tricks

For more details, please refer to [2.5.5 Swap Two Variables].

Tips

2.12 Strings

Q&A

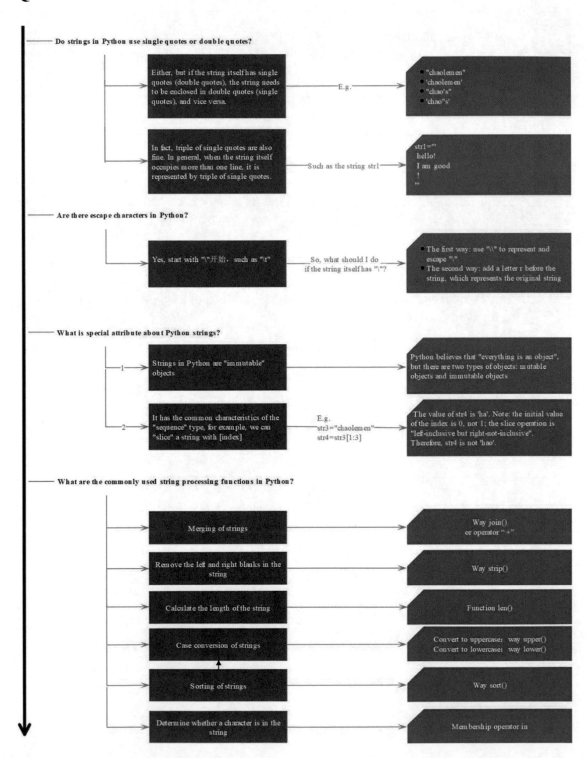

Do strings in Python use single quotes or double quotes?

Either, but if the string itself has single quotes (double quotes), the string needs to be enclosed in double quotes (single quotes), and vice versa.

E.g.

- "chaolemen"
- 'chaolemen'
- "chao's"
- 'chao"s'

In fact, triple of single quotes are also fine. In general, when the string itself occupies more than one line, it is represented by triple of single quotes.

Such as the string str1

str1='''
hello!
I am good
!
'''

Are there escape characters in Python?

Yes, start with "\"开始，such as "\t"

So, what should I do if the string itself has "\"?

- The first way: use "\\" to represent and escape "\"
- The second way: add a letter r before the string, which represents the original string

What is special attribute about Python strings?

1 Strings in Python are "immutable" objects

Python believes that "everything is an object", but there are two types of objects: mutable objects and immutable objects

2 It has the common characteristics of the "sequence" type, for example, we can "slice" a string with [index]

E.g.
str3="chaolemen"
str4=str3[1:3]

The value of str4 is 'ha'. Note: the initial value of the index is 0, not 1; the slice operation is "left-inclusive but right-not-inclusive". Therefore, str4 is not 'hao'.

What are the commonly used string processing functions in Python?

Merging of strings → Way join() or operator "+"

Remove the left and right blanks in the string → Way strip()

Calculate the length of the string → Function len()

Case conversion of strings → Convert to uppercase: way upper() Convert to lowercase: way lower()

Sorting of strings → Way sort()

Determine whether a character is in the string → Membership operator in

2.12.1 Defining strings

In[1]
```
print('abc')
print("abc")
```
Out[1] abc
        abc

Unlike in C and Java, the concepts of 'character' and 'string' are more closely unified in Python, resulting in fewer practical distinctions between them. In Python, a character is typically represented as a string of length 1, which allows it to be treated as a special case of a string.

Tips

Strings can be enclosed either with single quotes or double quotes in Python.

Tips

In[2]
```
print("abc'de'f")
```
Out[2] abc'de'f

When the string itself contains single quotes, it should be enclosed with double quotes, and vice versa.

Tips

In this case, the argument of the *print()* function is enclosed within single quotes.

Notes

In[3]
```
print('abc"de"f')
```
Out[3] abc"de"f

In this case, when using the *print()* function, the output is enclosed within double quotes.

Notes

In[4]
```
str1='''
Hello
world
!
'''
str1
```
Out[4] '\n Hello \n world \n !\n'

Triple quotes can also be used in Python to indicate strings with newlines. For more details, please refer to the official Python documentation on string literals.

Tips

2.12.2 Main features

In[5]
```
str1[1:4]="2222"
# Why that exception: TypeError: 'str' object does not support item assignment
```

Out[5]
```
---------------------------------------------------------------------------
TypeError                                 Traceback (most recent call last)
<ipython-input-5-d80a51ea9762> in <module>()
      1
----> 2 str1[1:4]="2222"
      3 # Why that exception: TypeError: 'str' object does not support item assignment
TypeError: 'str' object does not support item assignment
```

The first feature: Strings in Python are "immutable objects".

Tips

In[6]
```
str1="abc"
str1="defghijk"
str1[1:4]
```

Out[6] 'efg'

The execution of the above code will not raise an error, because Python is a dynamically typed language. Please refer to [2.2.2 Dynamically Typed Language].

Tips

"Immutable object" means that the value of the object cannot be altered locally, and "dynamically typed language" is a different concept from "Immutable object".

Notes

The second feature of strings in Python is that they are considered 'sequences'. This means that all operators and functions that support sequences can be used with strings. For instance, strings in Python support operations like slicing, which allows you to extract portions of a string by specifying a range of indices.

Tips

In[7] `'clm'[0:2]`

Out[7] 'cl'

Strings in Python support the operation of slicing. The rule for slicing is that it includes the beginning index but excludes the ending index. For example, when slicing a string, the resulting substring will include the element at index 0 but not the element at index 2.

Tips

In[8]
```
str3="chaolemen"
str4=str3[1:3]
str4
```
Out[8] 'ha'

In[9]
```
"chaolemen"[:6]
```
Out[9] 'chaole'

2.12.3 String operations

In[10]
```
'-'.join(['c', 'l'])
```
Out[10] 'c-l'

String concatenation in Python refers to the process of combining multiple strings into a single string. It is commonly achieved using the '+' operator or the 'str.join()' method.

Tips

In[11]
```
'c' + 'lm'
```
Out[11] 'clm'

In[12]
```
"chaolemen ".strip()
```
Out[12] 'chaolemen'

Removing whitespaces at the beginning and end of a string, such as spaces, newlines.

Tips

In[13]
```
'c' in 'clm'
```
Out[13] True

To check if a character or string appears within another string in Python, you can use the in keyword.

Tips

In[14]
```
len('clm')
```
Out[14] 3

Tips

To calculate the length of a string in Python, you can use the built-in function len().

In[15]
```
print(ord('A'))
print(chr(97))
```
Out[15]   65
          a

Tips

In Python, you can use the built-in function ord() to obtain the Unicode value of a character.

Notes

The built-in function *chr( )* in Python is indeed the counterpart of the *ord( )* function. It takes a Unicode value as an argument and returns the corresponding character string.

In[16]
```
print(ord('朝'))
print(chr(26397))
```
Out[16]   26397
          朝

Tips

By importing the sys module and calling the sys.getdefaultencoding() function from it, you can obtain the default character encoding used in Python.

In[17]
```
s='a\tbbc'
s
```
Out[17]   'a\tbbc'

Tips

Escape character.

In[18]   `print(s)`
Out[18]   a   bbc

Notes

When a string contains 'escape characters', there is a difference between the output of s and print(s). The difference is that the former does not interpret or process the escape characters, while the latter does perform the necessary escaping and displays the string accordingly.

In[19] `str(1234567)`

Out[19] `'1234567'`

Tips

The integer can be converted into a string using the *str()* function.

In[20] `"abc".upper()`

Out[20] `'ABC'`

Tips

To convert uppercase characters to lowercase, you can use the *lower()* method. Conversely, to convert lowercase characters to uppercase, you can use the *upper()* method.

Tips

When working with special characters and path strings in Python, it is important to be mindful of certain issues. For example, assigning a path string to a variable, such as s1 = "E:\SparkR\My\T", can lead to unexpected behavior due to the interpretation of backslashes as escape characters.

In[21] `s1="E:\SparkR\My\T"`
`s1`

Out[21] `'E:\\SparkR\\My\\T'`

Tips

In the Jupyter notebook, printing the string s1 directly is different from the output of the built-in function *print()*.

In[22] `s1=r"http://www.chaolemen.org"`
`s1`

Out[22] `'http://www.chaolemen.org'`

Notes

In Python, strings prefixed with r or R, such as r'...' or r"...", are referred to as raw strings.

Raw strings treat backslashes (\) as literal characters instead of escape characters. This means that they preserve the original backslashes and do not interpret them as escape sequences.

Tricks

Raw strings are commonly used when dealing with regular expressions, file paths, or any situation where backslashes need to be handled as literal characters.

Tips

In Python 3, the use of Unicode string literals (string literals prefixed by u) is no longer necessary. While they are still valid, they are primarily maintained for compatibility purposes with Python 2.

In[23]
```
sepStr = "-"
iterObj = ("a", "b", "c")
sepStr.join(iterObj)
```
Out[23]   'a-b-c'

Tips

The join() method in Python returns a string by concatenating all the elements of an iterable object (iterObj), separated by a specified string separator (sepStr). For more detailed information about iterable objects, please refer to the relevant sections on iterators and generators in the appropriate Python documentation.

Notes

The argument of the join() method in Python is a sequence, and the variable before the dot (referred to as seq_str here) represents the separator. The join() method concatenates all the elements of the sequence, using seq_str as the separator between them.

In[24]
```
str1=["abc","aaba","adefg","bb","c"]
str1.sort()
str1
```
Out[24]   ['aaba', 'abc', 'adefg', 'bb', 'c']

Tips

In Python, you can use the *set( )* function to convert a string into a set data structure.

In[28]
```
print("set(str1)=",set(str1))
```
Out[28]   set(str1)= {'c', 'adefg', 'bb', 'abc', 'aaba'}

Notes

The *re* module in Python provides support for regular expressions, including regular expression syntax, pattern matching, and various operations for working with patterns. It offers powerful tools for pattern matching, searching, substitution, and other advanced operations involving text processing based on regular expressions.

In[29]
```
import re
p1 = re.compile('[a-dA-D]')
r1 = p1.findall('chaolemen@ruc.edu.cn')
r1
```
Out[29]   ['c', 'a', 'c', 'd', 'c']

Tips

Useful functions of the re module:

- re.compile(): Compile a regular expression pattern into a regular expression object,,which can be used for matching using its findall(), search() and other methods.
- re.findall(): Return all non-overlapping matches of pattern in string, as a list of strings or tuples
- re.search(): Scan through string looking for the first location where the regular expression pattern produces a match, and return a corresponding match object.

Notes

The syntax of regular expressions in Python can be found in the official documentation. For Python 3, the documentation can be accessed at: https://docs.python.org/3/library/re.html.

2.13 Sequences

Q&A

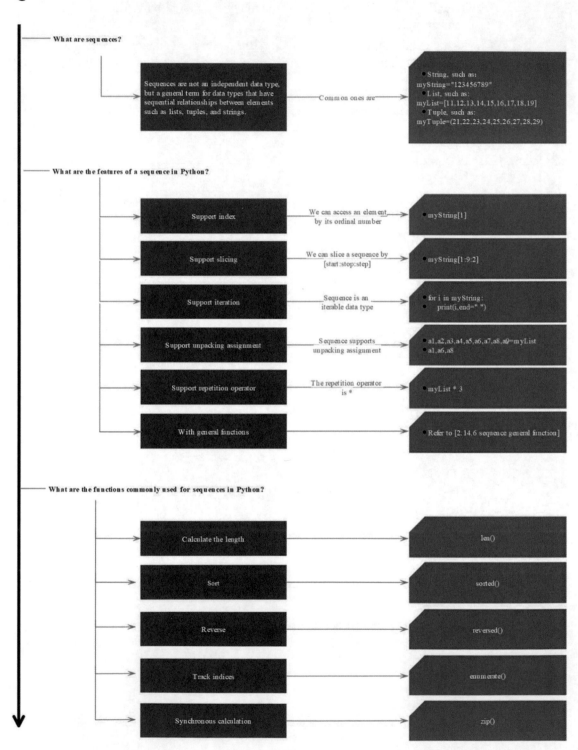

2.13.1 Indexing

Notes

In Python, a sequence is a positionally ordered collection of items
There are three basic sequence types: lists, tuples, and range objects

In[1]
```
myString="123456789"
myString[1]
```
Out[1] '2'

Tips

An element of sequence can be accessed by index/subscript.

In[2]
```
myList=[11,12,13,14,15,16,17,18,19]
myList[1]
```
Out[2] 12

In[3]
```
myTuple=(21,22,23,24,25,26,27,28,29)
myTuple[1]
```
Out[3] 22

2.13.2 Slicing

In[4]
```
myString="123456789"
myString[1:9:2]
```
Out[4] '2468'

Tips

Slicing can be used through [start: stop: step]. For further details, please refer to [2.10 Lists]

In[5]
```
myList=[11,12,13,14,15,16,17,18,19]
myList[1:9:2]
```
Out[5] [12, 14, 16, 18]

In[6]
```
myTuple=(21,22,23,24,25,26,27,28,29)
myTuple[1:9:2]
```
Out[6] (22, 24, 26, 28)

2.13.3 Iteration

In[7]
```
myString="123456789"
for i in myString:
    print(i,end=" ")
```

Out[7]   1 2 3 4 5 6 7 8 9

A sequence is an example of an iterable data type that can be iterated over using the for statement in Python.

Tips

In[8]
```
myList=[11,12,13,14,15,16,17,18,19]
for i in myList:
    print(i,end=" ")
```

Out[8]   11 12 13 14 15 16 17 18 19

In[9]
```
myTuple=(21,22,23,24,25,26,27,28,29)
for i in myTuple:
    print(i,end=" ")
```

Out[9]   21 22 23 24 25 26 27 28 29

2.13.4 Unpacking

In[10]
```
myString="123456789"
a1,a2,a3,a4,a5,a6,a7,a8,a9=myString
a1,a2,a3,a4,a5,a6,a7,a8,a9
```

Out[10]   ('1', '2', '3', '4', '5', '6', '7', '8', '9')

Sequences support "unpacking assignment", sometimes called "parallel assignment". The rule of assignment is "assigned by positions".

Tips

In[11]
```
myList=[11,12,13,14,15,16,17,18,19]
a1,a2,a3,a4,a5,a6,a7,a8,a9=myList
a1,a2,a3,a4,a5,a6,a7,a8,a9
```

Out[11]   (11, 12, 13, 14, 15, 16, 17, 18, 19)

In[12]
```
myTuple=(21,22,23,24,25,26,27,28,29)
a1,a2,a3,a4,a5,a6,a7,a8,a9=myTuple
a1,a2,a3,a4,a5,a6,a7,a8,a9
```

Out[12]   (21, 22, 23, 24, 25, 26, 27, 28, 29)

2.13.5 Repeat operator

In[13]
```
myString="123456789"
myString * 3
```

Out[13] '123456789123456789123456789'

The multiplication operator of sequences is *.

Tips

Notes

In Python, the * operator, when used with a sequence, performs a "repeat operation" rather than a "multiplication" operation. This means that the sequence is repeated a certain number of times to create a new sequence.

In[14]
```
myList=[11,12,13,14,15,16,17,18,19]
myList * 3
```

Out[14] [11,
12,
13,
14,
15,
16,
17,
18,
19,
11,
12,
13,
14,
15,
16,
17,
18,
19,
11,
12,
13,
14,
15,
16,
17,
18,
19]

```
In[15]   myTuple=(21,22,23,24,25,26,27,28,29)
         myTuple * 3
```

```
Out[15]  (21,
          22,
          23,
          24,
          25,
          26,
          27,
          28,
          29,
          21,
          22,
          23,
          24,
          25,
          26,
          27,
          28,
          29,
          21,
          22,
          23,
          24,
          25,
          26,
          27,
          28,
          29)
```

2.13.6 Basic Functions

```
In[16]   myString="123456789"
         myList=[11,12,13,14,15,16,17,18,19]
         myTuple=(21,22,23,24,25,26,27,28,29)
         len(myString),len(myList),len(myTuple)
```

```
Out[16]  (9, 9, 9)
```

Notes	In Python, all objects of "sequence", regardless of their data type (such as lists, tuples, strings), support common functions.

| Tips | In Python, the built-in function *len( )* is used to calculate the length of sequences. This function can be applied to various sequence types, such as lists, tuples, and strings, to determine the number of elements they contain. |

In[17] | sorted(myString),sorted(myList),sorted(myTuple)

Out[17] (['1', '2', '3', '4', '5', '6', '7', '8', '9'],
[11, 12, 13, 14, 15, 16, 17, 18, 19],
[21, 22, 23, 24, 25, 26, 27, 28, 29])

Tips

In Python, the *sorted( )* function is used to sort sequences. It takes an iterable as input and returns a new sorted list containing the elements of the original sequence.

In[18] | reversed(myString),reversed(myList),reversed(myTuple)

Out[18] (<reversed at 0x15bad2819a0>,
<list_reverseiterator at 0x15bad281070>,
<reversed at 0x15bad2d6af0>)

Tips

In Python, the *reversed()* function is used to reverse sequences. It takes an iterable as input and returns a reverse iterator object that can be converted into a reversed sequence or used in a loop.

In[19] | list(reversed(myString))

Out[19] ['9', '8', '7', '6', '5', '4', '3', '2', '1']

Notes

What the *reversed()* function returns is an iterator, which supports lazy evaluation, and can be converted into a list using the built-in function *list( )*.

In[20] | enumerate(myString),enumerate(myList),enumerate(myTuple)

Out[20] (<enumerate at 0x15bad2d1280>,
<enumerate at 0x15bad2cb500>,
<enumerate at 0x15bad2cb300>)

Tips

In Python, the *enumerate()* function is used to track and enumerate indexes while iterating over a sequence. It returns an iterator that generates pairs of index and value for each element in the sequence.

In[21] | list(enumerate(myString))

Out[21] [(0, '1'),
(1, '2'),
(2, '3'),
(3, '4'),
(4, '5'),
(5, '6'),
(6, '7'),
(7, '8'),
(8, '9')]

Notes   The *enumerate( )* function returns an iterator that can be converted to a list using *list( )*.

In[22]   `zip(myList,myTuple)`

Out[22]   `<zip at 0x15bad2d7600>`

Tips   In Python, the *zip( )* function is used to aggregate elements from two or more iterables into tuples. It takes multiple iterables as input and returns an iterator that generates tuples containing elements from each iterable, paired together.

In[23]   `list(zip(myList,myTuple))`

Out[23]   `[(11, 21),`
         `(12, 22),`
         `(13, 23),`
         `(14, 24),`
         `(15, 25),`
         `(16, 26),`
         `(17, 27),`
         `(18, 28),`
         `(19, 29)]`

Notes   The built-in function *zip( )* returns an iterator, which can be converted into a list using another built-in function list(). For details, please refer to [3.1 Iterators and Decorators].

Tips   In contrast with list, tuple, set, and dictionary, "sequence" is not an independent data type in Python, but a general term for multiple data types including list, tuple, and string.

2.14 Sets

Q&A

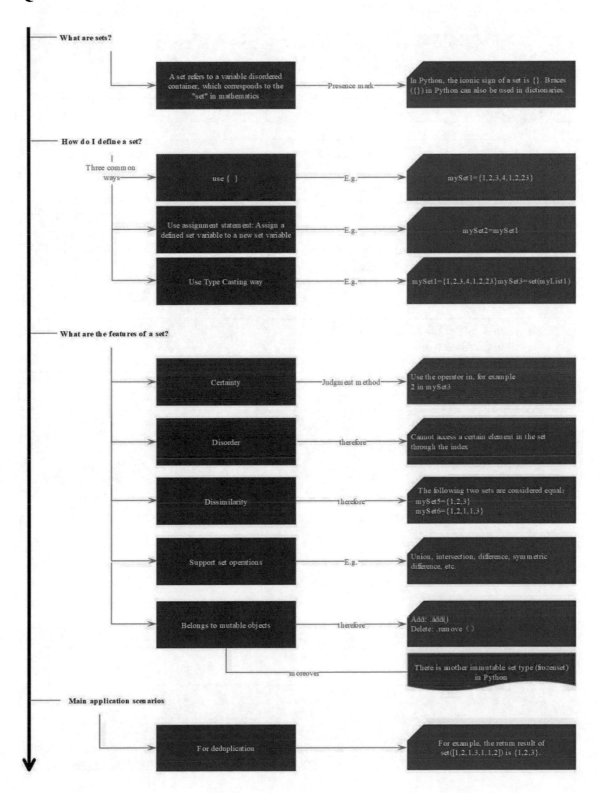

What are sets?

A set refers to a variable disordered container, which corresponds to the "set" in mathematics

— Presence mark → In Python, the iconic sign of a set is {}. Braces ({}) in Python can also be used in dictionaries.

How do I define a set?

Three common ways

use { } — E.g. → mySet1={1,2,3,4,1,2,23}

Use assignment statement: Assign a defined set variable to a new set variable — E.g. → mySet2=mySet1

Use Type Casting way — E.g. → mySet1={1,2,3,4,1,2,23}mySet3=set(myList1)

What are the features of a set?

Certainty — Judgment method → Use the operator in, for example 2 in mySet3

Disorder — therefore → Cannot access a certain element in the set through the index

Dissimilarity — therefore → The following two sets are considered equal: mySet5={1,2,3} mySet6={1,2,1,1,3}

Support set operations — E.g. → Union, intersection, difference, symmetric difference, etc.

Belongs to mutable objects — therefore → Add: .add() Delete: .remove ( )

— moreover → There is another immutable set type (frozenset) in Python

Main application scenarios

For deduplication → For example, the return result of set([1,2,1,3,1,1,2]) is {1,2,3}.

2.14.1 Defining sets

In[1]
```
mySet1={1,2,3,4,1,2,23}
mySet1
```

Out[1]   {1, 2, 3, 4, 23}

In Python, there are several methods to define sets. The first method involves directly defining a set using braces { }.

From this definition, it's clear that a set is essentially an unordered data structure consisting only of values with no keys.

Tips

In[2]
```
mySet2=mySet1
mySet2
```

Out[2]   {1, 2, 3, 4, 23}

The second method: use the assignment statement to assign values to new set variables from pre-existing defined set variables.

Tips

In[3]
```
myList1=[1,2,3,3,2,2,1,1]
mySet3=set(myList1)
mySet3
```

Out[3]   {1, 2, 3}

The third method: use the *set()* function to convert objects of other types into a set object.

Tips

In[4]
```
mySet4=set("chaolemen")
mySet4
```

Out[4]   {'a', 'c', 'e', 'h', 'l', 'm', 'n', 'o'}

2.14.2 Main features

In[5]
```
2 in mySet3
```

Out[5]   True

A key feature of a set is certainty: for any given set and any specific element, that element either belongs to the set or it does not. There is no ambiguity permitted.

Tips

```
In[6]   mySet4[2]
```

```
Out[6]   ----------------------------------------------------------------------
         TypeError                               Traceback (most recent call last)
         <ipython-input-6-78241c857f8a> in <module>
             1  # Unordered
             2  # The elements in the sets are unordered, so the elements in the
                # set cannot be accessed with indexes
         ----> 3  mySet4[2]  # Why that exception: TypeError: 'set' object does not support
                # indexing

         TypeError: 'set' object is not subscriptable
```

Tips

Unordered: The elements in sets are unordered, meaning they don't have a specific arrangement. Therefore, in Python, it's not possible to use indices to access elements within a set.

Notes

TypeError: 'set' object does not support indexing.
The reason of error: The set is disordered and can't be indexed.

```
In[7]   mySet5={1,2,3}
        mySet6={1,2,1,1,3}
        mySet5==mySet6
```

```
Out[7]   True
```

Tips

Uniqueness: The elements in a set are distinct from each other, meaning each element appears only once. Therefore, in Python, two sets with the same elements, regardless of their order, are considered equal.

2.14.3 Basic operations

```
In[8]    mySet7={1,3,5,10}
         mySet8={2,4,6,10}
```

```
In[9]    # Include
         3 in mySet7
```

```
Out[9]   True
```

```
In[10]   # Not include
         3 not in mySet7
```

```
Out[10]  False
```

```
In[11]   # Equal to
         mySet7 == mySet8
```

```
Out[11]  False
```

In[12]
```
# Not equal to
mySet7 != mySet8
```

Out[12]   True

In[13]
```
# Subset
{1,5} < mySet7
```

Out[13]   True

In[14]
```
# Union
mySet7|mySet8
```

Out[14]   {1, 2, 3, 4, 5, 6, 10}

In[15]
```
# Intersection
mySet7&mySet8
```

Out[15]   {10}

In[16]
```
# Difference
mySet7-mySet8
```

Out[16]   {1, 3, 5}

In[17]
```
# Symmetric difference
mySet7^mySet8
```

Out[17]   {1, 2, 3, 4, 5, 6}

In[18]
```
#To check whether one set is a subset of another set in Python
print({1,3}.issubset(mySet7))
```

Out[18]   True

In[19]
```
#To check whether one set is a superset of another set in Python
print({1,3,2,4}.issuperset(mySet7))
```

Out[19]   False

In[20]
```
mySet9={1,2,3,4}
mySet9.add(4)
mySet9.remove(1)
mySet9
```

Out[20]   {2, 3, 4}

Tips

In Python, there are two types of sets: set and frozenset.

The set type is mutable, meaning that after its creation, you can modify it by adding, removing, or changing elements.

In[21]
```
mySet10=frozenset({1,2,3,4})
mySet10
```

Out[21]   frozenset({1, 2, 3, 4})

The *frozenset* is an immutable type of set in Python. This means that once a frozenset is created, it cannot be modified – you can't add or remove elements from it.

Tips

In data science projects, to safeguard data from unintentional modifications during the analysis process, we typically employ immutable objects.

Notes

In[22] `mySet10.add(5)`

Out[22] --
AttributeError   Traceback (most recent call last)
<ipython-input-22-d051a89f1878> in <module>
----> 1 mySet10.add(5) # Why that exception: AttributeError: 'frozenset' object has no attribute 'add'

AttributeError: 'frozenset' object has no attribute 'add'

In Python, trying to modify a *frozenset* object, such as adding or removing elements, will raise an error since frozenset is an immutable object.

Notes

2.14.4 Sets and data science

In[23]
```python
myList=["d","a","t","a"]
mySet11=set(myList)
mySet11
```

Out[23] `{'a', 'd', 't'}`

Due to the uniqueness of elements in sets, they are commonly used to perform deduplication operations in data analysis and data science projects.

Tips

Python supports single-line expressions for certain constructs, commonly used as follows:

1. Single-line if statements, using ternary operators. Refer to section [2.7 If statements].
2. Single-line for statements, using list comprehensions. Refer to section [2.10 Lists].
3. Single-line function definitions, using lambda functions. Refer to section [2.20 Lambda functions].

These methods offer concise alternatives to their respective standard, multi-line constructs.

Notes

2.15 Dictionaries

Q&A

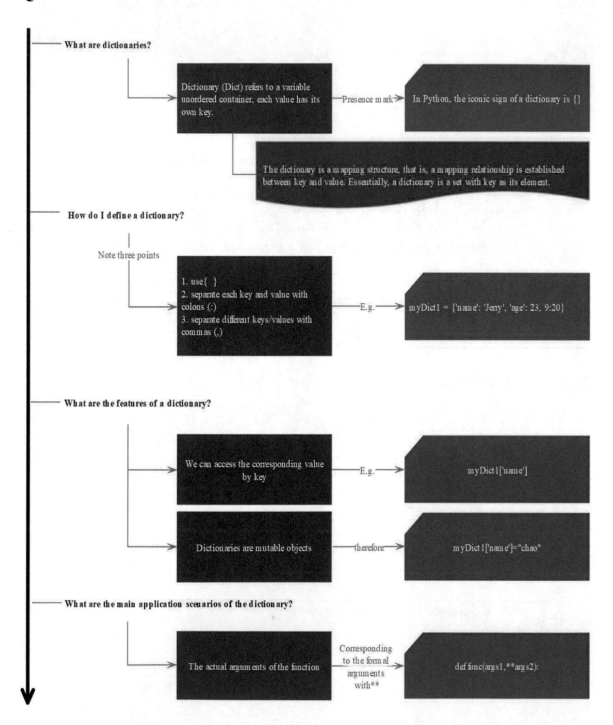

What are dictionaries?

Dictionary (Dict) refers to a variable unordered container, each value has its own key.

Presence mark → In Python, the iconic sign of a dictionary is {}

The dictionary is a mapping structure, that is, a mapping relationship is established between key and value. Essentially, a dictionary is a set with key as its element.

How do I define a dictionary?

Note three points

1. use{ }
2. separate each key and value with colons (:)
3. separate different keys/values with commas (,)

E.g. → myDict1 = {'name': 'Jerry', 'age': 23, 9:20}

What are the features of a dictionary?

We can access the corresponding value by key

E.g. → myDict1['name']

Dictionaries are mutable objects

therefore → myDict1['name']="chao"

What are the main application scenarios of the dictionary?

The actual arguments of the function

Corresponding to the formal arguments with** → def func(args1,**args2):

2.15.1 Defining dictionaries

Notes

A dictionary (dict) is a mapping structure, which is an unordered container where each key maps to its own value.

In[1] myDict1 = {'name': 'Jerry', 'age': 23,9:20}
       myDict1

Out[1] {'name': 'Jerry', 'age': 23, 9: 20}

Tips

A dictionary in Python is more equivalent to a named list in R.

Notes

When defining a dictionary in Python, you should:
1. Use braces { }.
2. Separate keys and values with a colon (:).
3. Separate different key-value pairs with a comma (,).

In[2] myDict3={"grade":2,"gender":"M","grade":15,"grade":5}
       myDict3

Out[2] {'grade': 5, 'gender': 'M'}

Tips

In Python dictionaries, duplicate keys are not allowed. If you provide duplicate keys, the value of the last key will be preserved, effectively overwriting previous assignments to that key.

2.15.2 Accessing dictionary items

Notes

We can access the items of a dictionary by referring to its key name.

In[3] myDict1['name']

Out[3] 'Jerry'

Notes

In Python, if the key of a dictionary is a string, it must be enclosed in single or double quotes. If the quotes are omitted, Python will interpret the key as a variable name. If there's no variable with such a name, Python will raise a NameError.

In[4]   `myDict1[name]`

Out[4]   --
NameError   Traceback (most recent call last)
<ipython-input-1-9f850ce95d5e> in <module>
    1 myDict2={2:2,2:3,4:5}
----> 2 myDict2[name]

NameError: name 'name' is not defined

Tips

There are two distinct approaches to correct this:

1. Enclose it in quotes, e.g.,   my_dict1['name'].

2. Declare it first, e.g.,
    a = 'name'
    my_dict1[a]

Notes

In Python, you can change the value of a specific item in a dictionary by referring to its key name and assigning a new value to it.

In[5]   `myDict1 = {'name': 'Jerry', 'age': 23,9:20}`
`myDict1['name']="chao"`
`myDict1`

Out[5]   {'name': 'chao', 'age': 23, 9: 20}

Tips

In Python, dictionary keys must be hashable. An object is considered hashable if it maintains a constant hash value throughout its lifetime. Immutable data types, such as tuple, frozenset, str, bytes, and numeric types, are all hashable. Note, however, that a tuple is considered hashable only if all its elements are hashable.

In[6]   `dct3={[2,3]:[4,4], 5:5}`

Out[6]   --
TypeError   Traceback (most recent call last)
<ipython-input-7-36fc453a24ae> in <module>
----> 1 dct3={[2,3]:[4,4], 5:5}

TypeError: unhashable type: 'list'

Tips

Here, the key [2,3] is a list (unhashable objects) so that the unhashable type error was raised.

| Tricks | In Python, a TypeError will be raised when an unhashable data type is used in code that requires hashable data. |

2.15.3 Dictionary and data science

In[7]
```python
def func(args1,**args2):
    print(args1)
    print(args2)
func("a",x1="b",x2="c",x3="d",x4="e",x5="f")
```

Out[7]   a
{'x1': 'b', 'x2': 'c', 'x3': 'd', 'x4': 'e', 'x5': 'f'}

| Tips | Dictionaries are widely utilized in data science projects for various purposes, including but not limited to storing temporary data, such as function arguments using **args. However, dictionaries have broader applications in tasks like data preprocessing, feature engineering, configuration parameter storage, categorical variable mapping, and efficient data retrieval. |

| Notes | In the formal parameters of a function, the parameters prefixed with * and ** respectively represent the formal parameters for receiving variable-length tuples (values without keys) and dictionaries (values with keys) as actual parameters. |

| Tips | In Python, when passing a dictionary as an actual parameter to a function, you must explicitly specify the corresponding key in the function call. This ensures that the function receives the correct value associated with the desired key from the dictionary. |

2.16 Functions

Q&A

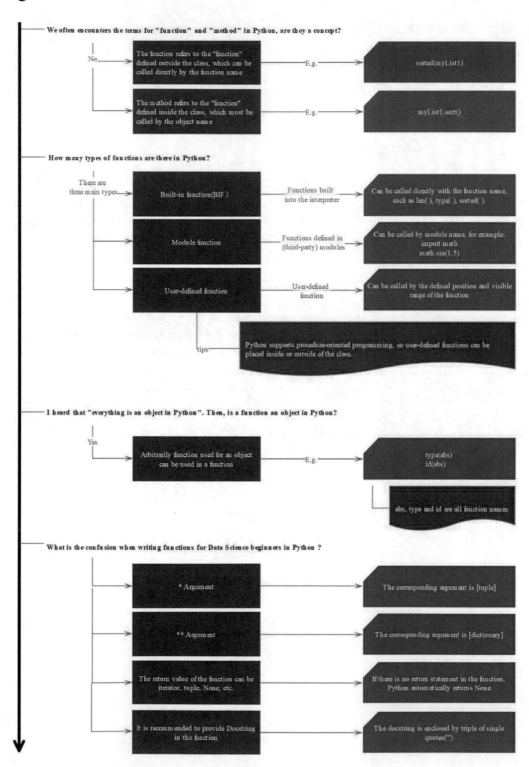

We often encounters the terms for "function" and "method" in Python, are they a concept?

No — The function refers to the "function" defined outside the class, which can be called directly by the function name — E.g. → sorted(myList1)

The method refers to the "function" defined inside the class, which must be called by the object name — E.g. → myList1.sort()

How many types of functions are there in Python?

There are three main types

Built-in function(BIF) — Functions built into the interpreter → Can be called directly with the function name, such as len( ), type( ), sorted( ).

Module function — Functions defined in (third-party) modules → Can be called by module name, for example: import math math.sin(1.5)

User-defined function — User-defined function → Can be called by the defined position and visible range of the function

tips — Python supports procedure-oriented programming, so user-defined functions can be placed inside or outside of the class.

I heard that "everything is an object in Python". Then, is a function an object in Python?

Yes → Arbitrarily function used for an object can be used in a function — E.g. → type(abs) id(abs)

abs, type and id are all function names

What is the confusion when writing functions for Data Science beginners in Python ?

* Argument → The corresponding argument is [tuple]

** Argument → The corresponding argument is [dictionary]

The return value of the function can be iterator, tuple, None, etc. → If there is no return statement in the function, Python automatically returns None

It is recommended to provide Docstring in the function → The docstring is enclosed by triple of single quotes(''')

2.16.1 Built-in functions

In[1]
```
i=20
type(i)
```
Out[1] int

Notes

There are three types of functions in Python: built-in functions, functions inside modules, and user-defined functions.

User-defined functions can be written as single-line functions, known as "lambda functions".

User-defined functions can be defined both inside and outside a class. This is because Python supports both object-oriented programming and procedural programming paradigms.

Tips

A built-in function (BIF) refers to a function that is included as part of the Python programming language. These functions are built into the Python interpreter and can be called directly by their function name.

Notes

For more details, please refer to [2.17 Built-in Functions].

2.16.2 Module Functions

In[2]
```
import math as mt
mt.sin(1.5)
```
Out[2] 0.9974949866040544

Tips

A function inside a module, also known as a module function, refers to a function that is defined within a Python module. To call a module function, you first need to import the module to which it belongs, and then you can use its name to invoke the function.

Notes

For more details, please refer to [2.18 Module functions].

2.16.3 User-defined functions

In[3]
```
def myFunc():
    j=0
    print('hello world')
myFunc()
```
Out[3] hello world

User-defined function" refers to a function defined by the user, allowing us to define custom functions in Python. These functions can be called directly by their function name, once they have been defined.

Tips

To define a user-defined function in Python, you use the def keyword. This keyword is followed by the name of the function, parentheses for any parameters, and a colon to indicate the start of the function block.

Notes

For more details, please refer to [2.19 User-defined functions].

Notes

In Python, user-defined functions can be written as single-line functions called "lambda functions." For more information, please refer to [2.20 Lambda functions].

Tips

Python supports both object-oriented and procedural programming paradigms. As a result, user-defined functions can be defined both inside or outside of a class. When defined inside a class, they are referred to as "methods," while functions defined outside of a class are simply called "functions." It is important for beginners to understand and distinguish between the concepts of "function" and "method." For more information, please refer to [3.9 Object-oriented programming].

Notes

2.17 Built-in functions

Q&A

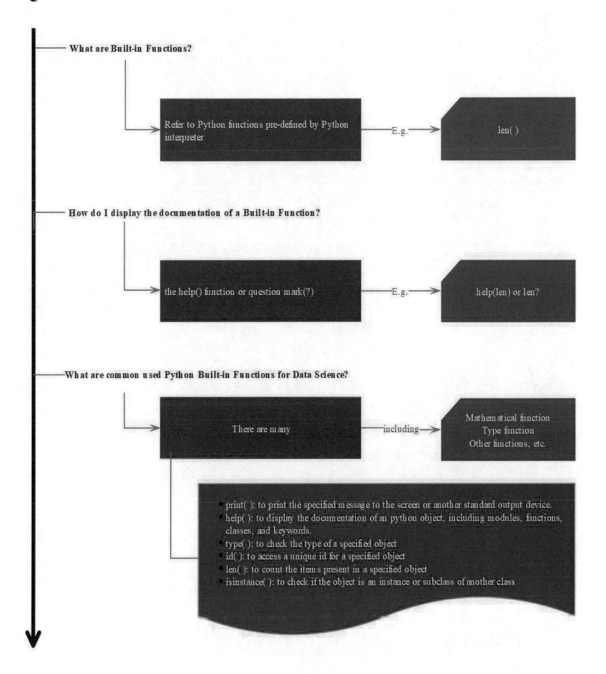

What are Built-in Functions?

Refer to Python functions pre-defined by Python interpreter

E.g. → len( )

How do I display the documentation of a Built-in Function?

the help() function or question mark(?)

E.g. → help(len) or len?

What are common used Python Built-in Functions for Data Science?

There are many

including → Mathematical function
Type function
Other functions, etc.

- print( ): to print the specified message to the screen or another standard output device.
- help( ): to display the documentation of an python object, including modules, functions, classes, and keywords.
- type( ): to check the type of a specified object
- id( ): to access a unique id for a specified object
- len( ): to count the items present in a specified object
- isinstance( ): to check if the object is an instance or subclass of another class

2.17.1 Calling built-in functions

In[1]
```
i=20
type(20)
```
Out[1]   int

Tips

An example of a built-in function is the *type()* function, which is used to determine the type of an object. You can call it directly by using the function name followed by parentheses and passing the object as an argument.

Notes

The difference between a method and a function is as follows: A method is a function in object-oriented programming that is associated with an object. It includes code that is called by the object's name. On the other hand, a function can be directly called by its name without being associated with an object.

In summary, a method is called by its name but is associated with an object, while a function can be called directly by its name.

Tips

To enhance performance and efficiency, many built-in functions in Python are implemented in languages like C or C++. This allows them to be executed at a lower level, closer to the system hardware, compared to pure Python code. By implementing critical parts of Python's functionality in lower-level languages, the built-in functions can often achieve faster execution times.

Tricks

To check the built-in function: the built-in function *dir()*.
dir(__builtins__)

2.17.2 Mathematical functions

In[2]   abs(-1)
Out[2]   1

Tips

Evaluating the absolute value.

In[3]   min([1,2,3])
Out[3]   1

Tips

Evaluating the minimum value.

In[4]   max([1,2,3])
Out[4]   3

Tips

Evaluating the maximum value.

In[5] `pow(2,10)`

Out[5] 1024

Tips

Evaluating 2 to the 10th power.

In[6] `round(2.991,2)`

Out[6] 2.99

Tips

The *round()* function in Python is used for rounding numbers. The second argument of the *round()* function specifies the number of decimal places to retain after rounding, rather than the number of digits after the decimal point.

2.17.3 Type conversion functions

In[7] `int(1.134)`

Out[7] 1

Tips

To cast to int (integer): int()

Notes

In general, the function names used for casting in Python are often similar to the names of the target data types.

In[8] `bool(1)`

Out[8] True

Tips

To cast to bool (boolean): bool()

In[9] `float(1)`

Out[9] 1.0

To cast to float (floating-point number): float()

In[10] `str(123)`

Out[10] '123'

To cast to str (string): str()

In[11] `list("chao")`

Out[11] ['c', 'h', 'a', 'o']

To cast to list: list()

In[12] `set("chao")`

Out[12] {'a', 'c', 'h', 'o'}

To cast to set: set()

In[13] `tuple("chao")`

Out[13] ('c', 'h', 'a', 'o')

To cast to tuple: tuple()

2.17.4 Other common used functions

In[14] `i=0`
`type(i)`

Out[14] int

To check data types: type()

In[15]   `isinstance(i, int)`

Out[15]   True

Tips

In Python, you can use the *isinstance( )* function to check the data type of an object. The isinstance() function takes two arguments: the object you want to check and the data type you want to compare it against. It returns True if the object is an instance of the specified data type, and False otherwise.

In[16]   `dir()`

Out[16]   ['In',
          'Out',
          '_',
          '_1',
          '_10',
          '_11',
          ……
          '_ih',
          '_ii',
          '_iii',
          '_oh',
          'exit',
          'get_ipython',
          'i',
          'quit']

Tips

To check the search path for a variable in Python, you can use the *dir( )* function or the magic commands %whos and %who in interactive environments like IPython or Jupyter Notebook.

In[17]   `help(dir)`

Out[17]   Help on built-in function dir in module builtins:

          dir(...)
              dir([object]) -> list of strings

              If called without an argument, return the names in the current scope.
              Else, return an alphabetized list of names comprising (some of) the attributes
              of the given object, and of attributes reachable from it.
              If the object supplies a method named __dir__, it will be used; otherwise
              the default dir() logic is used and returns:
                  for a module object: the module's attributes.
                  for a class object: its attributes, and recursively the attributes
                      of its bases.
                  for any other object: its attributes, its class's attributes, and
                      recursively the attributes of its class's base classes.

To ask for help: help()

In[18]   myList=[1,2,3,4,5]
          len(myList)
Out[18]   5

To evaluate length: len()

In[19]   range(1,10,2)
Out[19]   range(1, 10, 2)

To quickly generate sequences: range()

The range(1, 10, 2) function is used to generate an iterator that begins at 1 (inclusive), ends at 10 (exclusive), and increments by a step size of 2. Please refer to [2.10 Lists] for more details.

In[20]   list(range(1,10,2))
Out[20]   [1, 3, 5, 7, 9]

The *range()* function in Python returns an iterator object, which is a form of lazy evaluation. To evaluate and print the values of the iterator, you can use the list() function to convert the iterator into a list.

In[21]   callable(dir)
Out[21]   True

To check whether the function can be called: callable()

In[22] | `bin(8)`

Out[22] | `'0b1000'`

Tips

To convert decimal number to binary number: bin()

In[23] | `hex(8)`

Out[23] | `'0x8'`

Tips

To convert decimal number to hexadecimal number: hex()

Notes

Python and its third-party packages offer various features and programming concepts that better support the specific needs of data science projects compared to traditional software development. These features are outlined below, along with the corresponding references for further reading:

1. Interactive programming and interpreted language. For more information, please refer to [1.3 How to read and execute the code in this book].
2. Strongly typed language. For more information, please refer to [2.2.3 Strongly typed language (In[3])].
3. Dynamically typed language. For more information, please refer to [2.2.2 Dynamically Typed Language (In[2])].
4. Explicit indexing. For more information, please refer to [4.4 DataFrame (In[5])].
5. Duck typing. For more information, please refer to [3.4.5 dir() function (In[13])].
6. Ufunc and vectorized calculation. For more information, please refer to [4.2.6 Evaluation of ndarrays (In[69])].
7. Broadcasting mechanism. For more information, please refer to [4.2.9 Broadcasting ndarray (In[81])].
8. Lazy evaluation. For more information, please refer to [3.1 Iterators and Decorators (In[5])].
9. Data protection and in-place modification mechanism. For more information, please refer to [4.4 DataFrame (In[31])].
10. Slicing and list derivation methods. For more information, please refer to [2.10 Lists (In[27])].

These features and concepts, combined with the extensive capabilities of Python's third-party packages, make it a versatile language for data science projects.

2.18 Module functions

Q&A

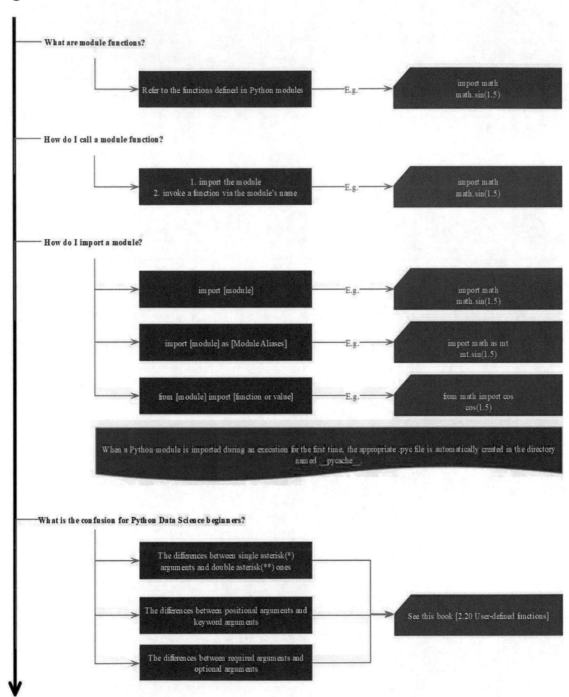

2.18.1 import module name

```
In[1]    import math
         math.sin(1.5)
Out[1]   0.9974949866040544
```

Tips

To call a module function, you can use the following method: *import* the module by its name.

Notes

To call the function in the module: module_name. function_name()

Notes

"Unlike built-in functions, functions inside a module are defined within packages or modules provided by third parties. To call these functions, you need to first import the module where the function is defined. The function is usually called using the module name followed by the function name.

Notes

In Python, there are multiple ways to import modules, and each method corresponds to a different way of calling functions from the imported modules.

Tricks

Before importing a third-party package or module, it is necessary to download it from PyPi or Conda server using tools like PIP or Conda. For more details, please refer to [3.3 Packages (In[2])] and [3.2 Modules (In[1])]. However, to facilitate programming, common packages in data science are often pre-installed in Jupyter Notebook. As a result, the packages mentioned in this book generally do not need to be downloaded and installed before importing.

In[2] `cos(1.5)`

Out[2] ---

NameError   Traceback (most recent call last)
<ipython-input-3-edeaf624fe76> in <module>
----> 1 cos(1.5) # Why that exception: NameError: name 'cos' is not defined

NameError: name 'cos' is not defined

Tips

NameError: name 'cos' is not defined.
The reason of error: When the *cos()* function is called, the module name "math" has not been imported.

In[3] `math.cos(1.5)`

Out[3] 0.0707372016677029

Tips

Workaround: <module_name>.<function_name>

The statement appears to suggest using a workaround to resolve a particular issue or problem. The recommended approach is to specify the module name followed by the function name, indicating that the function belongs to the specified module.

2.18.2 import module name as alias

In[4]	import math as mt mt.sin(1.5)

Out[4]   0.9974949866040544

The second method: *import* module name *as* alias

In principle, we have the flexibility to create our own "alias" when using the syntax "import module_name as alias". However, in the practice of data science, it is common to follow conventional "alias" names to ensure the readability of the source code.

To call the function in this module: alias.function_name()

2.18.3 from module name import function name

In[5]	from math import cos cos(1.5)

Out[5]   0.0707372016677029

The third method: from module name import function name

To call the functions imported in modules with this method: function_name()

It is recommended to carry out a comparative analysis with In[2]. The reason why the interpreter does not raise an error here is that the method of importing module has changed.

In[6]	from math import sin sin(1.5)

Out[6]   0.9974949866040544

By using the method of importing specific functions from a module, you can directly import the desired function and use it without needing to reference the module name.

2.19 User-defined functions

Q&A

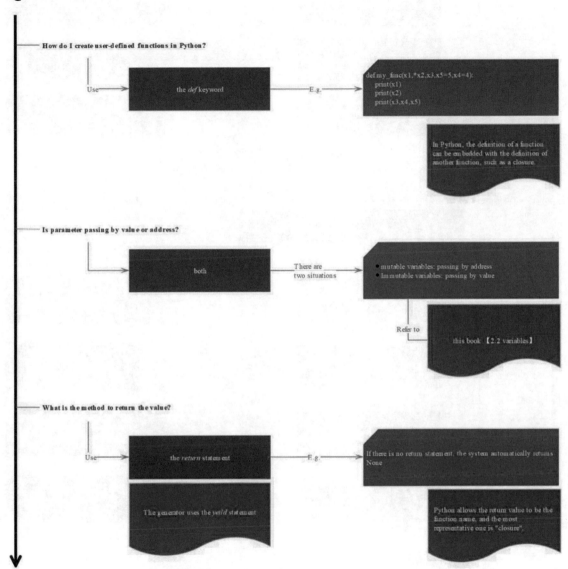

How do I create user-defined functions in Python?

Use → the *def* keyword

E.g. →
```
def my_func(x1,*x2,x3,x5=5,x4=4):
    print(x1)
    print(x2)
    print(x3,x4,x5)
```

In Python, the definition of a function can be embedded with the definition of another function, such as a closure.

Is parameter passing by value or address?

→ both

There are two situations →
- mutable variables: passing by address
- Immutable variables: passing by value

Refer to → this book 【2.2 variables】

What is the method to return the value?

Use → the *return* statement

The generator uses the *yield* statement

E.g. → If there is no return statement, the system automatically returns None

Python allows the return value to be the function name, and the most representative one is "closure".

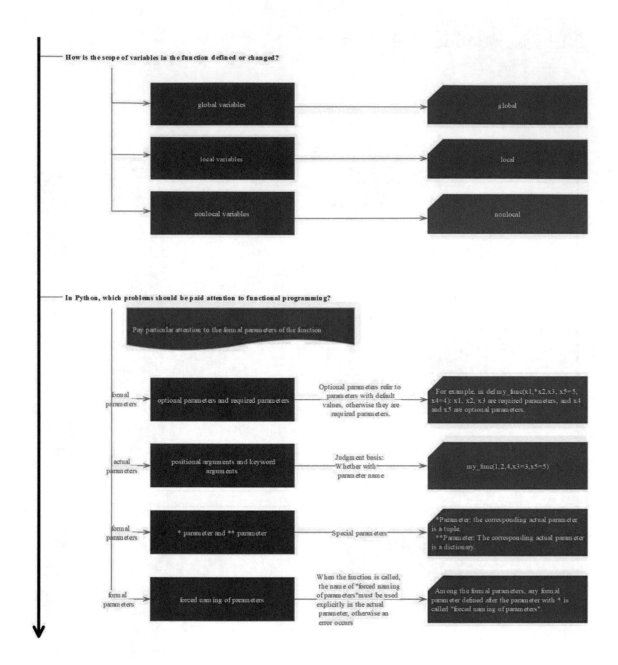

2.19.1 Defining user-defined functions

Notes

Unlike C and Java, a user-defined function is defined using the "def" keyword in Python.

Notes

Python supports the definition of "inner functions," which means that a function can be defined within another function. If the inner function, func2(), references a local variable (not a global variable) from the outer function, it is referred to as a "closure."

In[1]
```python
def func1():
    j=0
    print('hello world')

    def func2(i):
        print('pass'+str(i)+str(j))

    return func2
```

Tips

The inner function, *func2()*, is a local function that can only be accessed within the outer function, *func1()*. This means that *func2()* can only be called from within *func1()*. The return func2 statement in the outer function is used to return the inner function itself. Without this statement, *func2()* would not be executed since there are no other statements to call it.

Notes

The method of calling outer functions is as follows.

In[2]
```python
func1()
```

Out[2]
```
hello world
<function __main__.func1.<locals>.func2(i)>
```

Notes

The method of calling inner functions is as follows.

In[3]
```python
func1()(2)
```

Notes

According to the definition in [1], *func2* is the return value of *func1()*. Therefore, in terms of the running process, calling *func1()* with the argument 2 is similar to calling *func2(2)*.

Out[3]
```
hello world
pass20
```

Tips

When *func1()* is executed, the *return func2* statement will also be executed. As a result, *func2()* will be returned and can be subsequently executed. If the return statement is not present, the system will automatically return None, and an error will be raised with the message "TypeError: 'NoneType' object is not callable."

2.19.2 Function docStrings

When defining a function, it is recommended to include docstrings. Docstrings are used to provide a description of the function's purpose, behavior, and usage.

DocStrings need to be enclosed in three single quotes or three double quotes.

In[4]
```
def get_name(msg):
    '''Get the user name according to the user prompt msg. If the input is blank, the default is Anonymous User'''
    name = input(msg) or 'Anonymous User'
    return name
```

Docstrings serve as documentation for functions and can be accessed using either the built-in help() function or the ? symbol in certain Python environments, such as Jupyter Notebook or IPython.

In[5]
```
help(get_name)
```

Out[5]
```
Help on function get_name in module __main__:

get_name(msg)
    Get the user name according to the user prompt msg. If the input is blank, the default is Anonymous User
```

In[6]
```
get_name?
```

```
Signature: get_name(msg)
Docstring: Get the user name according to the user prompt msg. If the input is blank, the default is Anonymous User
File:      c:\users\szz\appdata\local\temp\ipykernel_22476\2916814581.py
Type:      function
```

2.19.3 Calling user-defined functions

To call a user-defined function, you can simply use the function name directly followed by parentheses.

In[7]
```
get_name('plz enter your name : ')
```

Out[7]
```
plz enter your name : chaolemen
'chaolemen'
```

Tricks

We can use the built-in function callable() to check whether the function is "callable".

In[8]
```python
print(callable(get_name))
```

Out[8]
```
True
```

2.19.4 Returning values

Notes

In Python, when defining a function, you have the option to use the return statement to specify the value or values that the function should return.

In[9]
```python
def myfunc(i,j=2):
    j=i+1
    return j
print(myfunc(3))
```

Out[9]
```
4
```

Notes

In Python, if a function does not have a return statement, the return value of the function is None. In Python, None is a special object that represents the absence of a value or a missing value.

In[10]
```python
def myfunc(i,j=2):
    j=i+1
print(myfunc(3))
```

Out[10]
```
None
```

Notes

When multiple values are returned, they are usually bundled together in a tuple data structure.

In[11]
```python
def myfunc(i,j=2):
    j=i+1
    return i,j
a,b =myfunc(3)
a,b
```

Out[11]
```
(3, 4)
```

2.19.5 Parameters and arguments

In[12]
```
def my_func(x1,*x2,x3,x5=5,x4=4):
    print(x1)
    print(x2)
    print(x3)
    print(x4)
    print(x5)
my_func(1,2,4,x3=3,x5=5)
```

Tips

From the perspective of function definition, formal parameters are divided into optional parameters and required parameters. The way to distinguish them is that the parameters with default values are called "optional parameters," which can be called without giving arguments, such as x4 and x5.

Tips

In Python, from the perspective of function calling methods, "arguments" are divided into "positional arguments" and "keyword arguments" (also known as named arguments). The way to distinguish them is by the presence of parameter names. For example, x3=3 and x5=5 are considered "keyword arguments," while 1, 2, and 4 are considered "positional arguments."

Notes

All "keyword arguments" must appear after "positional arguments" in Python; otherwise, an error will be raised with the message: "SyntaxError: positional argument follows keyword."

Out[12]
```
1
(2, 4)
3
4
5
```

Notes

In Python, a "parameter" refers to a variable listed in the function definition, while an "argument" refers to the actual value or expression that is passed to the function when it is called.

Notes

After the "formal parameters" corresponds to the "arguments", the remaining (2 and 4) become an element and pass in the arguments x2.

Tips

The **parameter syntax allows a function to accept a variable number of keyword arguments (key-value pairs) as a dictionary. Inside the function, the **parameter is treated as a dictionary that contains the keyword arguments passed during the function call.

In[13]   `my_func(1,2,x4=4,x3=3,x5=5)`

Tips

The header of the corresponding "function definition" is def my_func(x1,*x2,x3,x5 = 5, x4 = 4):

Out[13]
```
1
(2,)
3
4
5
```

Notes

From the perspective of function definition, any "formal parameters" defined after the *parameter in Python are called "forced named parameters." In the example def my_func(x1, *x2, x3, x5=5, x4=4):, the parameters x3, x5, and x4 are considered forced named parameters.

Notes

When calling a function with parameters defined after the *parameter (also known as a "starred parameter" or "splat parameter"), you must use explicit parameter names in the arguments. If you omit the parameter names, the Python interpreter will raise an error.

In[14]
```
my_func(1,2,4,x3=3,x5=5)
```

Out[14]
```
1
(2, 4)
3
4
5
```

2.19.6 Scope of variables

Notes

Local variables in Python are variables that are defined or declared inside a function's body. These variables have a local scope, meaning they can only be accessed and used within that specific function.

In[15]
```
x=0
def myFunc(i):
    x–i
    print(x)

myFunc(1)
print(x)
```

Tips

The second x is not the same one as the x in the first line. The second x is a local variable.

Out[15]
```
1
0
```

Notes

To convert a local variable to a global variable in Python, you can use the global keyword followed by the variable name. Simply declaring *global x* will make the variable x accessible and modifiable in the global scope.

In[16]
```
x=0
def myFunc(i):
    global x
#Then x is the global variable, not a local variable.
#
    x=i
    print(x)
myFunc(1)
print(x)
```

Tips

Here, the statement "*global x*" must be written on a single line and cannot be written as just "global" without specifying the variable name "x".

Out[16]
```
1
1
```

Notes

Similar to global variables, Python also has "nonlocal" variables, which are used in inner functions. The usage of nonlocal variables is similar to that of global variables, but they are specific to inner functions rather than being accessible globally.

In[17]
```
x=0
def myFunc(i):
    x=i
    def myF():
        nonlocal x    #this statement must be written on a single line.
        x=2
        print(x)
    print(x)
myFunc(1)
print(x)
```

Tips

Both the statements "*global x*" and "*nonlocal x*" must be written on a single line.

Out[17]
```
1
0
```

2.19.7 Pass-by-value and pass-by-reference

Notes

Argument passing rules in Python can be described as follows:

1. Immutable objects (int, float, str, bool, tuple): Pass-by-value. Changes to formal parameters do not affect the original arguments.

2. Mutable objects (list, set, dict): Pass-by-reference. Changes to formal parameters affect the original arguments.

Notes

(1) Pass-by-value: When the "argument" is an immutable object (int, float, str, bool, tuple), the "argument" and the "formal parameter" occupy different memory spaces, that is, when the "formal parameter" is modified by the "calling function", the value of the argument will not be changed.

In[18]
```python
i=100
def myfunc(j,k=2):
    j+=2
myfunc(i)
print(i)
```

Tips

In Python, parameters with default values are often referred to as "optional parameters". These parameters allow the function to be called without explicitly providing a value for them.

Out[18]
```
100
```

Notes

(2) Pass-by-reference: when the "argument" is a mutable object (list, set, dict), the argument and the "formal parameter" share the same memory space, that is, when the "formal parameter" is changed, the "argument" will also be changed.

In[19]
```python
i=[100]
def myfunc(j,k=2):
    j[0]+=2
myfunc(i)
print(i)
```

Out[19]
```
[102]
```

Notes

The principle of passing data between "arguments" and "formal parameters" is that "arguments" should correspond to "formal parameters" one by one. Except for the special parameters like "*self*" and "*cls*", they do not need to pass to the "arguments", such as:
def class_func(cls):
def __init__(self, name, age):

2.19.8 Arguments in functions

When using user-defined functions, we have to pay attention to the following three problems.

Firstly, "arguments" are divided into "positional arguments" and "keyword arguments". The distinction between them is not based on the presence of a default value. Instead, it lies in how the arguments are provided during function calls.

All "keyword arguments" must appear after "positional arguments" in Python; otherwise, an error is raised with the message: "SyntaxError: positional argument follows keyword".

In[20]
```python
def myfunc(j,k=2):
    j+=k
    j
d=myfunc(2,3)
d
```

If there is no return statement in a Python function, the return value of the function is None. In Python, the value None is commonly used to represent a missing or empty value.

In[21]
```python
def myfunc(k=2,j):
    j+=k
    j
d=myfunc(2,3)
d
```

Out[21]
```
  File "C:\Users\szz\AppData\Local\Temp\ipykernel_17668\2076857993.py", line 1
    def myfunc(k=2,j):
                  ^
SyntaxError: non-default argument follows default argument
```

Syntax error: non-default argument follows default argument.

The reason for this error is that in Python, when defining function parameters, non-default arguments (positional arguments) must come before default arguments (keyword arguments). The order should be: non-default arguments first, followed by default arguments.

Notes

Secondly, if a *return* statement is not explicitly written in a function, the default return value will be *None*. The value None can be displayed using the *print( )* function or by accessing it directly.

In[22]
```
def myfunc(j,k=2):
    j+=k
    j
#If there is no return statement, None will be returned automatically.
d=myfunc(3)
print(d)
#Output of None: If the built-in function print() is not used, None will not be displayed.
```

Out[22]
```
None
```

In[23]
```
d is None
```

Out[23]
```
True
```

Notes

Thirdly, functions are treated as objects in Python. This means that in Python, the language follows the philosophy of "everything is an object." Functions can be assigned to variables, passed as arguments to other functions, stored in data structures, and have attributes just like any other object in Python.

In[24]
```
myfunc=abs
print(type(myfunc))
#Like other objects, Python function names can be used as arguments of type (), and
the return value is the function type.
print(myfunc(-100))
```

Out[24]
```
<class 'builtin_function_or_method'>
100
```

2.20 Lambda functions

Q&A

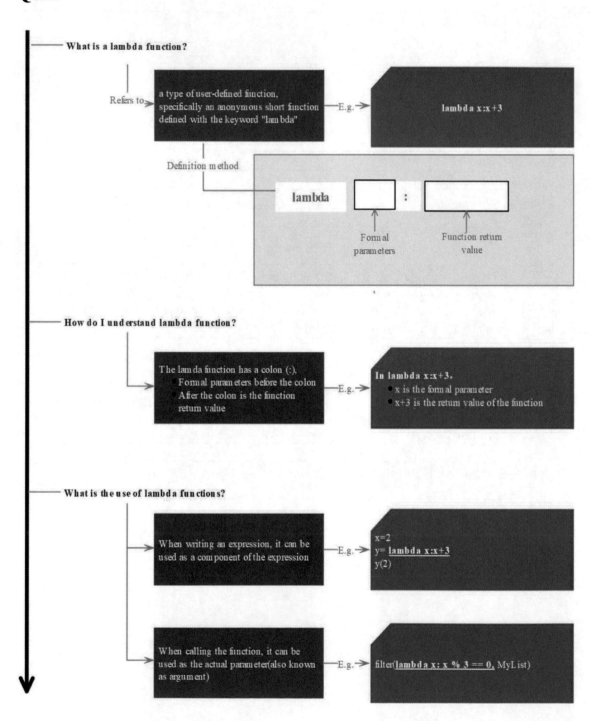

What is a lambda function?

Refers to → a type of user-defined function, specifically an anonymous short function defined with the keyword "lambda"

E.g. → lambda x:x+3

Definition method

lambda [ ] : [ ]

Formal parameters   Function return value

How do I understand lambda function?

The lamda function has a colon (:),
- Formal parameters before the colon
- After the colon is the function return value

E.g. → In lambda x:x+3,
- x is the formal parameter
- x+3 is the return value of the function

What is the use of lambda functions?

When writing an expression, it can be used as a component of the expression

E.g. →
x=2
y= lambda x:x+3
y(2)

When calling the function, it can be used as the actual parameter(also known as argument)

E.g. → filter(lambda x: x % 3 == 0, MyList)

2.20.1 Defining a lambda function

Notes

The essence of a lambda function in Python is that it is a single-line anonymous function. Lambda functions are defined using the lambda keyword and are typically used for creating small, one-time functions without explicitly naming them.

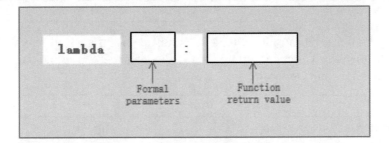

Tips

The lambda function has a colon (:). Before the colon are the formal parameters, and after the colon is the function's return value.

In[1]
```
x=2
y= lambda x:x+3
y(2)
```

Out[1] `5`

Notes

The lambda function in "in[1]" is equivalent to the following common function.

In[2]
```
x=2
def myfunc(x):
    return x+3
myfunc(2)
```

Out[2] `5`

2.20.2 Calling a lambda function

Notes

In data science projects, lambda functions are commonly used as arguments for other functions, with the *filter()* function being a common example.

In[3]
```
MyList = [1,2,3,4,5,6,7,8,9,10]
filter(lambda x: x % 3 == 0, MyList)
```

Tips

The *filter()* function uses an iterative reading mode, which reads the value of each element in the order of subscript from the second argument (e.g., MyList), and assigns it to the variable x in the first argument (a lambda function).

Out[3]   `<filter at 0xb656ac27f0>`

Notes

In Python, the return value of the *filter()* function is an iterator. This iterator's values can be displayed after converting it into a list. For more information, refer to section '3.1 Iterators and Generators'.

In[4]   `list(filter(lambda x: x % 3 == 0, MyList))`

Out[4]   `[3, 6, 9]`

Notes

Take the *map()* function as an example.

In[5]   `list(map(lambda x: x * 2, MyList))`

Out[5]   `[2, 4, 6, 8, 10, 12, 14, 16, 18, 20]`

Notes

Take the *reduce()* function as an example.

In[6]
```
from functools import reduce
reduce(lambda x, y: x + y, MyList)
```

Tips

The *reduce()* function is no longer a built-in function in Python since version 3. It has been moved to the functools module.

Out[6]   `55`

Exercises

[1] Which of the following is not a sequence type?
  A. list
  B. tuple
  C. set
  D. str

[2] Which of the following variables complies with the naming rules?
  A. 3q
  B. _
  C. while
  D. ds@

[3] Which of the following statements is illegal in Python?
  A. x = y = z = 1
  B. x = (y = z + 1)
  C. x,y = y,x
  D. x += y

[4] What is the output of the following program?
```
x = 20
y = True
print(x+y)
```

  A. 1
  B. True
  C. 21
  D. raise an exception

[5] Which of the following evaluates to False?
  A. 'abc' < 'ABC'
  B. 5 > 3 > 1
  C. 2 < 1 and 12 < 3 or 2 > 1
  D. (1 is 3) == 0

[6] Which of the following is false of Python
  A. Compound statements after *if* are indented instead of braces(curly brackets).
  B. Use *elif* instead of *else if* in Python.
  C. *If* can be written as a one line expression.
  D. There can be empty statements in the *if* statement.

[7] How many times will the following while loop be executed?
```
k – 100
while k > 1:
      print(k)
      k = k // 2
```

  A. 3
  B. 4
  C. 5
  D. 6

[8] What is the output of the following program?
```
lst1 = [3,4,5,6,7,8]
lst1.insert(2,3)
print(lst1)
```

    A. [3,4,5,3,6,7,8]
    B. [3,4,3,5,6,7,8]
    C. [3,4,5,6,7,8,[2,3]]
    D. [3,4,5,6,7,8,2,3]

[9] Which of the following is false of Python?
    A. Tuples are immutable, and usually contain a heterogeneous sequence of elements.
    B. Lists are mutable, and their elements are usually homogeneous.
    C. Elements inside tuples can be sorted with the *sort* method.
    D. The frequency of elements inside tuples can be executed with the *count* method.

[10] Which of the following is not used in Python 3 to solve the problem of special characters in the path?
    A. s = "D:\test"
    B. s = r"D:\test"
    C. s = u"D:\test"

[11] What is the output of the following program?
```
lst = [1,2,3]
tpl = 1,2,3
print(list(zip(lst,tpl)))
```

    A. [(1, 1), (2, 2), (3, 3)]
    B. ([1,1],[2,2],[3,3])
    C. [2,4,6]
    D. (2,4,6)

[12] Which of the following data structures is unordered?
    A. list
    B. tuple
    C. set
    D. string

[13] Which of the following data structures is normally used to duplicate removal in Python?
    A. list
    B. tuple
    C. set
    D. string

[14] Which of the following cannot be used as keys in the dictionary?
    A. number
    B. string
    C. tuple
    D. list

[15] Which of the following is true of calling method of the built-in functions?
    A. First import the module to which it belongs, and then call through the module name.
    B. Call directly with the function name.
    C. Call with the def keyword.

[16]   What will the following program print out?
set("happy")

A. ['h','a','p','p','y']
B. ('h','a','p','p','y')
C. {'h','a','p','p','y'}

[17]   Which of the following code will run with errors?
A. import time
    time.localtime()
B. import time as ti
    ti.localtime()
C. import time as ti
    localtime()
D. from time import localtime
    localtime()

[18]   What is the output of the following program?
```
def InputInt( a ):
     a = 15
b = 2
InputInt(b)
print( b )
```
A. 15
B. 2
C. raise an exception

[19]   Which of the following statements about the *user-defined* function is wrong?
A. The mutable variable of the *user-defined* function is passed by position
B. Immutable variables of the *user-defined* function are passed by value.
C. The *user-defined* functions cannot be placed in a class.
D. The *user-defined* functions can be written as single line functions.

[20]   Which of the following statements about the *lambda* function is wrong?
A. Small anonymous functions can be created with the the *lambda* keyword.
B. Like nested function definitions,the *lambda* functions can reference variables from the containing scope.
C. The *lambda* functions are syntactically restricted to a single expression.
D. All of the above

3. Advanced Python Programming for Data Science

This chapter will introduce the advanced Python programming concepts and skills necessary to excel as a data scientist. The topics we will cover include:

- Iterators and generators
- Modules
- Packages
- Help documentations
- Exception and errors
- Debugging
- Search path
- Current working directory
- Object-oriented programming

3.1 Iterators and generators

Q&A

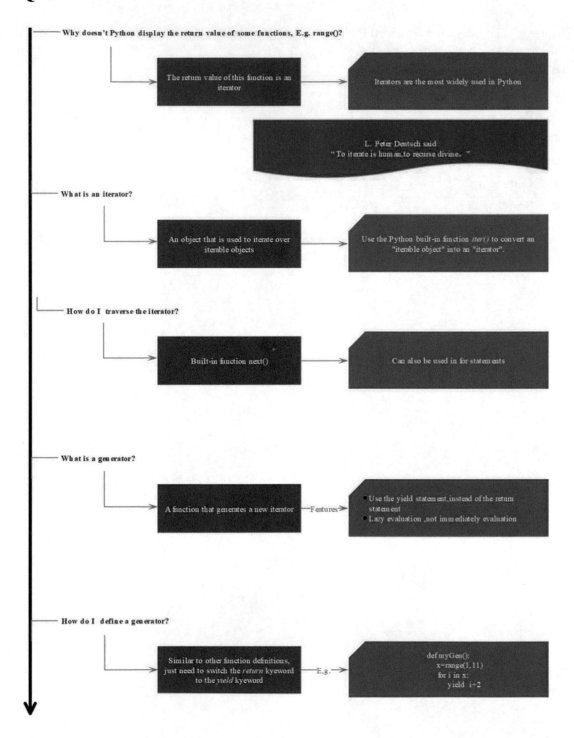

3.1.1 Iterable objects vs. iterators

Notes

In Python, an iterator is an object that is obtained by passing an iterable object to the built-in *iter()* function. Not only can functions that accept iterable objects receive iterators, but they can also use the *iter()* function to convert iterable objects into iterators directly.

Tips

1. Iterable object: An object that can be used directly in a loop statement, such as a '*for*' loop.

2. Iterator: An object that can be called by the built-in *next()* function and will continuously return the next value in sequence.

Notes

(1) While all iterators are iterable, the converse is not necessarily true. That is, iterable objects are not always iterators.

In[1]
```python
myList=[1,2,3,4,5]
next(myList)
```

Out[1]
```
TypeError        Traceback (most recent call last)
~\AppData\Local\Temp\ipykernel_3880\2514634475.py in <module>
        1 myList=[1,2,3,4,5]
----> 2 next(myList)

TypeError: 'list' object is not an iterator
```

Tips

Report errors: TypeError: 'list' object is not an iterator.
Cause analysis: Although *myList* is an iterable object, it is not an iterator.

Notes

To test whether an object is an iterable, use the built-in *isinstance()* function in conjunction with the *collections* module.

In[2]
```python
myList=[1,2,3,4,5]
from collections.abc import Iterable
result = isinstance(myList, Iterable)
```

Notes

(2) The built-in *iter()* function in Python is used to convert iterable objects into iterators.

In[3]
```
myIterator=iter(myList)
print(next(myIterator))
print(next(myIterator))
print(next(myIterator))
```

Tips

The built-in *next( )* function in Python is a method used to traverse items in an iterator, retrieving them one at a time.

Out[3]
```
1
2
3
```

3.1.2 Generator vs. iterators

Notes

A generator in Python is a special kind of function that returns a generator iterator. The key differences between a generator and a regular function are:

1. Generators use the yield keyword instead of the return keyword.
2. Instead of immediate execution, generators use a 'lazy execution' strategy. This means that when a *generator* function is called, it isn't executed immediately. Instead, execution is deferred until each element needs to be processed."

Notes

(1) In Python, a generator is a special type of function that does not return a single value. Instead, it returns an iterator object that generates a sequence of values. This is accomplished by using *yield* statements instead of *return* statements.

In[4]
```
def myGen():
    x=range(1,11)
    for i in x:
        yield  i+2
```

Notes

(2) Generators in Python exhibit a characteristic known as 'lazy execution.' This means they do not compute the results immediately when they're defined. Instead, they generate each value on-the-fly as you iterate over them. This feature allows them to represent potentially infinite data structures and also saves memory usage for large sequences.

In[5] `myGen()`

Tips

In this case, the output is <generator object myGen at 0x00000213EA679E58>. This is the representation of a generator object in Python, rather than a specific return value.

Out[5] `<generator object myGen at 0x00000213EA679E58>`

Notes

(3) One of the key features of a generator is that its elements are executed only when they are accessed or called. This behavior is part of the 'lazy execution' model followed by generators in Python.

In[6]

```
for x in myGen():
    print(x,end=",")
```

Tricks

"To directly display the items produced by a generator, use the *print()* function with the unpacking operator (*), as in the following example: *print(*mygen())*.

Out[6]   3,4,5,6,7,8,9,10,11,12,

3.2 Modules

Q&A

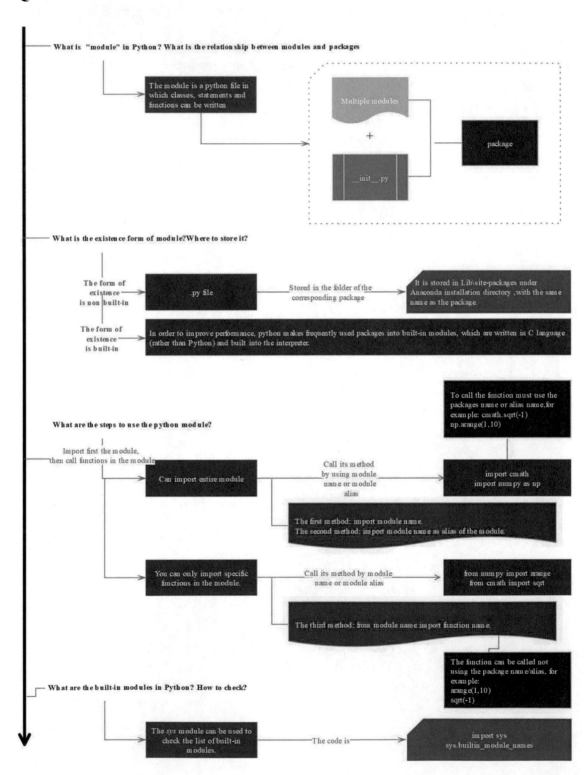

What is "module" in Python? What is the relationship between modules and packages

The module is a python file in which classes, statements and functions can be written

Multiple modules

+

__init__.py

package

What is the existence form of module? Where to store it?

The form of existence is non built-in — .py file — Stored in the folder of the corresponding package — It is stored in Lib\site-packages under Anaconda installation directory ,with the same name as the package.

The form of existence is built-in — In order to improve performance, python makes frequently used packages into built-in modules, which are written in C language (rather than Python) and built into the interpreter.

What are the steps to use the python module?

Import first the module, then call functions in the module

Can import entire module — Call its method by using module name or module alias — import cmath / import numpy as np — To call the function must use the packages name or alias name,for example: cmath.sqrt(-1) np.arange(1,10)

The first method: import module name. The second method: import module name as alias of the module.

You can only import specific functions in the module. — Call its method by module name or module alias — from numpy import arange / from cmath import sqrt

The third method: from module name import function name.

The function can be called not using the package name/alias, for example: arange(1,10) sqrt(-1)

What are the built-in modules in Python? How to check?

The sys module can be used to check the list of built-in modules. — The code is — import sys sys.builtin_module_names

3.2.1 Importing and using modules

Tips

In Python, we can import a module into our code using the import statement. The import statement performs two operations: searching for the named module and binding the search results to a name in the local scope.

There are three types of the import statements:
- import module_name
- import module_name as alias_name
- from module_name import function_name

Notes

Step 1: Importing a module:
import module_name

Step 2: Calling functions in the module:
module_name.function_name()

In[1]
```python
import math
math.sin(1.5)
```

Out[1]
```
0.9974949866040544
```

In[2]
```python
cos(1.5)
```

out[2]
```
NameError        Traceback (most recent call last)
~\AppData\Local\Temp\ipykernel_25560\176693822.py in <module>
----> 1 cos(1.5)
NameError: name 'cos' is not defined
```

Tips

NameError: name 'cos' is not defined.
To use the cos() function, which calculates the cosine of a value, you need to specify the module name math.

Notes

Step 1: Importing a module with an alias:
import module_name as alias

Step 2: Calling functions in the module using the alias:
alias.function_name()

In[3]
```python
import math as mt
mt.sin(1.5)
```

Out[3]
```
0.9974949866040544
```

	Step 1: Importing a function from a module: from module_name import function_name Step 2: Calling the imported function: function_name()

Notes

In[4]
```
from math import cos
cos(1.5)
```

Out[4]   0.0707372016677029

3.2.2 Checking built-in modules list

	sys.builtin_module_names() is a function in Python's sys module that returns a tuple of strings. This tuple contains the names of all modules that are compiled into the Python interpreter.

Notes

In[5]
```
import sys
print(sys.builtin_module_names)
```

Out[5]   ('_abc', '_ast', '_bisect', '_blake2', '_codecs', '_codecs_cn', '_codecs_hk', '_codecs_iso2022', '_codecs_jp', '_codecs_kr', '_codecs_tw', '_collections', '_contextvars', '_csv', '_datetime', '_functools', '_heapq', '_imp', '_io', '_json', '_locale', '_lsprof', '_md5', '_multibytecodec', '_opcode', '_operator', '_pickle', '_random', '_sha1', '_sha256', '_sha3', '_sha512', '_signal', '_sre', '_stat', '_statistics', '_string', '_struct', '_symtable', '_thread', '_tracemalloc', '_warnings', '_weakref', '_winapi', '_xxsubinterpreters', 'array', 'atexit', 'audioop', 'binascii', 'builtins', 'cmath', 'errno', 'faulthandler', 'gc', 'itertools', 'marshal', 'math', 'mmap', 'msvcrt', 'nt', 'parser', 'sys', 'time', 'winreg', 'xxsubtype', 'zlib')

3.3 Packages

Q&A

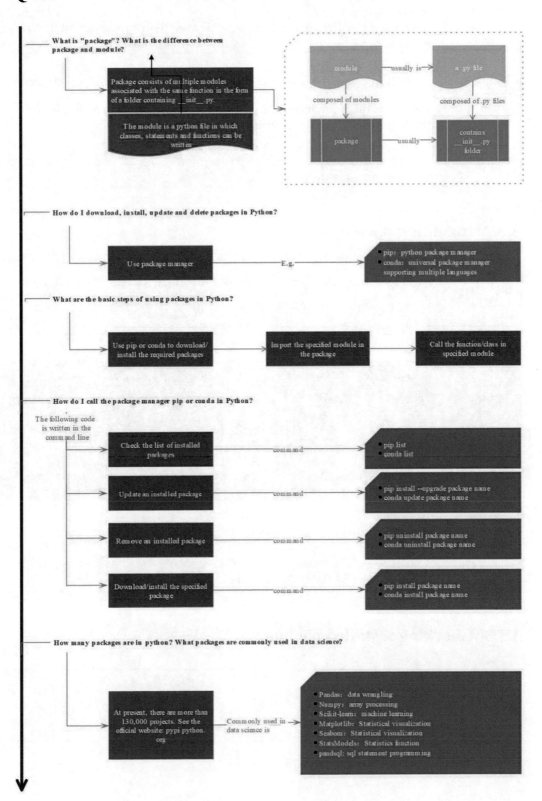

What is "package"? What is the difference between package and module?

Package consists of multiple modules associated with the same function in the form of a folder containing __init__.py.

The module is a python file in which classes, statements and functions can be written

module —— usually is —→ a .py file

composed of modules   composed of .py files

package —— usually —→ contains __init__.py folder

How do I download, install, update and delete packages in Python?

Use package manager —— E.g. —→
- pip: python package manager
- conda: universal package manager supporting multiple languages

What are the basic steps of using packages in Python?

Use pip or conda to download/install the required packages → Import the specified module in the package → Call the function/class in specified module

How do I call the package manager pip or conda in Python?

The following code is written in the command line

Check the list of installed packages —— command —→
- pip list
- conda list

Update an installed package —— command —→
- pip install --upgrade package name
- conda update package name

Remove an installed package —— command —→
- pip uninstall package name
- conda uninstall package name

Download/install the specified package —— command —→
- pip install package name
- conda install package name

How many packages are in python? What packages are commonly used in data science?

At present, there are more than 130,000 projects. See the official website: pypi.python.org —— Commonly used in data science is —→
- Pandas: data wrangling
- Numpy: array processing
- Scikit-learn: machine learning
- Matplotlib: Statistical visualization
- Seaborn: Statistical visualization
- StatsModels: Statistics function
- pandsql: sql statement programming

3.3.1 Packages vs modules

Notes

In Python:

1. A module is a file with a .py extension that contains a collection of functions and global variables. It serves as a reusable component that can be imported into other Python programs.
2. A package is a directory that contains a collection of related modules. It provides a way to organize and structure code by grouping related functionality together.

Notes

The two most commonly used tools for managing Python packages or modules are:

1. Pip: Pip is the recommended tool by the Python Packaging Authority for installing packages from the Python Package Index (PyPI).
2. Conda: Conda is a cross-platform package and environment manager that not only installs and manages conda packages from the Anaconda repository but also supports packages from the Anaconda Cloud.

3.3.2 Installing packages

Notes

To install packages, you can use either pip or conda depending on your package management setup. Here's the syntax for installing packages with each tool:

1. Using pip:pip install package_name
2. Using conda:conda install package_name

```
Anaconda Prompt (Anacoda)                                                    —    □

(base) C:\Users\szz>pip install scipy
WARNING: Ignoring invalid distribution -umpy (d:\anacoda\lib\site-packages)
WARNING: Ignoring invalid distribution -ip (d:\anacoda\lib\site-packages)
WARNING: Ignoring invalid distribution -umpy (d:\anacoda\lib\site-packages)
WARNING: Ignoring invalid distribution -ip (d:\anacoda\lib\site-packages)
Requirement already satisfied: scipy in d:\anacoda\lib\site-packages (1.7.3)
Requirement already satisfied: numpy<1.23.0,>=1.16.5 in d:\anacoda\lib\site-packages (from scipy) (1.21.5)
WARNING: Ignoring invalid distribution -umpy (d:\anacoda\lib\site-packages)
WARNING: Ignoring invalid distribution -ip (d:\anacoda\lib\site-packages)
WARNING: Ignoring invalid distribution -umpy (d:\anacoda\lib\site-packages)
WARNING: Ignoring invalid distribution -ip (d:\anacoda\lib\site-packages)
WARNING: Ignoring invalid distribution -umpy (d:\anacoda\lib\site-packages)
WARNING: Ignoring invalid distribution -ip (d:\anacoda\lib\site-packages)
```

Notes

In Python, when you run the command *pip install scipy*, it prompts "Requirement already satisfied: scipy in c:\anaconda\lib\site-packages". This indicates that the scipy package is already installed and there is no need to reinstall it. However, when you run the command *pip install orderPy*, there is no such prompt.

3.3.3 Checking installed packages

Notes

pip list
or
conda list

🖳 Anaconda Prompt (Anacoda)

```
(base) C:\Users\szz>conda list
# packages in environment at D:\Anacoda:
#
# Name                    Version                   Build  Channel
_anaconda_depends         2021.11                   py37_0    defaults
_ipyw_jlab_nb_ext_conf    0.1.0                     py37_0    defaults
absl-py                   0.9.0                     pypi_0    pypi
alabaster                 0.7.12                      py_0    conda-forge
anaconda                  custom                    py37_1    defaults
anaconda-client           1.7.2                     py37_0    defaults
anaconda-navigator        1.9.12                    py37_0    defaults
anaconda-project          0.8.3                       py_0    defaults
aniso8601                 9.0.1                     pypi_0    pypi
anyio                     3.5.0              py37h03978a9_0    conda-forge
appdirs                   1.4.4               pyh9f0ad1d_0    conda-forge
argcomplete               2.0.0               pyhd8ed1ab_0    conda-forge
argh                      0.26.2          pyh9f0ad1d_1002    conda-forge
argon2-cffi               21.3.0              pyhd8ed1ab_0    conda-forge
argon2-cffi-bindings      21.2.0            py37hcc03f2d_1    conda-forge
arrow                     1.2.2               pyhd8ed1ab_0    conda-forge
articutapi                1.1.6                     pypi_0    pypi
```

3.3.4 Updating or removing installed packages

Notes

To update installed packages:
    pip install --upgrade a package's name
    or
    conda update a package's name

```
(base) C:\Users\szz>conda update scipy
Collecting package metadata (current_repodata.json): done
Solving environment: \
Warning: 10 possible package resolutions (only showing differing packages):
...
## Package Plan ##
```

Tips

Run *pip uninstall* and *conda uninstall* to remove the package installed.

Notes

To remove installed packages, you can use either pip or conda, depending on your package management setup. Here's the syntax for uninstalling packages with each tool:

1. Using pip: pip uninstall package_name

2. Using conda:conda uninstall package_name

3.3.5 Importing packages or modules

(1) Import a module: Use a conventional aliase followed by as.

In[1] `import pandas as pd`

(2) Import multiple modules: Separate them with commas.

In[2] `import pandas as pd, numpy as np, math as math`

To import multiple modules and provide aliases, you should use separate import statements for each module and alias.

Tips

(3) Only import specific functions in a module.
In *"from pandas import DataFrame"*, the first argument *pandas* is the module name, the second argument *DataFrame* is a function name in this module.

In[3] `from pandas import DataFrame`

(4) Import packages with the hierarchical filesystem structure:Use dots to represent the hierarchical relationship.

In[4] `import Graphics.Primitive.fill`

If you are unable to download or install a package using pip or conda commands, you can visit the official website of the package. From there, you can download the package and follow the installation steps outlined in the official documentation.

3.3.6 Checking Package Version

To check the version of a package using its built-in attributes and methods, you can typically access the __version__ attribute of the package.

In[5] `pd.__version__`

3.3.7 Commonly used Packages

Notes

In data science projects, commonly used basic packages include the following:

1. Pandas: For handling data frames (relational tables) and series
2. NumPy: For multidimensional array (matrix) processing
3. Scikit-learn, TensorFlow, and PyTorch: For machine learning
4. Matplotlib: For statistical visualization
5. Seaborn: For enhanced data visualization
6. StatsModels: For statistical analysis
7. Pandasql: For SQL programming with pandas
8. Scrapy: For web scraping
9. PySpark: For programming with Apache Spark
10. NLTK, spaCy: For natural language processing in English
11. pynlpir, Jieba: For natural language processing in Chinese
12. Wordcloud: For generating word clouds
13. Random: For generating random numbers

3.4 Help documentation

Q&A

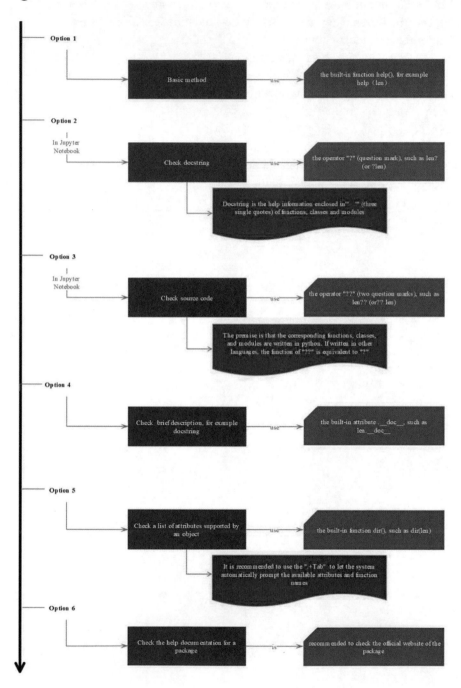

3.4.1 The *help* function

Notes — The most basic and generic way to check help information is the built-in *help()* function.

In[1] | `help(len)`

Out[1] | Help on built-in function len in module builtins:

len(obj, /)
    Return the number of items in a container.

3.4.2 DocString

Notes — In IPython, a convenient way to access help information for objects, functions, or modules is to use the question mark (?) character.

In[2] | `len?`

Tips — The IPython (or IPython-based Jupyter Notebook/Lab) system displays help information as follows:

```
Signature: len(obj, /)
Docstring: Return the number of items in a container.
Type:      builtin_function_or_method
```

Notes — The syntax to check help information using the question mark character (?) is a functionality provided by IPython, an enhanced interactive Python shell, and is not a syntax inherent to the Python language.

In[3] | `myList1=[1,2,3,4]`
`myList1.append?`

Tips — The help information printed is as follows.

```
Signature: myList1.append(object, /)
Docstring: Append object to the end of the list.
Type:      builtin_function_or_method
```

Notes

The help document consulted by *docstring* is a multiple-lines explanatory text bounded by three instances of a quotation mark (")

In[4]
```
def testDocString():
    """This is docString,
    You can use "?" to view the help information"""
    return(1)

testDocString?
```

Notes

The iPython (or iPython-based Jupyter Notebook/Lab, etc.) system display help information as following:

```
Signature: testDocString()
Docstring:
此处为docString,
即用 " ? " 能查看得到的帮助信息
File:      c:\users\szz\appdata\local\temp\ipykernel_5248\4037377024.py
Type:      function
```

In[5] `?testDocString`

Tips

The iPython (or iPython-based Jupyter Notebook/Lab, etc.) system display the same help information as In[4].

3.4.3 Checking source code

Notes

The ?? syntax, when used in Python environments such as IPython or Jupyter Notebook/Lab, allows you to access the source code of a function or object.

In[6] `testDocString??`

Tips

The help information printed by the system is consistent with In[4].

Notes

Prerequisite: The target object must be written in Python, as the source code cannot be checked if it is not. In such cases, the functionality of ?? becomes the same as ?.

Notes

To check the help information for the built-in *len()* function, we can use len?

In[7]   `len?`

Notes

The iPython (or iPython-based Jupyter Notebook/Lab, etc.) system display help information as following:

```
Signature: len(obj, /)
Docstring: Return the number of items in a container.
Type:      builtin_function_or_method
```

In[8]   `len??`

Tips

"len??" has the same output as "len?".
Reason analysis: The built-in *len()* function is not written in Python.

3.4.4 The *doc* attribute

Notes

The __*doc*__ attribute, enclosed by double underscores (__), is a default attribute automatically added to each class in Python's object-oriented programming method. It contains the documentation string (docstring) for the class. For more details, refer to section '3.9 Object-oriented programming.

In[9]   `testDocString.__doc__`

Out[9]   `'This is docString,\nYou can use "?" to view the help information'`

In[10]   `len.__doc__`

Out[10] `'Return the number of items in a container.'`

3.4.5 The *dir()* function

Notes

The *dir()* function is used to retrieve a list of all attributes and methods available in the specified object.

In[11]   `dir(print)`

Out[11]
```
['__call__',
 '__class__',
 '__delattr__',
 '__dir__',
 '__doc__',
 '__eq__',
 '__format__',
 '__ge__',
 '__getattribute__',
 '__gt__',
 '__hash__',
 '__init__',
 '__le__',
 '__lt__',
 '__module__',
 '__name__',
 '__ne__',
 '__new__',
 '__qualname__',
 '__reduce__',
 '__reduce_ex__',
 '__repr__',
 '__self__',
 '__setattr__',
 '__sizeof__',
 '__str__',
 '__subclasshook__',
 '__text_signature__']
```

In[12]   `dir(len)`

Out[12]
```
['__call__',
 '__class__',
 '__delattr__',
 '__dir__',
 '__doc__',
 '__eq__',
 '__format__',
 '__ge__',
 '__getattribute__',
 '__gt__',
 '__hash__',
 '__init__',
 '__init_subclass__',
 '__le__',
 '__lt__',
 '__module__',
 '__name__',
 '__ne__',
 '__new__',
 '__qualname__',
 '__reduce__',
 '__reduce_ex__',
 '__repr__',
 '__self__',
 '__setattr__',
 '__sizeof__',
 '__str__',
 '__subclasshook__',
 '__text_signature__']
```

In[13]   `dir?`

Tips

Python follows a principle called 'duck typing' in its programming style. The term 'duck typing' refers to a concept that focuses on an object's behavior rather than its specific type or class. In other words, if an object walks like a duck (supports certain attributes and methods) and quacks like a duck (exhibits expected behavior), then it is considered a 'duck', regardless of its actual class or type.

3.5 Exception and errors

Q&A

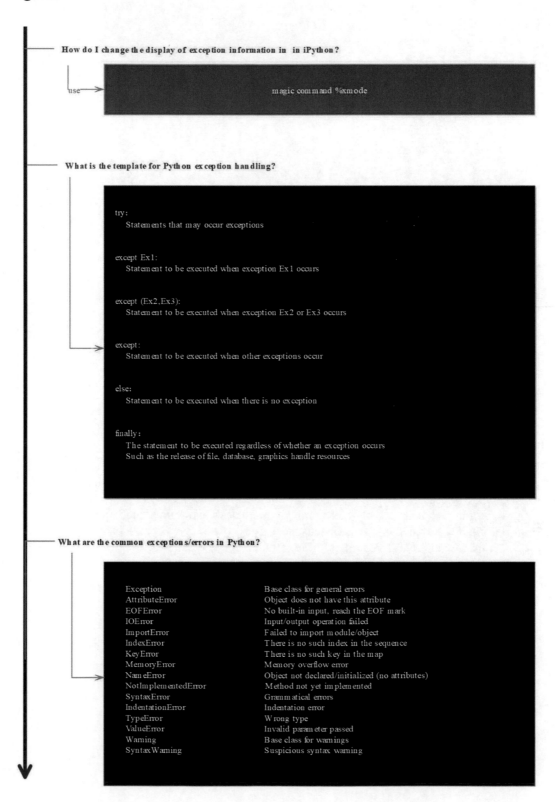

How do I change the display of exception information in in iPython?

use → magic command %xmode

What is the template for Python exception handling?

```
try:
    Statements that may occur exceptions

except Ex1:
    Statement to be executed when exception Ex1 occurs

except (Ex2,Ex3):
    Statement to be executed when exception Ex2 or Ex3 occurs

except:
    Statement to be executed when other exceptions occur

else:
    Statement to be executed when there is no exception

finally:
    The statement to be executed regardless of whether an exception occurs
    Such as the release of file, database, graphics handle resources
```

What are the common exceptions/errors in Python?

Exception	Base class for general errors
AttributeError	Object does not have this attribute
EOFError	No built-in input, reach the EOF mark
IOError	Input/output operation failed
ImportError	Failed to import module/object
IndexError	There is no such index in the sequence
KeyError	There is no such key in the map
MemoryError	Memory overflow error
NameError	Object not declared/initialized (no attributes)
NotImplementedError	Method not yet implemented
SyntaxError	Grammatical errors
IndentationError	Indentation error
TypeError	Wrong type
ValueError	Invalid parameter passed
Warning	Base class for warnings
SyntaxWarning	Suspicious syntax warning

3.5.1 Try/Except/Finally

In Python, Errors that occur at runtime (after passing the syntax test) are called exceptions.

In Python's *try/except/finally* statements, a colon (:) is placed after try, except, and finally to signify the start of a code block associated with each statement.

In[1]
```python
try:
    f=open('myfile.txt','w')
    while True:
        s=input("please enter Q")
        if s.upper()=='Q':break
        f.write(s+'\n')
except KeyboardInterrupt:
    print("program interruption")
finally:
    f.close()
```

The *finally* section refers to the code that will be executed regardless of whether an exception occurs or not. The finally block is useful for releasing resources and performing cleanup operations.

Unlike the C and Java languages, in Python, the else statement can be added to exception handling constructs even when no exceptions occur.

Out[1]
```
please enter Qa
please enter QQ
```

The syntax template for try/except/finally statements in Python is as follows:

```python
try:
    # Statements that may raise exceptions
except Ex1:
    # Statement to be executed when exception Ex1 occurs
except (Ex2, Ex3):
    # Statement to be executed when exception Ex2 or Ex3 occurs
except:
    # Statement to be executed when other exceptions occur
else:
    # Statement to be executed when there is no exception
finally:
    # Statement to be executed regardless of whether an exception occurs, such as
    #     releasing file, database, or graphics handle resources
```

3.5.2 Exception reporting mode

Notes

IPython or Jupyter Notebook provides us with a magic command %xmode to switch modes for the exception handlers.

%xmode takes a single argument, the mode, and there are four modes: Plain, Context, Verbose, and Minimal. The default mode is Context.

Notes

To switch the exception reporting mode to "Plain":
　%xmode Plain

In[2]
```
%xmode Plain
x=1
x1
```

Out[2]
```
Exception reporting mode: Plain
Traceback (most recent call last):

  File "C:\Users\szz\AppData\Local\Temp\ipykernel_4976\3044902845.py", line 3, in <module>
    x1

NameError: name 'x1' is not defined
```

Notes

To switch the exception reporting mode to "Verbose":
　%xmode Verbose

In[3]
```
%xmode Verbose
x=1
x1
```

Out[3]
```
Exception reporting mode: Verbose
---------------------------------------------------------------------------
NameError                Traceback (most recent call last)
~\AppData\Local\Temp\ipykernel_4976\719643460.py in <module>
      1 get_ipython().run_line_magic('xmode', 'Verbose')
      2 x=1
----> 3 x1
        global x1 = undefined

NameError: name 'x1' is not defined
```

Tips

Python defines a wide range of exception classes (Exceptions) and error classes (Errors). More detailed information about these classes can be obtained from the Python official website's tutorial on errors and exceptions: https://docs.python.org/3/tutorial/errors.html.

Notes

To switch the exception reporting mode to "Context":
   %xmode Context

In[4]
```
%xmode Context
x=1
x1
```

Out[4]
```
Exception reporting mode: Context
-------------------------------------------------------------------------
NameError                      Traceback (most recent call last)
~\AppData\Local\Temp\ipykernel_4976\320895153.py in <module>
       1 get_ipython().run_line_magic('xmode', 'Context')
       2 x=1
----> 3 x1

NameError: name 'x1' is not defined
```

3.5.3 Assertion

Notes

In data science projects, Assertion is mainly used to set Check Points and to test if certain assumptions remain true.

Notes

When encountering an *assert* statement, Python evaluates the accompanying expression, which is expected to be true. If the expression evaluates to false, Python raises an AssertionError exception.

In[5]
```
a=1
b=2
assert b!=0 , "The denominator can't equal 0"
```

Notes

When encountering an *assert* statement, Python evaluates the accompanying expression, which is expected to be true. If the expression evaluates to false, Python raises an AssertionError exception, optionally displaying an error message.

In[6]
```
a=1
b=0
assert b!=0 , "The denominator can't equal 0"
```

Out[6]
```
-------------------------------------------------------------------------
AssertionError     Traceback (most recent call last)
~\AppData\Local\Temp\ipykernel_4976\796219993.py in <module>
       1 a=1
       2 b=0
----> 3 assert b!=0 , "The denominator can't equal 0"

AssertionError: The denominator can't equal 0
```

3.6 Debugging

Q&A

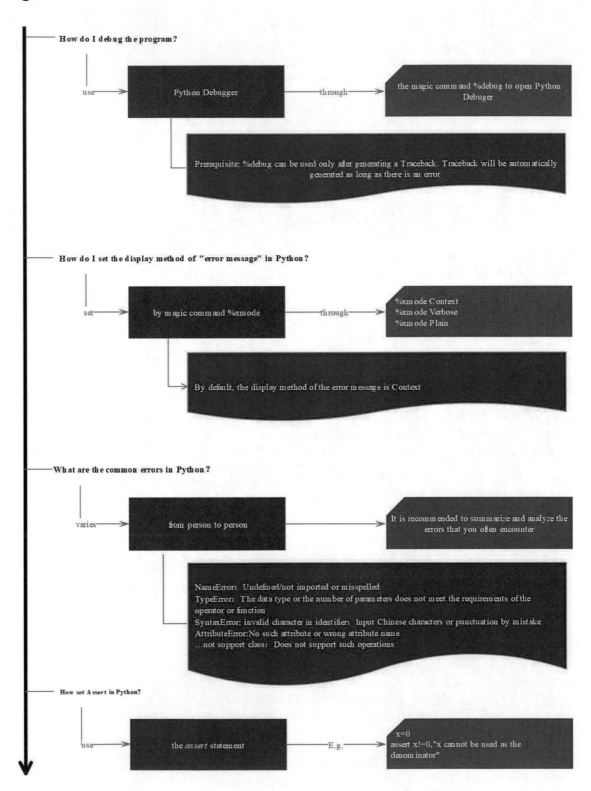

How do I debug the program?

use → Python Debugger

through → the magic command %debug to open Python Debuger

Prerequisite: %debug can be used only after generating a Traceback. Traceback will be automatically generated as long as there is an error

How do I set the display method of "error message" in Python?

set → by magic command %xmode

through → %xmode Context
%xmode Verbose
%xmode Plain

By default, the display method of the error message is Context

What are the common errors in Python?

varies → from person to person

It is recommended to summarize and analyze the errors that you often encounter

NameError: Undefined/not imported or misspelled
TypeError: The data type or the number of parameters does not meet the requirements of the operator or function
SyntaxError: invalid character in identifier: Input Chinese characters or punctuation by mistake
AttributeError:No such attribute or wrong attribute name
...not support class: Does not support such operations

How set Assert in Python?

use → the *assert* statement

E.g. → x=0
assert x!=0,"x cannot be used as the denominator"

3.6.1 Enabling the Python Debugger

Notes

When Python raises an exception or error message, it is recommended to use the Python Debugger (PDB) to debug the program.

In[1]
```
x=1
x1
```

Tips

Here, a NameError is raised that name 'x1' is not defined

Out[1]
```
---------------------------------------------------------------------
NameError        Traceback (most recent call last)
~\AppData\Local\Temp\ipykernel_19180\372800001.py in <module>
      1 x=1
----> 2 x1

NameError: name 'x1' is not defined
```

Notes

To open the Python Debugger (PDB), you can type the magic command %debug in IPython or Jupyter Notebook.

In[2]
```
%debug
```

Notes

To exit the Python Debugger (PDB), you can press 'q' or type 'quit' while in the debugger mode.

Tips

In addition to PDB, Pylint and Pychecker is commonly used Python debuggers.

Out[2]
```
> c:\users\szz\appdata\local\temp\ipykernel_19180\372800001.py(2)<module>()

ipdb> x
1
ipdb> x1
*** NameError: name 'x1' is not defined
ipdb> x
1
ipdb> q
```

3.6.2 Changing exception reporting modes

Notes

> %xmode toggles between different modes of exception handling in IPython, including plain, context, and verbose.

In[3]
```
%xmode Plain
y=1
Y
```

Out[3]
```
Exception reporting mode: Plain
Traceback (most recent call last):

  File "C:\Users\szz\AppData\Local\Temp\ipykernel_19180\265797083.py", line 3, in <module>
    Y

NameError: name 'Y' is not defined
```

In[4]
```
%xmode Verbose
y=1
Y
```

Out[4]
```
Exception reporting mode: Verbose
---------------------------------------------------------------------------
NameError         Traceback (most recent call last)
~\AppData\Local\Temp\ipykernel_19180\3286916471.py in <module>
          1 get_ipython().run_line_magic('xmode', 'Verbose')
          2 y=1
----> 3 Y

      global Y = undefined

NameError: name 'Y' is not defined
```

In[5]
```
%debug
```

Out[5]
```
> c:\users\szz\appdata\local\temp\ipykernel_19180\3286916471.py(3)<module>()

ipdb> y
1
ipdb> Y
*** NameError: name 'Y' is not defined
ipdb> y
1
ipdb> quit
```

3.6.3 Working with checkpoints

Notes

In data science, assertions (or assert statements) can be used as checkpoints to validate assumptions and ensure data integrity.

In[6]
```
a=1
b=0
assert b!=0,"The denominator can't equal 0"
```

Tips

If the condition is false, an AssertionError is raised.

Notes

When coding an assert statement in Python, don't forget to include a comma (,) to separate the expression being evaluated from an optional error message.

Out[6]
```
---------------------------------------------------------------------
AssertionError     Traceback (most recent call last)
~\AppData\Local\Temp\ipykernel_19180\3245325190.py in <module>
    1 a=1
    2 b=0
----> 3 assert b!=0,"The denominator can't equal 0"
      global b = 0

AssertionError: The denominator can't equal 0
```

In[7]
```
%debug
```

Out[7]
```
> c:\users\szz\appdata\local\temp\ipykernel_19180\3245325190.py(3)<module>()

ipdb> a
ipdb> b
ipdb> a
ipdb> quit
```

3.7 Search path

Q&A

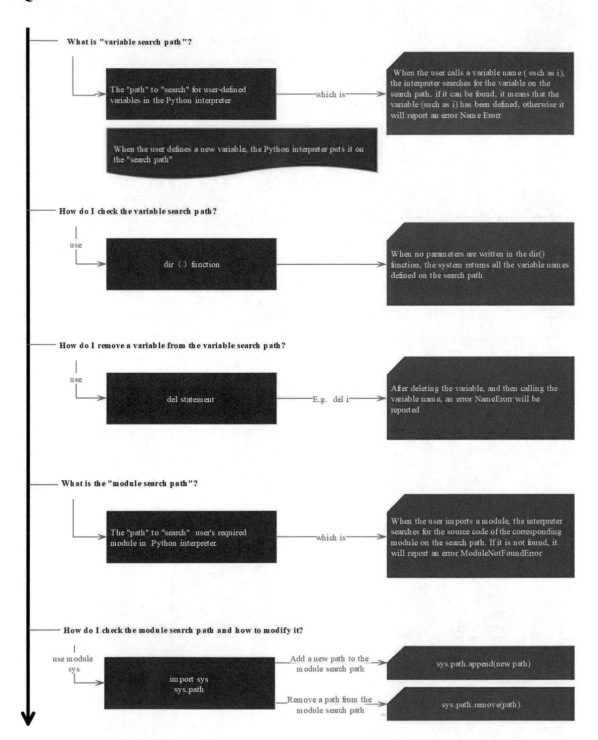

3.7.1 The variable search path

Notes

To see all variables that exist in the search path of the Python interpreter, you can use the built-in *dir()* function or the magic commands %whos and %who.

In[1]
```
myList=[1,2,3,4,5]
next(myList)
```

Out[1]
```
['In',
 'Out',
 '_',
 '__',
 '___',
 '__builtin__',
 '__builtins__',
 '__doc__',
 '__loader__',
 '__name__',
 '__package__',
 '__spec__',
 '_dh',
 '_i',
 '_i1',
 '_ih',
 '_ii',
 '_iii',
 '_oh',
 'exit',
 'get_ipython',
 'quit']
```

Tips

To add a variable to the search path, you can define a new variable using an assignment statement. For example:

In[2]
```
vi=1
```

Tips

To display the search path in Python and check whether the newly defined variable "vi" is present, you can use the *dir()* function or the %whos magic command in IPython.

In[3]
```
dir()
```

Out[3]
```
['In',
 'Out',
 '_',
 '_1',
 '_2',
 '_3',
 '__',
 '___',
 '__builtin__',
 '__builtins__',
 '__doc__',
 '__loader__',
 '__name__',
 '__package__',
 '__spec__',
 '_dh',
 '_i',
 '_i1',
 '_i2',
 '_i3',
 '_i4',
 '_i5',
 '_ih',
 '_ii',
 '_iii',
 '_oh',
 'exit',
 'get_ipython',
 'quit',
 'vi']
```

Notes To remove a variable from the search path, use the *del* statement followed by the variable name.

In[4] `del vi`

Tips Delete the *vi* variable.

Notes In Python data science projects, the common cause of a "NameError" is when a variable is not found in the search path or the current scope.

In[5] `vi`

Tips

NameError: name 'vi' is not defined.

The reason for this error is that the variable 'vi' has been deleted or is not defined in In[4].

Out[5]

```
------------------------------------------------------------------------
NameError   Traceback (most recent call last)
<ipython-input-5-c5bfa1c921c4> in <module>()
----> 1 vi

NameError: name 'vi' is not defined
```

3.7.2 The module search path

Notes

To check the module search *path* in Python, you can use the path attribute provided by the sys module and the *python -m site* command in the Anaconda prompt.

In[6]

```
import sys
sys.path
```

Notes

"*sys.path*" is an attribute in Python and should not be treated as a method. It cannot be parenthesized.

Out[6]

```
['',
 'C:\\Anaconda\\python36.zip',
 'C:\\Anaconda\\DLLs',
 'C:\\Anaconda\\lib',
 'C:\\Anaconda',
 'C:\\Anaconda\\lib\\site-packages',
 'C:\\Anaconda\\lib\\site-packages\\win32',
 'C:\\Anaconda\\lib\\site-packages\\win32\\lib',
 'C:\\Anaconda\\lib\\site-packages\\Pythonwin',
 'C:\\Anaconda\\lib\\site-packages\\IPython\\extensions',
 'C:\\Users\\soloman\\.ipython']
```

Notes

To add a new path to the module search path in Python, you can use the *sys.path. append()* method.

In[7]

```
import sys
sys.path.append('H:\\Python\\Anaconda')
```

In[8]

```
sys.path
```

To display the module search path in Python and check whether the newly added path from In[7] has appeared, you can use the sys.path attribute. Here's an example of how you can do it:

Out[8]
```
['C:\\Users\\szz',
 'D:\\Anacoda\\python37.zip',
 'D:\\Anacoda\\DLLs',
 'D:\\Anacoda\\lib',
 'D:\\Anacoda',
 '',
 'C:\\Users\\szz\\AppData\\Roaming\\Python\\Python37\\site-packages',
 'D:\\Anacoda\\lib\\site-packages',
 'D:\\Anacoda\\lib\\site-packages\\pyquery-1.4.3-py3.7.egg',
 'D:\\Anacoda\\lib\\site-packages\\cssselect-1.1.0-py3.7.egg',
 'D:\\Anacoda\\lib\\site-packages\\pip-21.1.1-py3.7.egg',
 'D:\\Anacoda\\lib\\site-packages\\win32',
 'D:\\Anacoda\\lib\\site-packages\\win32\\lib',
 'D:\\Anacoda\\lib\\site-packages\\Pythonwin',
 'D:\\Anacoda\\lib\\site-packages\\IPython\\extensions',
 'C:\\Users\\szz\\.ipython',
 'H:\\Python\\Anaconda']
```

To remove a path from the module search path, you can use the *sys.path.remove()* method.

In[9]   `sys.path.remove('H:\\Python\\Anaconda')`

In[10]   `sys.path`

We can display the module search path again and check whether the path that was removed in In[9] is no longer displayed on the module search path.

Out[10]
```
['C:\\Users\\szz',
 'D:\\Anacoda\\python37.zip',
 'D:\\Anacoda\\DLLs',
 'D:\\Anacoda\\lib',
 'D:\\Anacoda',
 '',
 'C:\\Users\\szz\\AppData\\Roaming\\Python\\Python37\\site-packages',
 'D:\\Anacoda\\lib\\site-packages',
 'D:\\Anacoda\\lib\\site-packages\\pyquery-1.4.3-py3.7.egg',
 'D:\\Anacoda\\lib\\site-packages\\cssselect-1.1.0-py3.7.egg',
 'D:\\Anacoda\\lib\\site-packages\\pip-21.1.1-py3.7.egg',
 'D:\\Anacoda\\lib\\site-packages\\win32',
 'D:\\Anacoda\\lib\\site-packages\\win32\\lib',
 'D:\\Anacoda\\lib\\site-packages\\Pythonwin',
 'D:\\Anacoda\\lib\\site-packages\\IPython\\extensions',
 'C:\\Users\\szz\\.ipython']
```

3.8 Current working directory

Q&A

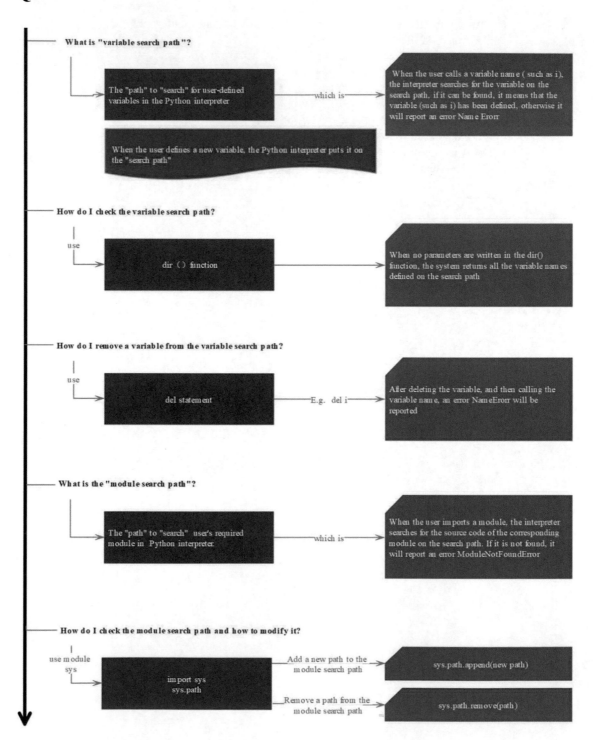

3.8.1 Getting current working directory

| Notes | The "current working directory" in Python refers to the default path where files and folders are read from or written to. For instance, in the book [4.44 DataFrame and Pandas], when referring to an external file such as "bc_data.csv," it needs to be placed in the "current working directory" beforehand to be accessed without specifying the full file path. |

| Notes | To obtain the current working directory in Python, you can use the *getcwd()* method provided by the *os* module. |

In[1]	import os print(os.getcwd())
Out[1]	C:\Users\szz

3.8.2 Resetting current working directory

| Notes | To change the current working directory in Python, you can use the *chdir()* function from the *os* module. |

| Tips | Before changing the current working directory, you need to create a new working directory to replace the original current working directory. For example, you can create a new directory named 'Python projects' on the E: drive. |

In[3]	os.chdir('E:\PythonProjects') print(os.getcwd())
Out[3]	E:\PythonProjects

3.8.3 Reading/writing current working directory

| Notes | The data analyst needs to choose the appropriate file import method based on the type of the target data file and the requirements of the analysis work. There are various methods available, including using the built-in *open()* function or utilizing the *read_csv()* and *read_excel()* functions from the third-party extension package Pandas. |

| Notes | For example, read the file "bc_data.csv" from the current working directory into the *data* dataframe. |

In[4] |
```
from pandas import read_csv
data = read_csv('bc_data.csv')
data.head(5)
```

Notes

Here, executing the statement *read_csv('bc_data.csv')* assumes that the target file 'bc_data.csv' has been placed in the current working directory, such as "*E:\Python projects*".

Tips

Readers can find the data file 'bc_data.csv' in the supporting resources provided with this book.

	id	diagnosis	radius_mean	texture_mean	perimeter_mean	area_mean	smoothness_mean	compactness_mean	conc:
0	842302	M	17.99	10.38	122.80	1001.0	0.11840	0.27760	
1	842517	M	20.57	17.77	132.90	1326.0	0.08474	0.07864	
2	84300903	M	19.69	21.25	130.00	1203.0	0.10960	0.15990	
3	84348301	M	11.42	20.38	77.58	386.1	0.14250	0.28390	
4	84358402	M	20.29	14.34	135.10	1297.0	0.10030	0.13280	

5 rows × 32 columns

3.9 Object-oriented programming

Q&A

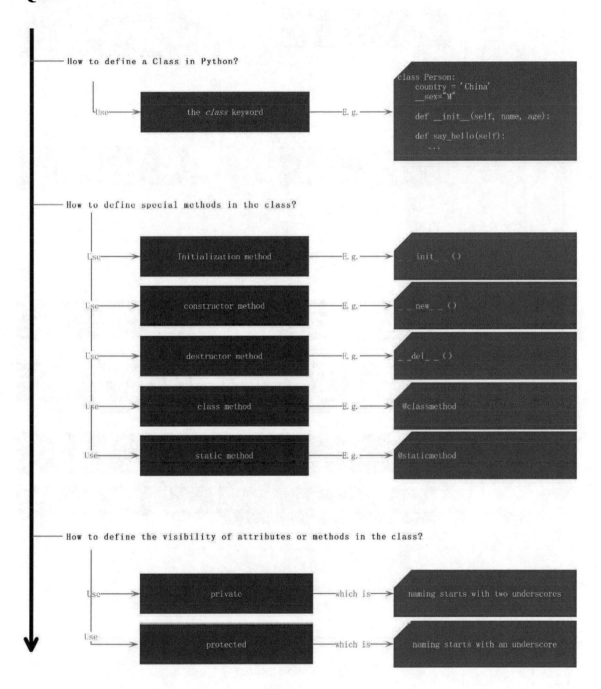

How to define a Class in Python?

Use → the *class* keyword — E. g. →

```
class Person:
    country = 'China'
    __sex="M"

    def __init__(self, name, age):

    def say_hello(self):
        ...
```

How to define special methods in the class?

Use → Initialization method — E. g. → __init__ ()

Use → constructor method — E. g. → __new__ ()

Use → destructor method — E. g. → __del__ ()

Use → class method — E. g. → @classmethod

Use → static method — E. g. → @staticmethod

How to define the visibility of attributes or methods in the class?

Use → private — which is → naming starts with two underscores

Use → protected — which is → naming starts with an underscore

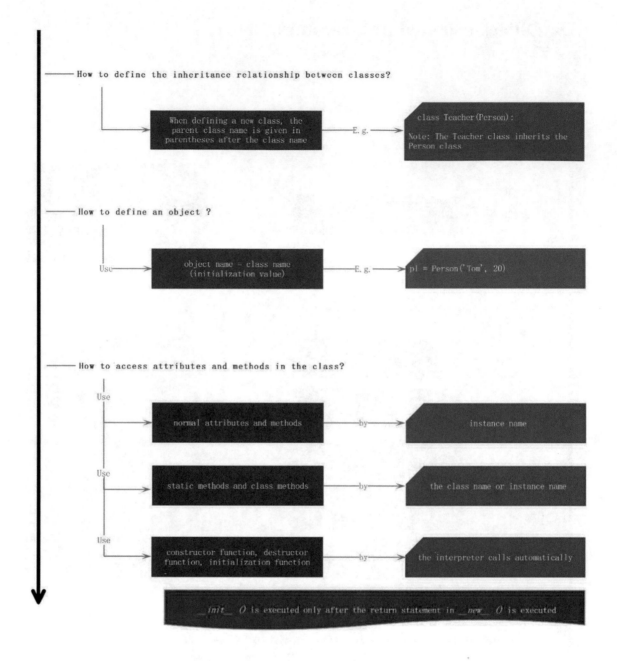

How to define the inheritance relationship between classes?

When defining a new class, the parent class name is given in parentheses after the class name —— E. g. ——

class Teacher(Person):

Note: The Teacher class inherits the Person class

How to define an object ?

Use —— object name = class name (initialization value) —— E. g. —— p1 = Person('Tom', 20)

How to access attributes and methods in the class?

Use —— normal attributes and methods —— by —— instance name

Use —— static methods and class methods —— by —— the class name or instance name

Use —— constructor function, destructor function, initialization function —— by —— the interpreter calls automatically

__init__ () is executed only after the return statement in __new__ () is executed

3.9.1 Classes

Python is a versatile programming language that supports multiple programming paradigms, including object-oriented programming (OOP) and functional programming (FP). This chapter does not aim to provide an introduction to the object-oriented programming paradigm itself.

In Python, class definitions begin with the keyword "class," followed by the name of the class and a colon.

In[1]
```python
class Person:
        nationality = 'China'  #Define nationality/nationality as a public attribute here
        _deposit=10e10  #Python protected attribute names start with an underscore. Here, the
                    deposit quantity / deposit is defined as the protected attribute.
        __gender="M" #Python private attribute names start with two underscores.
                Here, gender is defined as the private attribute.

        def __init__(self, name, age):
            self.name = name #Instance attribute
            age = age # local variable

        def say_hi(self):
            print(self.name)

p1 = Person('Tom', 30)
p1.say_hi()
```

The method of defining attribute and method visibility in Python differs from that of languages like C++, C#, and Java. In Python, the convention is to use one underscore or two underscores at the beginning of the name to indicate different levels of visibility, distinguishing between protected and private attributes and methods.

Person ('Tom', 30) does two things: create a new object and initialize it to return the instance P1.

The three essential methods in Python are as follows:

1. __init__(): Initialization function or constructor
2. __new__(): Constructor function (rarely used)
3. __del__(): Destructor function

Out[1]   Tom

3.9.2 Methods

Notes

The difference between a method and a function lies in their relationship to object-oriented programming. In object-oriented programming, a method is a function that is associated with a class or object.

Notes

In Python, there are three types of the user-defined methods: instance methods, class methods and static methods.

In[2]
```python
class Person:
    """

        Here is the docString of class Person

    """
    nationality = 'China'
    _deposit=10e10
    __gender="M"


    def __init__ (self, name, age):
        age = age #age is a local variable in the function __ init__ ()
        self.name = name #Unlike the age variable, self.name is the instance attribute
# The definition syntax of an instance is similar to that of a general function, except
for formal parameters.
# The first parameter of the instance method must be the positional parameter self.
Otherwise, TypeError is raised "TypeError: * * * () function has a positive arguments
error".
#self :A reference of the current instance, indicating that the method is an "instance
method".
#The instance method can be accessed in the form of "instance name. function name".
    def say_hi(self):
        print(self.name)
# Class method: add a line @ classmethod in front of a method.
# In the definition of class method, the first parameter must be "class reference cls",
that is, #the function can be called through the class name.
    @classmethod
    def class_func(cls):
        cls.nationality = 'CHINA'
        print('I live in {0}'. Format(cls.nationality))
# Static method: add a line @ staticmethod in front of a method.
# Characteristics of static method: no cls or self in the formal parameters, or even no
# parameters

# Functions without any parameters are generally defined as "static methods".
    @staticmethod
    def static_func(x, y):
        print(x+y)

p1 = Person('Tom', 20)
p1.say_hi()
```

Out[2] | Tom

Notes

A static method can be called from either a class or object reference.

In[3] | Person.static_func(200,300) # use class name to call "static method".

Out[3] | 500

In[4] | p1.static_func(200,300) # use instance name to call "static method".

Out[4] | 500

Tips

A class method can be called from either a class or object reference

In[5] | Person.class_func() # use class name to call "class method".

Out[5] | I live in CHINA

In[6] | p1.class_func()   # use instance name to call "class method".

Out[6] | I live in CHINA

3.9.3 Inheritance

Notes

In Python, the syntax for specifying inheritance between classes is unique. When defining a class, you can indicate its parent class or classes by putting the parent class name(s) in parentheses after the class name.

In[7]
```python
class Teacher(Person):
    pass

t1=Teacher("zhang",20)
```

In[8] | Person.class_func()

Out[8] | I live in CHINA

In[9] | t1.class_func()

Tips

As you can see from the above output, the class *Teacher* has inherited its parent class Person's class_func () method.

Out[9] | I live in CHINA

In[10] | t1.static_func(1,10)

Out[10] | 11

In[11] | Person.static_func(2,10)

Out[11] | 12

In[12] | t1._deposit

Tips

A subclass can inherit the protected attribute from its parent class, such as the *_deposit* attribute in In[12].

Out[12] | 100000000000.0

In[13] | t1. _ _gender #AttributeError: 'Teacher' object has no attribute '__gender'

Tips

A subclass can not inherit the private attribute from its parent class, such as the *__gender* attribute in In[2].

Out[13] |
```
---------------------------------------------------------------------------
AttributeError     Traceback (most recent call last)
~\AppData\Local\Temp\ipykernel_18396\514368724.py in <module>
----> 1 t1.__gender

AttributeError: 'Teacher' object has no attribute '__gender'
```

Notes

Use the following operations to check the docString of the *Teacher* class and its parent class *Person*.

In[14] |
```
Person?
Teacher?
```

Notes

To check the name of a class in Python, you can use the *__name__* attribute.

In[15] | Person.__name__

Out[15] | 'Person'

Notes

In Python, theSystem-defined names are also known as "dunder" names. These names are defined by the interpreter and its implementation (including the standard library. Commonly used dunder attributes are as follows:

- __name__: Return the class name
- __doc__: Return the docString of the class
- __bases__: Return the tuple of all parent classes of the class
- __dict__: Return a list of all attributes and methods of a class
- __module__: Return the name of the module where the class definition is located
- __class__: Return the class corresponding to the instance

3.9.4 Attributes

Notes

Unlike Java and C++, Python does not use the private keyword to define *private* variables. Instead, the convention in Python is to use "double underscores" at the beginning of variable names to indicate privacy, although it does not enforce true encapsulation.

In[16]

```
class Student:
    __name="Zhang"

#__name is a private variable, but age is not.
    age=18
    @property
    def get_name(self):
#If self is not written here, the arguments mismatch error will be thrown: "TypeError:
#get_name() take s 0 positional arguments but 1 was given".
        print(self.__name)
#If self is not written here, error will be thrown: "NameError: name '_Student__
#name' is not defined".

#Private variables can be called neither by class name nor by instance.
stdnt1=Student()

#@property decorator calls a method or function as an attribute.
stdnt1.get_name
```

Notes

A function decorated with the @property decorator in Python cannot be called using (), and it must be accessed as an attribute. If you attempt to call a property-decorated function with parentheses, you will encounter a TypeError stating that the function takes no positional arguments.

Out[16]

Zhang

3.9.5 Self and Cls

Notes

In Python, self and cls are passed to the methods in the first argument. The self and cls means a references to an instance and a class, respectively.

- Always use self for the first argument to instance methods.
- Always use cls for the first argument to class methods.

For instance, when defining a class, *self* stands for "instance reference", as is often used in __ *init__* (); *cls* stands for "a reference to a class", as often used in __ *new__* ().

In[17]
```
class Student:
    age=0
    name="z"
    def __init__(self):
#The self can only appear in formal parameters.
        self.name="zhang"
#The self. name is an instance variable, which is different from another class variable
#name.
        age=10
#The age here is a local variable in "__init__ ()".
s1=Student()
s2=Student()
s1.name="song"
s1.age=30
Student.age=20
#The age is a class attribute.
Student.name="li"
# The name is a class attribute.
s1.name, s1.age,s2.name, s2.age
```

Tips

In Python object-oriented programming, class attributes (such as *name*) and instance attributes (such as *age*) occupy their own independent storage space in memory without mutual influence, and the search rule of instance attributes is "first search the memory of instance attributes to find the corresponding attributes, it can't be found such as *s2.age*. The class attribute value will replace the instance attribute value with the same name". Readers are advised to use Python general attribute ".__*dic__*" to track the attributes and attribute values of each class and instance, such as s1.__*dict__* or Student.__*dict__*.

Out[17]   ('song', 30, 'zhang', 20)

3.9.6 __new__ () and __init__()

Notes

It is important to note that if the __new__() method of your class does not return an instance of the class (cls), the __init__() method will not be called. This means that the initialization step will be skipped, and the object will not be properly initialized.

In[18]
```python
class Student:
    name="wang"
    __age=16

    def __new__(cls,name,age):
        print('__new__() is called')

    def __init__(self,name,age):
        print('__init__() is called')
        self.name = name
        self.age = age
    def sayHi(self):
        print(self.name,self.age)

s1= Student("zhang", 18)
```

Out[18]   __new__() is called

In[19]   print(s1)

Notes

There is no return statement in *__new_ ()*, Hence, the value of s1 is NoneType.

Tips

In Python, the *__new__()* method is called when an object is created, and it is responsible for creating and returning a new instance of the class. The *__init__()* method, on the other hand, is called after the *__new__()* method and is used to initialize the newly created object.

Out[19]   None

Tips

The *__new__()* function is used to produce an "object";
The *__init__()* function is used to produce an "instance".

Out[19]   None

Tips

The output result is <generator object myGen at 0x00000213EA679E58>, not a specific return value.

In[20] | `s1.sayHi()`

Tips | Here, the Python interpreter will raise an AttributeError that 'NoneType' object has no attribute 'sayHi'

Out[20] |
```
-------------------------------------------------------------
AttributeError     Traceback (most recent call last)
~\AppData\Local\Temp\ipykernel_18396\2394443593.py in <module>
----> 1 s1.sayHi()

AttributeError: 'NoneType' object has no attribute 'sayHi'
```

Tips | *The AttributeError is raised in that there is no return statement in the __new__() function. To modify: Add return object. __new__() (cls) to the __new__() function.*

In[21] |
```python
class Student:
    name="wang"
    __age=16

    def __new__(cls,*args, **kwargs):
        print('__new__() is called')
        return object.__new__(cls)

    def __init__(self,name,age):
        print('__init__() is called')
        self.name = name
        self.age = age

    def sayHi(self):
        print(self.name,self.age)

s1= Student("zhang", 18)
s1.sayHi()
```

Tips | Adding a return statement (return object.__new__(cls)) in the __new__() method will ensure that the __init__() method is invoked. By calling object.__new__(cls), you are explicitly creating a new instance of the class.

Out[21] |
```
__new__() is called
__init__() is called
zhang 18
```

Exercises

[1] Which of the following statements about the *iterable* object and the *iterator* object in Python is wrong?
A. Functions that can receive the *iterator* objects can receive the *iterable* objects.
B. The *iterator* object can be called by the *next* function, constantly returning the object of the next value.
C. The *iter* function can convert the *iterable* object into the *iterator* object.
D. The *iterable* objects are not necessarily the *iterator* objects.

[2] Which of the following is true of Python?
A. Calling the *range* function returns to the *generator* object.
B. The *return* statements are generally used in the *generator* objects to return results.
C. The result will not be returned immediately when the generator is called, because the generator follows lazy calculation.
D. The *generator* objects contain the *iterator* objects.

[3] Which of the following is a benefit of using modules in python?
A. It greatly improves the maintainability of the code.
B. Writing code does not have to start from scratch to improve efficiency.
C. Avoid conflicts between function names and variable names.
D. All of the above

[4] Which of the following statements about modules is wrong?
A. Modules are normally .py file.
B. The search order of modules is: modules already loaded in memory- > built-in modules
  - >The module contained in the sys.path.
C. The user cannot customize the module.
D. No matter how many times *import* is executed, the single module in the whole program will be imported only once.

[5] Which of the following statements about the relationship between modules and packages is false?
A. Packages can be used to group a set of modules under a common package name.
B. A package can only correspond to one module.
C. Each package directory will have an init.py, and init.py itself is a module.

[6] Which of the following is not a built-in module?
A. sys
B. random
C. os
D. image

[7] Which of the following will run with errors?
A. from file1.file2 import test
B. import file1.file2.test as test
C. import seaborn,jieba as sns,jieba
D. import seaborn as sns,jieba as jieba

[8] Which of the following is false of package?
A. It is a folder that always contain__ init__. py module.
B. Packages are a way of organizing and managing code.
C. Other modules and subpackages are generally contained.
D. The package cannot be customized.

[9]   Which of the following has a syntax error?
  A. dir([])
  B. dir(?)
  C. dir('')
  D. dir()

[10] Which of the following statements about help documents is false?
  A. __ doc__ is preceded and followed by a short underline.
  B. When using *help (module_name)*, we need to import the module first.
  C. The object in *help (object)* is the content that needs help.
  D. If we use *help (object)* or *help ('object')*, press *q* directly when exiting.

[11] Which of the following is true?
  A. The *try, except* and *finally* statements always be used at the same time.
  B. The *finally* statement has the same capacity as the *else* clauses.
  C. The *assert* statement is mainly used to set checkpoint. When the check condition is true, AssertionError will be raised.
  D. The assertion contents of the *assert* statement can be empty.

[12] SyntaxError indicates( )
  A. suspicious syntax warning
  B. invalid arguments passed in
  C. syntax error
  D. indentation error

[13] Which of the following will appear when an error occurred while encoding Unicode?
  A. UnicodeError
  B. UnicodeDecodeError
  C. UnicodeEncodeError
  D. UnicodeTranslateError

[14] If Chinese characters or punctuation are mistakenly typed in the code, the system will prompt ( )
  A. Not ImplementedError
  B. IndentationError
  C. EOFError
  D. SyntaxError

[15] What will the following program print out?
```
import math
def f(n):
    assert n>0,'n must be positive'
    return math.sqrt(n)
f(4)
```

  A. 2.0
  B. AssertionError: n must be positive
  C. AssertionError: n must be positive
      2.0

[16] Which of the following is false of Python Pdb?
  A. The **prompt** of debugger is Pdb.
  B. The debugger is not extensible.
  C. The *pdb* module defines an interactive source code debugger for Python programs.
  D. pdb supports post debugging, which can be imported under program control.

[17] Which of the following statements about object-oriented technology is false?
    A. Class is used to specify a set of objects with the same attributes and methods.
    B. Class variables are common throughout the instantiated objects.
    C. The functions defined in the class are called variables.
    D. Instances of data structures defined by classes are called objects.

[18] Which of the following statements about variables in a class is true?
    A. *self* represents an instance of a class which is required when defining methods of a class.
    B. The value of a class variable cannot be shared among all instances of this class.
    C. Class variables can be accessed directly in internal or external classes.
    D. *self* is a keyword in Python and cannot be modified.

[19] What is the output of the following program?

```
x=1
y=2
del y
z=x*y
```

    A. NameError
    B. SyntaxError
    C. ValueError
    D. AssertionError

[20] Which of the following statements about the current working directory is false?
    A. The *getcwd* function in the *os* module is used to check the current working directory.
    B. Current working path can be modified with *os.chdir(path)*.
    C. The current working directory is the search path, which refers to the default read-write path of files and folders in Python.
    D. The *open* function is a common file import function.

4. Data wrangling with Python

Data wrangling is the process of transforming and mapping data from one raw data form into another format with the intent of making it more appropriate and valuable for data science purposes. This chapter will introduce the essential data wrangling skills for data scientists, including:

1. Random number generation
2. Multidimensional arrays
3. Series
4. DataFrames
5. Date and time manipulation
6. Data visualization

These skills are crucial for data scientists to effectively manipulate, analyze, and visualize data in their projects.

C. Borjigin, *Python Data Science,* https://doi.org/10.1007/978-981-19-7702-2_4

4.1 Random number generation

Q&A

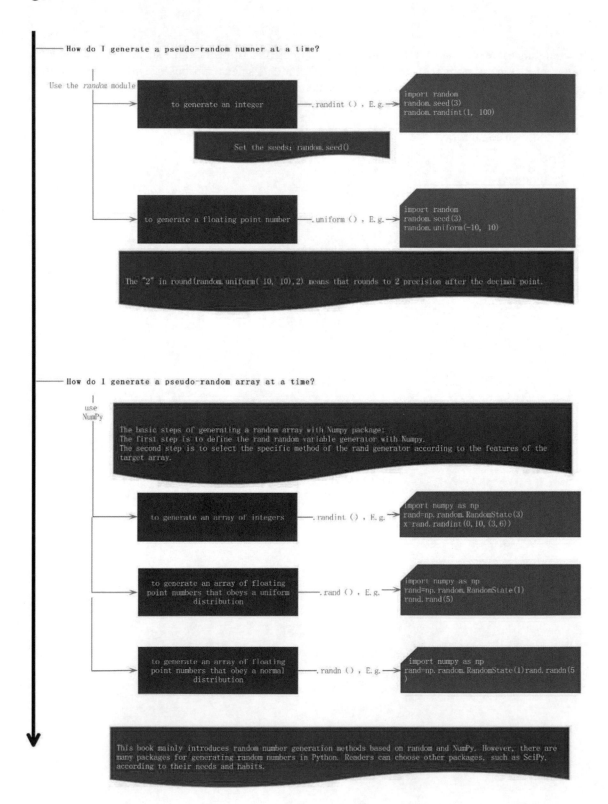

How do I generate a pseudo-random numner at a time?

Use the *random* module

to generate an integer → .randint ( ) , E.g. →
```
import random
random.seed(3)
random.randint(1, 100)
```

Set the seeds: random.seed()

to generate a floating point number → .uniform ( ) , E.g. →
```
import random
random.seed(3)
random.uniform(-10, 10)
```

The "2" in round(random.uniform(-10, 10),2) means that rounds to 2 precision after the decimal point.

How do I generate a pseudo-random array at a time?

use NumPy

The basic steps of generating a random array with Numpy package:
The first step is to define the rand random variable generator with Numpy.
The second step is to select the specific method of the rand generator according to the features of the target array.

to generate an array of integers → .randint ( ) , E.g. →
```
import numpy as np
rand=np.random.RandomState(3)
x=rand.randint(0, 10, (3,6))
```

to generate an array of floating point numbers that obeys a uniform distribution → .rand ( ) , E.g. →
```
import numpy as np
rand=np.random.RandomState(1)
rand.rand(5)
```

to generate an array of floating point numbers that obey a normal distribution → .randn ( ) , E.g. →
```
import numpy as np
rand=np.random.RandomState(1)rand.randn(5)
```

This book mainly introduces random number generation methods based on random and NumPy. However, there are many packages for generating random numbers in Python. Readers can choose other packages, such as SciPy, according to their needs and habits.

4.1.1 Generating a random number at a time

Tips

There are two common methods for generating random numbers from a computer: Pseudo-Random Number Generators (PRNGs) and True Random Number Generators (TRNGs).

PRNGs rely on a seed number and an algorithm to generate numbers that appear to be random but are actually predictable. They are widely used in computer programs and simulations.

In contrast, TRNGs generate randomness from physical phenomena using hardware and integrate it into a computer. These generators provide a higher level of true randomness compared to PRNGs.

Notes

The Python standard library provides a module called *random* that offers a suite of functions for generating pseudo random numbers.

In[1]
```
import random
random.seed(3)
```

Tricks

random.seed(): Initialize the random number generator. The random number generator needs a number to start with (a seed value), to be able to generate a random number. By default the random number generator uses the current system time.

Tips

The random package is not the only package in Python that generates random numbers. Other packages such as NumPy, SciPy, and scikit-learn also provide functions for generating random numbers.

Notes

The random module contains several functions that allows you to generate random numbers. For instance, the randint(a,b) function generates random integers from a (inclusive) to b (exclusive).

In[2]
```
import random
random.seed(3)
random.randint(1, 100)
```

Out[2]   31

Notes

Random.uniform(a,b): Generates a random floating point number from a uniform distribution.

```
In[3]   import random
        random.seed(3)
        random.uniform(-10, 10)
```

Out[3]   -5.240707458162173

Notes

The "2" in "round(random.uniform(-10, 10),2)" means that the round function will return random.uniform(-10, 10) rounded to 2 precision after the decimal point.

```
In[4]   random.seed(3)
        round(random.uniform(-10, 10),2)
```

Out[4]   -5.24

4.1.2 Generating a random array at a time

Tips

The basic steps of generating a random array with Numpy package:
The first step is to define random variable generator (e.g rand) with Numpy.
The second step is to select the specific method of the *rand* generator according to the features of the target array (such as uniform distribution or normal distribution), including randint(), rand(), or randn().

```
In[6]   # to create a container for pseudo-random number generator

        import numpy as np
        rand=np.random.RandomState(32)
```

Notes

numpy.random.RandomState(seed):Container for the Mersenne Twister pseudo-random number generator. Here, the seed is used to initialize the pseudo-random number generator.

```
In[7]   # to generate a random array

        x=rand.randint(0,10,(3,6))
        x
```

Out[7]   array([[7, 5, 6, 8, 3, 7],
               [9, 3, 5, 9, 4, 1],
               [3, 1, 2, 3, 8, 2]])

Notes

RandomState.randint(a, b, shape)：Return random integers from a (inclusive) to b (exclusive) with the output shape.

4.2 Multidimensional arrays

Q&A

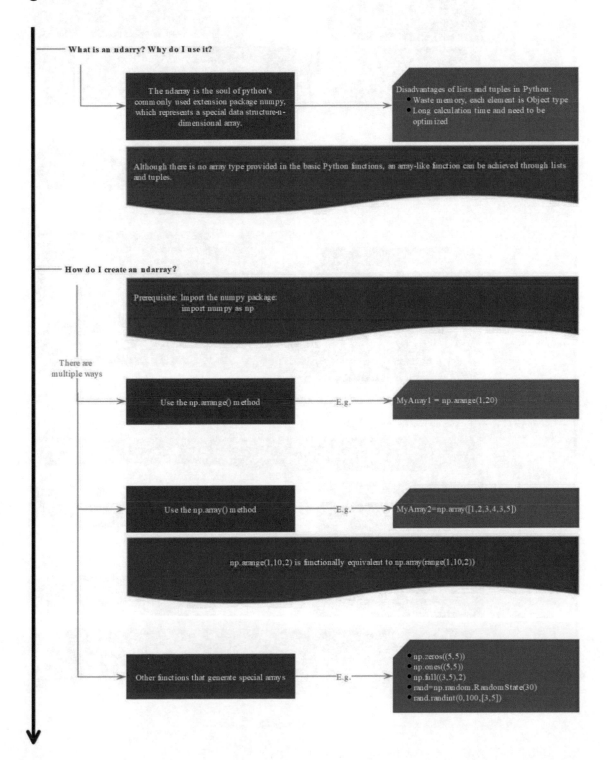

What is an ndarry? Why do I use it?

The ndarray is the soul of python's commonly used extension package numpy, which represents a special data structure-n-dimensional array.

Disadvantages of lists and tuples in Python:
- Waste memory, each element is Object type
- Long calculation time and need to be optimized

Although there is no array type provided in the basic Python functions, an array-like function can be achieved through lists and tuples.

How do I create an ndarray?

Prerequisite: Import the numpy package:
import numpy as np

There are multiple ways

Use the np.arange() method   E.g.   MyArray1 = np.arange(1,20)

Use the np.array() method   E.g.   MyArray2=np.array([1,2,3,4,3,5])

np.arange(1,10,2) is functionally equivalent to np.array(range(1,10,2))

Other functions that generate special arrays   E.g.
- np.zeros((5,5))
- np.ones((5,5))
- np.full((3,5),2)
- rand=np.random.RandomState(30)
- rand.randint(0,100,[3,5])

What are the special features of ndarray?

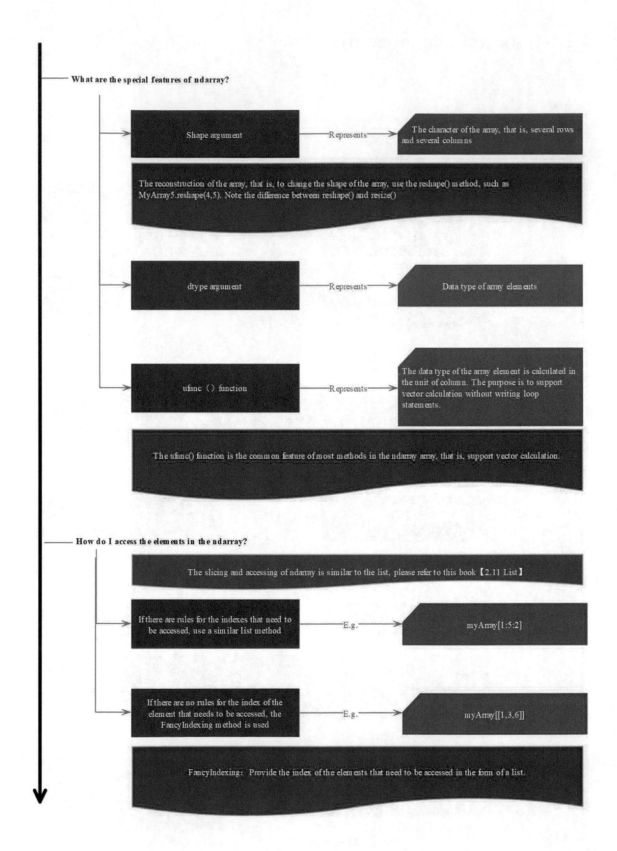

Shape argument — Represents → The character of the array, that is, several rows and several columns

The reconstruction of the array, that is, to change the shape of the array, use the reshape() method, such as MyArray5.reshape(4,5). Note the difference between reshape() and resize()

dtype argument — Represents → Data type of array elements

ufunc ( ) function — Represents → The data type of the array element is calculated in the unit of column. The purpose is to support vector calculation without writing loop statements.

The ufunc() function is the common feature of most methods in the ndarray array, that is, support vector calculation.

How do I access the elements in the ndarray?

The slicing and accessing of ndarray is similar to the list, please refer to this book 【2.11 List】

If there are rules for the indexes that need to be accessed, use a similar list method — E.g. → myArray[1:5:2]

If there are no rules for the index of the element that needs to be accessed, the FancyIndexing method is used — E.g. → myArray[[1,3,6]]

FancyIndexing: Provide the index of the elements that need to be accessed in the form of a list.

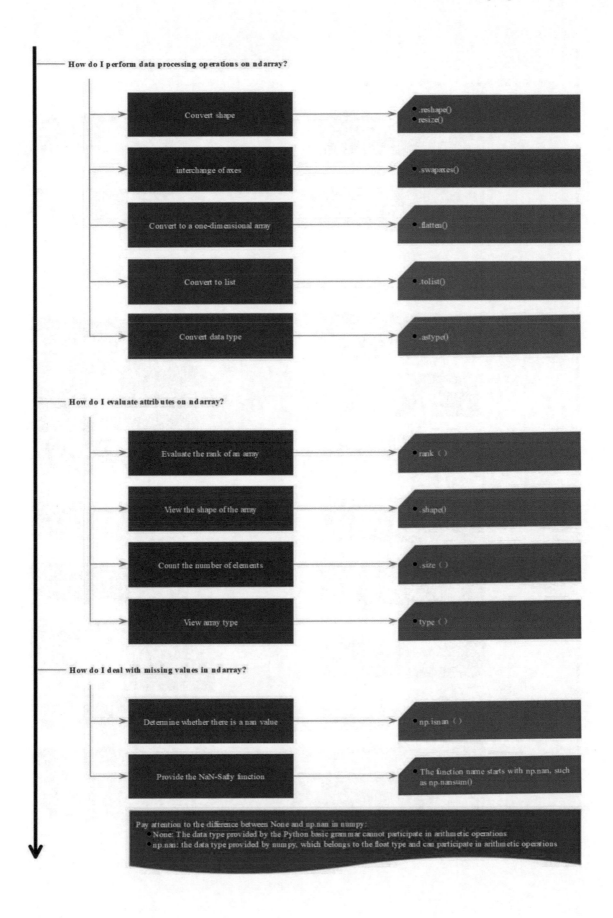

How do I perform data processing operations on ndarray?

Convert shape → • .reshape() • .resize()

interchange of axes → • .swapaxes()

Convert to a one-dimensional array → • .flatten()

Convert to list → • .tolist()

Convert data type → • .astype()

How do I evaluate attributes on ndarray?

Evaluate the rank of an array → • .rank（）

View the shape of the array → • .shape()

Count the number of elements → • .size（）

View array type → • type（）

How do I deal with missing values in ndarray?

Determine whether there is a nan value → • np.isnan（）

Provide the NaN-Safty function → • The function name starts with np.nan, such as np.nansum()

Pay attention to the difference between None and np.nan in numpy:
• None: The data type provided by the Python basic grammar cannot participate in arithmetic operations
• np.nan: the data type provided by numpy, which belongs to the float type and can participate in arithmetic operations

What is the difference between resize and reshape?

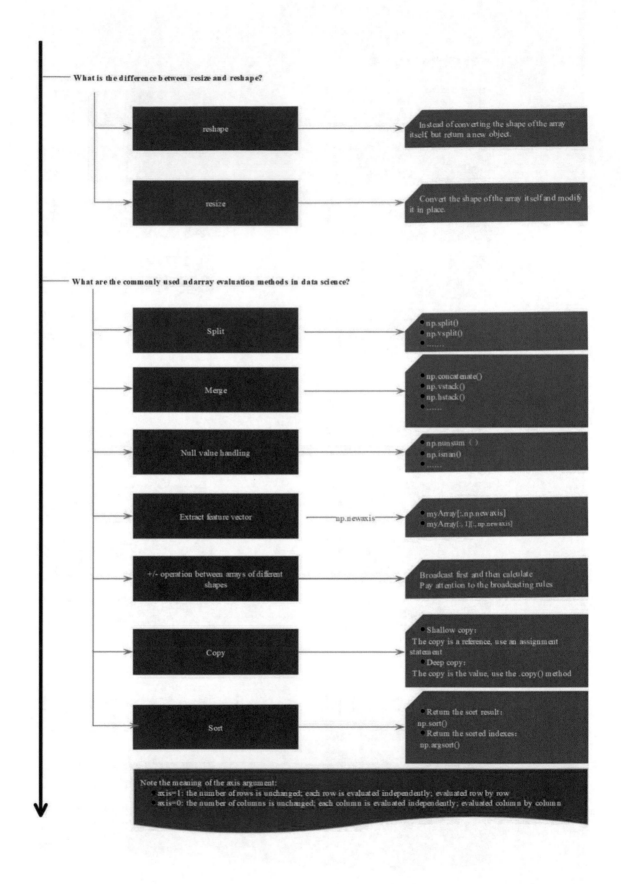

reshape — Instead of converting the shape of the array itself but return a new object.

resize — Convert the shape of the array itself and modify it in place.

What are the commonly used ndarray evaluation methods in data science?

Split
- np.split()
- np.vsplit()
- ......

Merge
- np.concatenate()
- np.vstack()
- np.hstack()
- ......

Null value handling
- np.nunsum ( )
- np.isnan()
- ......

Extract feature vector — np.newaxis
- myArray[:,np.newaxis]
- myArray[:, 1][:,np.newaxis]

+/- operation between arrays of different shapes
- Broadcast first and then calculate
- Pay attention to the broadcasting rules

Copy
- Shallow copy:
  The copy is a reference, use an assignment statement
- Deep copy:
  The copy is the value, use the .copy() method

Sort
- Return the sort result:
  np.sort()
- Return the sorted indexes:
  np.argsort()

Note the meaning of the axis argument:
- axis=1: the number of rows is unchanged; each row is evaluated independently; evaluated row by row
- axis=0: the number of columns is unchanged; each column is evaluated independently; evaluated column by column

4.2.1 Createting ndarrays

Notes

NumPy offers powerful N-dimensional arrays(ndarray) that support linear algebra routines, comprehensive mathematical functions, random number generators, and more.

In[1] | # To import the NumPy module

import numpy as np

Notes

An ndarray object represents a multidimensional, homogeneous array of fixed-size items.

Notes

Ndarray can be created in several ways, one of which is using the np.arange () function. For instance, numpy.arange(a,b) returns evenly spaced values within the half-open interval [a, b). In other words, the interval including a but excluding b.

In[2] | MyArray1 = np.arange(1,20)
MyArray1

Out[2] | array([1, 2, 3, 4, 5, 6, 7, 8, 9, 10, 11, 12, 13, 14, 15, 16, 17, 18, 19])]

Tricks

The difference between range() and numpy.arange():
- range() is a built-in function in Python that returns a range object, as described in [2.8 The For Statement].
- numpy.arange() is a function in the third-party model NumPy, which returns the ndarray of NumPy.

For integer arguments, the numpy.arange() function is equivalent to the Python built-in range() function, but returns an ndarray rather than a list.

Tips

numpy.arange() :return evenly spaced values within the half-open interval [start, stop). In other words, the interval including start but excluding stop.

In[3] | # to call the python built-in function range()

range(1,10,2)

Out[3] | range(1, 10, 2)

Notes

In Python 2, the python built-in function range() creates a list, and it is effectively eagerly evaluated. In Python 3, it creates a range object, whose individual values are lazily evaluated. In other words, In Python2, range() returns a list, which is equivalent to list(range()) in Python3.

In[4] | # to convert a Range object to a List object
list(range(1,10,2))

Out[4] | [1, 3, 5, 7, 9]

Notes

numpy.arange() returns an ndarray object.
In contrast to Python's built-in data types such as lists or tuples, ndarray objects consume less memory and are convenient to use.

In[5] | np.arange(1,10,2)

Out[5] | array([1, 3, 5, 7, 9])

Notes

The second way to create an ndarray is by calling the *np.array()* function from the *NumPy* module.

In[6] | MyArray2=np.array([1,2,3,4,3,5])
MyArray2

Out[6] | array([1, 2, 3, 4, 3, 5])

Tips

The expression np.array(range(1,10,2)) is equivalent to np.arange(1,10,2) in NumPy. Both expressions generate an ndarray containing the values [1, 3, 5, 7, 9].

In[7] | np.array(range(1,10,2))

Out[7] | array([1, 3, 5, 7, 9])

Notes

The third way to create an ndarray is by calling functions like np.zeros(), np.ones(), and others provided by NumPy. These functions allow you to create arrays filled with zeros, ones, or specific values.

In[8] | MyArray3=np.zeros((5,5))
MyArray3

Out[8] | array([[0., 0., 0., 0., 0.],
       [0., 0., 0., 0., 0.],
       [0., 0., 0., 0., 0.],
       [0., 0., 0., 0., 0.],
       [0., 0., 0., 0., 0.]])

Notes

In np.zeros((5,5)), the argument (5,5) represents the shape of the target array, which is an array of 5 rows and 5 columns.

In[9]
```
MyArray4=np.ones((5,5))
MyArray4
```

Out[9]
```
array([[1., 1., 1., 1., 1.],
       [1., 1., 1., 1., 1.],
       [1., 1., 1., 1., 1.],
       [1., 1., 1., 1., 1.],
       [1., 1., 1., 1., 1.]])
```

Notes

numpy.full (shape, fill_value, dtype=None):
    Return a new array of given shape and data type(dtype), filled with fill_value.

In[10]
```
# To create a new array with 3 rows and 5 columns, filled with 2

np.full((3,5),2)
```

Out[10]
```
array([[2, 2, 2, 2, 2],
       [2, 2, 2, 2, 2],
       [2, 2, 2, 2, 2]])
```

Notes

To generate random arrays using np.random(), please refer to section [4.1.2 Generating a random array at a time] for detailed instructions and examples.

In[11]
```
rand=np.random.RandomState(30)
MyArray5=rand.randint(0,100,[3,5])
MyArray5
```

Out[11]
```
array([[37, 37, 45, 45, 12],
       [23,  2, 53, 17,  46],
       [ 3, 41,  7, 65,  49]])
```

Notes

Here, 0 and 100 represent the range of the random value, and [3,5] represents the shape of the target array with 3 rows and 5 columns.

Notes

Two important features of the ndarray in NumPy:
    (1) shape: the shape of a multidimensional array
        Its value is a tuple or a list.
        For instance, shape = (2,15) represents an array with 2 rows and 15 columns.
    (2) dtype: The data type of the element in the multidimensional array
        Its value is the data type provided by the *NumPy* module such as np.int.
        For instance, dtype = np.int represents that the data type of the array elements
        is *int* in *NumPy*.
NumPy supports a much greater variety of numerical types than Python does, including numpy.int, numpy.short, numpy.int_ and numpy.longlong.

In[12]
```
import numpy as np
MyArray4=np.zeros(shape=(2,15) ,dtype=np.int)
MyArray4
```

Out[12]   array([[0, 0, 0, 0, 0, 0, 0, 0, 0, 0, 0, 0, 0, 0, 0],
            [0, 0, 0, 0, 0, 0, 0, 0, 0, 0, 0, 0, 0, 0, 0]])

Tricks

MyArray4 = np.zeros((2, 15), dtype=np.int)

In this statement, the phrase "shape =" can be omitted, and the np.int data type does not require double quotes.

Notes

The shape argument represents the shape of the array, and its value can be a tuple, such as (3,5).

In[13]   np.ones((3,5),dtype=float)

Out[13]   array([[1., 1., 1., 1., 1.],
            [1., 1., 1., 1., 1.],
            [1., 1., 1., 1., 1.]])

Notes

The value of the shape argument can also be specified as a list, such as [3, 5].

In[14]   np.ones([3,5],dtype=float)

Out[14]   array([[1., 1., 1., 1., 1.],
            [1., 1., 1., 1., 1.],
            [1., 1., 1., 1., 1.]])

4.2.2 Slicing and indexing ndarrays

Notes

Both Lists in Python and ndarrays in NumPy allow slicing and indexing, and they share a similar syntax.

In[15]   # to create the test dataset

import numpy as np
myArray=np.array(range(1,10))

myArray

Out[15]   array([1, 2, 3, 4, 5, 6, 7, 8, 9])

Notes

(1) The index of the first item/element is 0.

In[17] `myArray[0]`

Out[17] 1

Notes

(2) Python supports negative indexes, please refer to [2.10 Lists] for details.

In[18] `myArray[-1]`

Out[18] 9

Notes

(3) Several ways of indexing items/elements

In[19]
```
# to create and show the current value of the variable myArray
import numpy as np
myArray=np.array(range(0,10))

print("myArray=",myArray)
```

Out[19] myArray= [0 1 2 3 4 5 6 7 8 9]

Tips

Slicing means taking elements from one given index to another given index.

Notes

1, 9 and 2 are the start, end and step index of the slicing respectively.

In[20] `print("myArray[1:9:2]=",myArray[1:9:2])`

Out[20] myArray[1:9:2]= [1 3 5 7]

Notes

The start index can be omitted.

In[21] `print("myArray[:9:2]=",myArray[:9:2])`

Out[21] myArray[:9:2]= [0 2 4 6 8]

Notes

The start and stop index can be omitted.

In[22] `print("myArray[::2]=",myArray[::2])`

Out[22] myArray[::2]= [0 2 4 6 8]

The start, stop and step index can all be omitted.

In[23] `print("myArray[::]=",myArray[::])`

Out[23] myArray[::]= [0 1 2 3 4 5 6 7 8 9]

The start and stop index can be omitted.

In[24] `print("myArray[:8:]=",myArray[:8:])`

Out[24] myArray[:8:]= [0 1 2 3 4 5 6 7]

The step index can be omitted.

In[25] `print("myArray[:8]=",myArray[0:8])`

Out[25] myArray[:8]= [0 1 2 3 4 5 6 7]

The stop and step index can be omitted.

In[26] `print("myArray[4::]=",myArray[4::])`

Out[26] myArray[4::]= [4 5 6 7 8 9]

The value of the step index can be negative.

In[27] `print("myArray[9:1:-2]=",myArray[9:1:-2])`
`print("myArray[::-2]=",myArray[::-2])`

Out[27] myArray[9:1:-2]= [9 7 5 3]
myArray[::-2]= [9 7 5 3 1]

Fancy indexing refers to the practice of using an array of indices to access multiple elements of an array simultaneously.

Notes Fancy Indexing is a very flexible way of slicing, which means to support a non-iterative way to slice the elements irregularly. The notation of fancy indexing is the nesting of [], that is, another [] appears in the []. For example, myArray[[2,5,6]] means to locate the three elements with indexes 2, 5 and 6.

In[28] `print("myArray[[2,5,6]]=",myArray[[2,5,6]])`

Out[28]   myArray[[2,5,6]]= [2 5 6]

 Notes In NumPy, it is possible to use an expression containing the array name itself as an index, which acts as a filtering condition. For more details, please refer to In[29].

In[29] `print("myArray[myArray>5]=",myArray[myArray>5])`

Out[29]   myArray[myArray>5]= [6 7 8 9]

 Notes In slicing, the start index is inclusive (e.g., "0" in this code), but the stop index is exclusive (e.g., "2" in this code). This is because the slicing rule in Python is "including the start but excluding the stop".

In[30] `myArray[0:2]`

Out[30]   array([0, 1])

 Notes When slicing an ndarray, it will return a view of the elements in the original array, not a shallow copy. This means that any modifications made to the sliced array will affect the original array as well.

In[31] `myArray`

Out[31]   array([0, 1, 2, 3, 4, 5, 6, 7, 8, 9])

 Notes (4) To access non-consecutive elements of an array, you can use slicing. Please refer to [2.10 Lists] for more details.

In[32] `myArray=np.array(range(1,11))`
`myArray`

Out[32]   array([1, 2, 3, 4, 5, 6, 7, 8, 9, 10])

 Notes When the index is irregular, an error will be raised if fancy indexing is not used. Fancy indexing refers to passing an array of indices to access multiple array elements at once. For more details, please refer to the section on Fancy Indexing in [4.2 Multidimensional arrays].

In[33]   myArray[1,3,6]

IndexError   Traceback (most recent call last)
<ipython-input-30-13b1cd8a6af6> in <module>()
      1
----> 2 myArray[1,3,6]
      3

IndexError: too many indices for array

Raise an exception: too many indices for array.
To correct this exception, please use Fancy Indexing as follows:

Tricks

In[34]   myArray[[1,3,6]]
Out[34]   array([2, 4, 7])

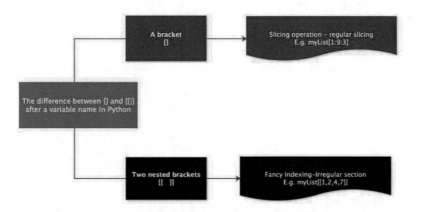

In data science projects, it is often necessary to generate a special matrix called a "feature matrix". From the output above, the current value of myArray is a row of records, which does not meet the requirements of a feature matrix and needs to be normalized.

Notes

In[35]   myArray
Out[35]   array([1, 2, 3, 4, 5, 6, 7, 8, 9, 10])

In NumPy, the np.newaxis is an alias for the Python constant None, hence, wherever we use np.newaxis we could also use None:

Tricks

In[36] | `myArray[:,np.newaxis]`

Out[36]
```
array([[ 1],
       [ 2],
       [ 3],
       [ 4],
       [ 5],
       [ 6],
       [ 7],
       [ 8],
       [ 9],
       [10]])
```

Tricks

Here, the np.newaxis is generally used with slicing. It indicates that you want to add an additional dimension to the array. In addition, the colon (:) cannot be omitted here.

Tips

Here, the codes of In[39] are equivalent to those of In[40].

Notes

To get the shape of a given ndarray, you can use the .shape attribute. For example, if arr is an ndarray, you can access its shape using arr.shape.

In[37] | `myArray[:,np.newaxis].shape`

Out[37]   (10, 1)

Notes

To convert the shape of an ndarray in NumPy, you can use the numpy.reshape() function. It allows you to reshape an array into a specified shape while keeping the same elements.

In[38]
```
myArray2=np.arange(1,21).reshape([5,4])
myArray2
```

Out[38]
```
array([[ 1,  2,  3,  4],
       [ 5,  6,  7,  8],
       [ 9, 10, 11, 12],
       [13, 14, 15, 16],
       [17, 18, 19, 20]])
```

Notes

An example of slicing an ndarray is myArray2[[2,4],3].

In[39] `myArray2[[2,4],3]`

Out[39] array([12, 20])

Tips

Here, the codes of In[39] are equivalent to those of In[40].

In[40]
```
x=[2,4]
myArray2[x,3]
```

Out[40] array([12, 20])

4.2.3 Shallow copy and deep copy

Tips

Assignment statements in Python do not copy objects, they create bindings between a target and an object. Hence, the numpy provides two distinct methods: generic shallow and deep copy operations
- A shallow copy means the copied array contains only a reference to the original array.
- A deep copy means copying each element of the original array into the copied array

In[41]
```
import numpy as np
myArray1=np.array(range(0,10))
myArray2=myArray1
myArray2[1]=100
myArray1
```

Out[41] array([0, 100, 2, 3, 4, 5, 6, 7, 8, 9])

Tricks

Here, the value of myArray has changed in that myArray1 and myArray2 share the same memory adrrress

Notes

Deep copy: A deep copy creates a new array object with its own separate copy of the original array's data. Any modifications made to the data in one array will not affect the other. You can create a deep copy using the numpy.copy() function.

In[42]
```
import numpy as np
myArray1=np.array(range(0,10))
myArray2=myArray1.copy()
myArray2[1]=200
myArray1
```

Out[42] array([0, 1, 2, 3, 4, 5, 6, 7, 8, 9])

Tricks

The myArray1 here has not changed. The reason is that 'myArray2 = myArray1.copy()' creates a deepcopy, resulting in myArray1 and myArray2 being mutually independent.

4.2.4 Shape and reshape

Notes

Reshape means returning a transformed array with the new shape specifies in the numpy method reshpe().

In[43] | import numpy as np
MyArray5=np.arange(1,21)
MyArray5

Out[43] | array([1, 2, 3, 4, 5, 6, 7, 8, 9, 10, 11, 12, 13, 14, 15, 16, 17, 18, 19, 20])

Notes

In numpy, to check the shape of an array, you can use the attribute ndarray.shape.

In[44] | MyArray5.shape

Out[44] | (20,)

Notes

(1) to change the shape of ndarray:
ndarray.reshape() or ndarray.resize()

In[45] | MyArray6=MyArray5.reshape(4,5)
MyArray6

Out[45] | array([[1, 2, 3, 4, 5],
         [6, 7, 8, 9, 10],
         [11, 12, 13, 14, 15],
         [16, 17, 18, 19, 20]])

Notes

In numpy, the numpy.reshape() function does not modify an array in place. Instead, it returns a new reshaped array while leaving the original array unchanged.

In[46] | MyArray5.shape
MyArray5

Out[46] | (20,)
array([1, 2, 3, 4, 5, 6, 7, 8, 9, 10, 11, 12, 13, 14, 15, 16, 17, 18, 19, 20])

Tips

The numpy.reshape() function returns a new array with a modified shape but preserves the original data of the array. It does not modify the array in place.

In[47] | MyArray5.reshape(5,4)

Out[47] array([[1, 2, 3, 4],
        [5, 6, 7, 8],
        [9, 10, 11, 12],
        [13, 14, 15, 16],
        [17, 18, 19, 20]])

Notes

ValueError: cannot reshape array of size 20 into shape (5,5).

In[48] | MyArray5.reshape(5,4)

ValueError   Traceback (most recent call last)
<ipython-input-46-8920a583f59a> in <module>()
----> 1 MyArray5.reshape(5,5)
     2

ValueError: cannot reshape array of size 20 into shape (5,5)

Tips

Here, a value error is raised in that the python interpreter cannot reshape array of size 20 into shape (5,5).

In[49] | MyArray5

Out[49] array([1, 2, 3, 4, 5, 6, 7, 8, 9, 10, 11, 12, 13, 14, 15, 16, 17, 18, 19, 20])

Notes

The *resize()* method in NumPy can be used to change the shape of an array in-place. Unlike reshape(), resize() modifies the array itself rather than returning a new array.

In[50] | MyArray5.resize(4,5)
       MyArray5

Out[50] array([[1, 2, 3, 4, 5],
        [6, 7, 8, 9, 10],
        [11, 12, 13, 14, 15],
        [16, 17, 18, 19, 20]])

Tips

The main difference between resize() and reshape() in NumPy is that resize() performs in-place modification, meaning it modifies the array itself, while reshape() returns a new array with the specified shape without modifying the original array.

Notes

(3) The *swapaxes()* method in NumPy allows you to interchange two axes of an array.

In[51]   `MyArray5.swapaxes(0,1)`

Out[51]   array([[1, 6, 11, 16],
             [2, 7, 12, 17],
             [3, 8, 13, 18],
             [4, 9, 14, 19],
             [5, 10, 15, 20]])

Notes

Swapaxes(0,1) does not change the array itself.

In[52]   `MyArray5`

Out[52]   array([[1, 2, 3, 4, 5],
             [6, 7, 8, 9, 10],
             [11, 12, 13, 14, 15],
             [16, 17, 18, 19, 20]])

Tricks

In data science, it is important to pay attention to whether the evaluation of a data object changes the data itself or returns a copy of the new value.

Notes

(4) Use the *flatten()* method to convert a multidimensional array into a one-dimensional array.

In[53]   `MyArray5.flatten()`

Out[53]   array([1, 6, 11, 16, 2, 7, 12, 17, 3, 8, 13, 18, 4, 9, 14, 19, 5, 10, 15, 20])

Tips

ndarray.flatten( ):
    Return a copy of the array collapsed into one dimension.

Notes

(5) Use the *tolist()* method to convert the multidimensional array to a nested list.

In[54] | MyArray5.tolist()

Out[54] [[1, 6, 11, 16],
         [2, 7, 12, 17],
         [3, 8, 13, 18],
         [4, 9, 14, 19],
         [5, 10, 15, 20]]

ndarray.tolist():
    Return the array as an a.ndim-levels deep nested list of Python scalars.

Tips

(6) The data type of array elements can be reset.

Notes

In[55] | MyArray5.astype(np.float)

Out[55] array([[1., 6., 11., 16.],
            [2., 7., 12., 17.],
            [3., 8., 13., 18.],
            [4., 9., 14., 19.],
            [5., 10., 15., 20.]])

numpy.ndarray.astype():
    Returns a copy of the array, cast to a specified type.

Tips

When executing MyArray5.astype(np.float), the array MyArray5 itself does not change, but a new array of the specified data type (in this case, np.float) is returned.

Notes

In[56] | MyArray5

Out[56] array([[1, 6, 11, 16],
            [2, 7, 12, 17],
            [3, 8, 13, 18],
            [4, 9, 14, 19],
            [5, 10, 15, 20]])

4.2.5 Dimension and size

(1) To evaluate the number of array dimensions: rank() or ndim().

Notes

In[57] `np.rank(MyArray5)`

> C:\Anaconda\lib\site-packages\ipykernel_launcher.py:3: VisibleDeprecationWarning: 'rank' is deprecated; use the 'ndim' attribute or function instead. To find the rank of a matrix see 'numpy.linalg.matrix_rank'.
> This is separate from the ipykernel package so we can avoid doing imports until

Out[57] 2

Tricks

The system prompts "'rank' is deprecated", indicating that this method has been deprecated. The system prompts "use the 'ndim' attribute or function instead".
Variations of this naming convention are common among Python third-party packages.

In[58] `np.ndim(MyArray5)`
Out[58] 2

Notes

There are two usages of ndim in numpy: as an attribute (MyArray5.ndim) and as a method (np.ndim(MyArray5)).

In[59] `MyArray5.ndim`
Out[59] 2

Notes

(2) To get the shape of the array: the *shape()* method or the *shape* attribute.

In[60] `np.shape(MyArray5)`
Out[60] (5, 4)

Notes

In NumPy, the *shape* attribute supports functional calls. For example, np.shape(MyArray4) is equivalent to MyArray4.shape.

In[61] `MyArray5.shape`
Out[61] (5, 4)

Tips

numpy.shape() is the equivalent function to ndarray.shape, and numpy.ndim() is the equivalent function to ndarray.ndim(). They both provide the same functionality to retrieve the shape and number of dimensions of a NumPy array.

(3) In NumPy, the numpy.size function can be used to evaluate the number of elements in an array. It returns the total number of elements present in the array, regardless of its shape or dimensions.

Notes

In[62]　MyArray5.size

Out[62]　20

In NumPy, the ndarray.shape attribute returns a tuple of array dimensions, indicating the size of each dimension of the array.

The ndarray.size attribute returns the total number of elements in the array, providing the overall size or length of the array.

Tips

(4) To check the type of the array:
　　the built-in function type().

Notes

In[63]　type(MyArray5)

Out[63]　numpy.ndarray

Here, the type() function is a built-in function in Python and not specific to NumPy. Therefore, you do not need to prefix it with np when using it to determine the type of a NumPy array.

Tips

4.2.6 Evaluation of ndarrays

(1) Multiplication with arrays.

Notes

In[64]　MyArray5*10

Out[64]　array([[10, 60, 110, 160],
　　　　　　　[20, 70, 120, 170],
　　　　　　　[30, 80, 130, 180],
　　　　　　　[40, 90, 140, 190],
　　　　　　　[50, 100, 150, 200]])

There are three common used ways to multiply NumPy ndarrays in data science:
- numpy.dot(array a, array b) : returns the dot product of two arrays.
- numpy.multiply(array a, array b) : returns the element-wise matrix multiplication of two arrays.
- numpy.matmul(array a, array b) : returns the matrix product of two arrays.

Tips

Notes

(2) Horizontal split: the *split( )* method.
[3,5] is the index of the split position.

In[65]
```
x=np.array([11,12,13,14,15,16,17,18])
x1,x2,x3=np.split(x,[3,5])
print(x1,x2,x3)
```

Out[65]   [11 12 13] [14 15] [16 17 18]

Notes

The *np.vsplit( )* method is used to perform a vertical split of an array. Here, MyArray5. reshape(4, 5) is split into two parts at index 2 along the vertical axis. The resulting splits are assigned to the variables upper and lower using unpacking assignment.

In[66]
```
upper,lower=np.vsplit(MyArray5.reshape(4,5),[2])
print("The upper part is\n",upper)
print("\n\nThe lower part is\n",lower)
```

Out[66]   The upper part is
```
[[ 1  6 11 16  2]
 [ 7 12 17  3  8]]

The lower part is
[[13 18  4  9 14]
 [19  5 10 15 20]]
```

Notes

(3) To merge the arrays: np.concatenate().

In[67]   `np.concatenate((lower,upper),axis=0)`

Out[67]
```
array([[13, 18,  4,  9, 14],
       [19,  5, 10, 15, 20],
       [ 1,  6, 11, 16,  2],
       [ 7, 12, 17,  3,  8]])
```

Tricks

Here, axis = 0 means that the axis along which the arrays will be joined. If axis is None, arrays are flattened before use. Default is 0.

Notes

(4) np.vstack() and np.hstack() support horizontal or vertical merging(stacking) respectively.
The premise of calling np.vstack(): the number of columns of the arrays is the same.

In[68]   `np.vstack([upper,lower])`

Out[68]   array([[1, 6, 11, 16, 2],
                [7, 12, 17, 3, 8],
                [13, 18, 4, 9, 14],
                [19, 5, 10, 15, 20]])

Notes

The premise of calling np.hstack(): the number of rows of the arrays is the same.

In[69]   `np.hstack([upper,lower])`

Out[69]   array([[1, 6, 11, 16, 2, 13, 18, 4, 9, 14],
                [7, 12, 17, 3, 8, 19, 5, 10, 15, 20]])

Tips

- numpy.vstack() : Stack arrays in sequence vertically (row wise).
- numpy.vsplit() : Split an array into multiple sub-arrays vertically (row-wise).
- numpy.hstack() : Stack arrays in sequence horizontally (column wise).
- numpy.hsplit() : Split an array into multiple sub-arrays horizontally (column-wise).

Notes

In NumPy, function evaluations on arrays are commonly implemented as "ufunc functions," which operate element-wise on entire arrays. These ufunc functions allow for efficient vectorized computations without the need for explicit loop statements.

In[70]   `np.add(MyArray5,1)`

Out[70]   array([[2, 7, 12, 17],
                [3, 8, 13, 18],
                [4, 9, 14, 19],
                [5, 10, 15, 20],
                [6, 11, 16, 21]])

Tricks

The same function, which is summing the elements of an array, can be achieved using both the built-in Python function sum() and the NumPy function numpy.sum().

Tips

A ufunc (universal function) is a function that operates on ndarrays in an element-by-element fashion. That is, a ufunc is a "vectorized" wrapper for a function that takes a fixed number of specific inputs and produces a fixed number of specific outputs

4.2.7 Insertion and deletion

Notes
To delete a specific element in a NumPy array, you can use the np.delete() function.

In[71]
```
import numpy as np
myArray1=np.array([11,12,13,14,15,16,17,18])
np.delete(myArray1,2)
```

Out[71] array([11, 12, 14, 15, 16, 17, 18])

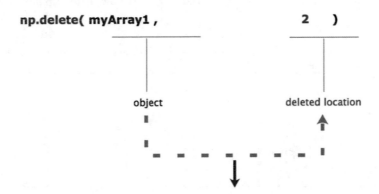

Delete the element with subscript 2 in myArray1

Tips
numpy.delete(arr, obj, axis=None) is a function that returns a new array with sub-arrays along a specified axis deleted. The arr parameter represents the input array, obj specifies the indices or slice objects of the elements to be deleted, and axis (optional) indicates the axis along which the deletion should occur.

Notes
To insert a specific element: np.insert().

In[72]   `np.insert(myArray1,1,88)`

Out[72]   array([11, 88, 12, 13, 14, 15, 16, 17, 18])

Tips
numpy.insert(arr, obj, values, axis=None) is a function that inserts values into an array along a specified axis before the given indices.

4.2.8 Handling missing values

To check if each element of an array is a missing value: np.isnan().

In[73]   np.isnan(myArray)

Out[73]   array([False, False, False, False, False, False, False, False, False, False])

To check if there is at least one missing value in the array: np.any().

In[74]   np.any(np.isnan(myArray))

Out[74]   False

To check if all elements in an array are missing values: np.all().

In[75]   np.all(np.isnan(myArray))

Out[75]   False

numpy.isnan: to test element-wise for NaN and return result as a boolean array.
Numpy.all(): to test whether all array elements along a given axis evaluate to True.
Numpy.any(): to test whether any array element along a given axis evaluates to True.

In many function evaluations, if missing values are encountered, an error may be raised or a NaN (Not a Number) value may be obtained as the result. To handle missing values in such cases, you can use *NaN-safe* functions provided by NumPy, such as np.nansum().

In[76]   MyArray=np.array([1,2,3,np.nan])
         np.nansum(MyArray)

Out[76]   6.0

The difference between np.nan and None.:
- None is a data type provided by Python syntax and cannot participate in arithmetic operations.
- The *np.nan* data type is provided by NumPy, which belongs to the *float* type and can participate in arithmetic operations.

In[77]   np.sum(MyArray)

Out[77]   nan

4.2.9 Broadcasting ndarray

Tips

In NumPy, broadcasting refers to the mechanism by which arrays with different shapes are treated during arithmetic operations. When performing operations between arrays of different shapes, NumPy automatically adjusts the shapes of the arrays to make them compatible, following a set of rules or constraints.

Notes

Rule 1: If the number of dimensions is the same, but the size of at least one dimension is different, broadcasting is performed by replicating the array along the dimension with a smaller size. The operation is completed by iterating over the arrays in a loop.

In[78]
```
import numpy as np
A1=np.array(range(1,10)).reshape([3,3])
A1
```

Out[78]
```
array([[1, 2, 3],
       [4, 5, 6],
       [7, 8, 9]])
```

Notes

A1 and A2 have the same number of columns and different number of rows.

In[79]
```
A2=np.array([10,10,10])
A2
```

Out[79]
```
array([10, 10, 10])
```

Notes

Before A1+A2 is executed, the operation of broadcasting is performed row by row. After A1 and A2 are converted to the same structure, the evaluation will be executed.

In[80]
```
A1+A2
```
Out[80]
```
array([[11, 12, 13],
       [14, 15, 16],
       [17, 18, 19]])
```

Notes

Rule 2: If the shapes of the arrays being operated on are not compatible, meaning they have different numbers of dimensions and the size of at least one dimension is different (except when one of the dimensions is 1).

In[81]
```
A3=np.arange(10).reshape(2,5)
A3
```

Out[81]
```
array([[0, 1, 2, 3, 4],
       [5, 6, 7, 8, 9]])
```

Notes	A3 is 2 rows x 5 columns, and A4 is 4 rows x 4 columns.

In[82]
```
A4=np.arange(16).reshape(4,4)
A4
```
Out[82]
```
array([[ 0,  1,  2,  3],
       [ 4,  5,  6,  7],
       [ 8,  9, 10, 11],
       [12, 13, 14, 15]])
```

Notes	An error is raised: ValueError: operands could not be broadcast together with shapes (2,5) (4,4)

In[83]
```
A3+A4
```

ValueError   Traceback (most recent call last)
<ipython-input-86-0fe8480883de> in <module>()
----> 1 A3+A4
      2 **ValueError: operands could not be broadcast together with shapes (2,5) (4,4)**

ValueError: operands could not be broadcast together with shapes (2,5) (4,4)

4.2.10 Sorting an ndarray

Notes	(1) To return a sorted copy of an array np.sort().

In[84]
```
import numpy as np
myArray=np.array([11,18,13,12,19,15,14,17,16])
myArray
```
Out[84]   array([11, 18, 13, 12, 19, 15, 14, 17, 16])

In[85]   np.sort(myArray)
Out[85]   array([11, 12, 13, 14, 15, 16, 17, 18, 19])

Notes	(2) To return the indices that would sort an array: np.argsort().

In[86]   np.argsort(myArray)
Out[86]   array([0, 3, 2, 6, 5, 8, 7, 1, 4], dtype=int64)

Tricks

In NumPy, multidimensional arrays can be sorted along a specified axis by using the *axis* parameter in the np.sort() function.

In[87] | MyArray=np.array([[21, 22, 23, 24,25],
                          [35, 34,33, 32, 31],
                          [1, 2, 3, 100, 4]])
        np.sort(MyArray,axis=1)

Out[87] | array([[21, 22, 23, 24, 25],
               [31, 32, 33, 34, 35],
               [1, 2, 3, 4, 100]])

Tips

Here, axis = 1 means the axis along which to sort. If None, the array is flattened before sorting. The default is −1, which sorts along the last axis.

In[88] | np.sort(MyArray,axis=0)

Out[88] | array([[1, 2, 3, 24, 4],
               [21, 22, 23, 32, 25],
               [35, 34, 33, 100, 31]])

4.3 Series

Q&A

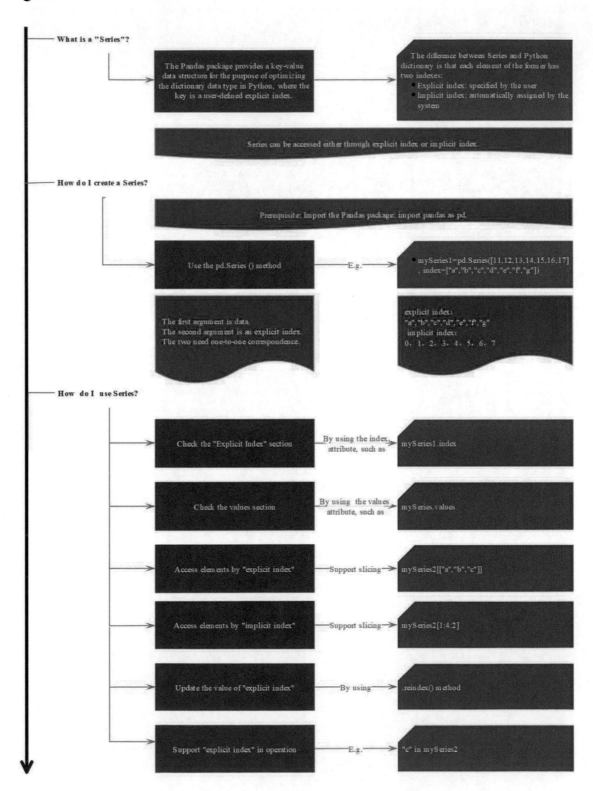

What is a "Series"?

The Pandas package provides a key-value data structure for the purpose of optimizing the dictionary data type in Python, where the key is a user-defined explicit index.

The difference between Series and Python dictionary is that each element of the former has two indexes:
- Explicit index: specified by the user
- Implicit index: automatically assigned by the system

Series can be accessed either through explicit index or implicit index.

How do I create a Series?

Prerequisite: Import the Pandas package: import pandas as pd.

Use the pd.Series () method

E.g.
- mySeries1=pd.Series([11,12,13,14,15,16,17], index=["a","b","c","d","e","f","g"])

The first argument is data.
The second argument is an explicit index.
The two need one-to-one correspondence.

explicit index:
"a","b","c","d","e","f","g"
implicit index:
0, 1, 2, 3, 4, 5, 6, 7

How do I use Series?

Check the "Explicit Index" section — By using the index attribute, such as — mySeries1.index

Check the values section — By using the values attribute, such as — mySeries.values

Access elements by "explicit index" — Support slicing — mySeries2[["a","b","c"]]

Access elements by "implicit index" — Support slicing — mySeries2[1:4:2]

Update the value of "explicit index" — By using — .reindex() method

Support "explicit index" in operation — E.g. — "c" in mySeries2

4.3.1 Creating Series

Notes

Pandas Series is a one-dimensional array of indexed data. It can be thought of as a special type of Python dictionary. It is a data structure that maps typed keys to a set of typed values. The keys of a Series are explicitly defined indexes that can be of any data type. The values of the Series correspond to these indexes and can also be of any data type.

Tricks

Series in Pandas can be thought of as enhanced versions of Dict in Python. Both of them stored data in Key-Value data model.

Notes

There are two main arguments in pandas.Series( ):
- data：Contains data stored in a Series. the argument data should be array-like, Iterable, dict, or scalar value.
- index：Contains the explicit index of data stored in the Series. Values must be hashable and have the same length as data. Non-unique index values are allowed.

Tips

Series has two types of index.
- The explicit index is defined with typed label names when creating a series.
- The implicit index is defined automatically with an ordered sequence of numbers like "0,1,2,3...".

Unlike software development projects, explicit index is usually used instead of implicit index in data science projects, because the implicit index is difficult to locate if the dataset is large.

```
In[1]   import pandas as pd
        mySeries1=pd.Series(data = [11,12,13,14,15,16,17], index=["a","b","c","d","e","f","g"])
        mySeries1
```

```
Out[1]  a    11
        b    12
        c    13
        d    14
        e    15
        f    16
        g    17
        dtype: int64
```

Tricks

When defining a Series in Pandas, the length of the index and the length of the data should be the same. If the lengths do not match, an exception will be raised indicating the mismatch between the index and data lengths.

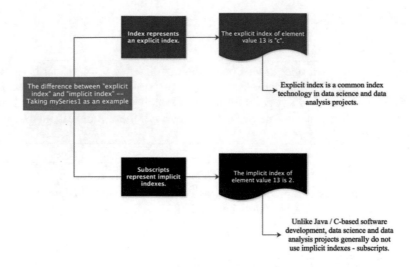

| In[2] | `import pandas as pd`
`mySeries1=pd.Series([11,12,13,14,15,16,17], index=[a,b,c,d,e,f,g])`

`mySeries1` |

```
NameError          Traceback (most recent call last)
<ipython-input-3-88cdcb222886> in <module>()
      1 import pandas as pd
----> 2 mySeries1=pd.Series([11,12,13,14,15,16,17],
          index=[a,b,c,d,e,f,g])
      3
      4 mySeries1

NameError: name 'a' is not defined
```

Here, a NameError is raised because we missing the quotation marks of the string 'a'. Strings in python should be surrounded by either single quotation mark, or double quotation marks.

Tips

If the "data" parameter is only one value, the pd.*series()* method will assign the same value to each index.

Notes

| In[3] | `mySeries2=pd.Series(10, index=["a","b","c","d","e","f","g"])`
`mySeries2` |

```
Out[3]  a    10
        b    10
        c    10
        d    10
        e    10
        f    10
        g    10
        dtype: int64
```

Notes

When defining a Series in Pandas, if the "data" parameter contains more than one value, the length of both the data values and the index should be the same. This ensures that each data value is paired with a corresponding index value. If the lengths do not match, an exception will be raised.

In[4]
```
mySeries3=pd.Series([1,2,3,4,5], index=["a","b","c"])
mySeries3
```

```
ValueError                    Traceback (most recent call last)
<ipython-input-5-e8a37d3e2b30> in <module>()
----> 1 mySeries3=pd.Series([1,2,3,4,5], index=["a","b","c"])
      2 mySeries3
     91
     92    @property

ValueError: Wrong number of items passed 5, placement implies 3
```

Tricks

There is another kind of exception: ValueError: Wrong number of items passed 5, placement implies 3.
The reason that this exception raised is the length of the indexes is not same as data values.

4.3.2 Working with Series

Notes

(1) Getting the index labels of the given Series object.

In[5]
```
import pandas as pd
mySeries4=pd.Series([21,22,23,24,25,26,27], index=["a","b","c","d","e","f","g"])
mySeries4.index
```
Out[5]   Index(['a', 'b', 'c', 'd', 'e', 'f', 'g'], dtype='object')

Tricks

The returned data type is index, which is a special type defined in Pandas.

Notes

(2) Getting all the values in the given Series object.

In[6]   `mySeries4.values`
Out[6]   array([21, 22, 23, 24, 25, 26, 27], dtype=int64)

(3) Slicing a Series with its explicit index

In[7]   `mySeries4['b']`

Out[7]   22

The Series also supports Fancy Indexing to pass an array of indices to access multiple elements at once.

In[9]   `mySeries4[["a","b","c"]]`

Out[9]   a   21
         b   22
         c   23
         dtype: int64

In NumPy, explicit indexes can be used as start and stop positions for slicing operations. Unlike in Python, both the start and stop indices will be included in the returned result. This means that the sliced array will contain elements starting from the start index up to and including the stop index.

In[10]   `mySeries4["a":"d"]`

Out[10] a   21
         b   22
         c   23
         d   24
         dtype: int64

(4) Slicing a Series with its implicit index.

In[11]   `mySeries4[1:4:2]`

Out[11] b   22
         d   24
         dtype: int64

In[12]   `mySeries4`

Out[12] a   21
         b   22
         c   23
         d   24
         e   25
         f   26
         g   27
         dtype: int64

Tips

Notice that when slicing with an explicit index (i.e. mySeries4["a":"d"), the final index is included in the slice, while when slicing with an implicit index (i.e. mySeries4[1:4:2]), the final index is excluded from the slice.

Notes

(5) Checking whether a value is an element of the explicit index(labels) of a series or not.

In[13] `"c" in mySeries4`

Out[13] True

In[14] `"h" in mySeries4`

Out[14] False

Notes

(6) The *series.reindex()* method is used to reset the explicit index.

In[15]
```
import pandas as pd
mySeries4=pd.Series([21,22,23,24,25,26,27], index=["a","b","c","d","e","f","g"])
mySeries5=mySeries4.reindex(index=["b","c","a","d","e","g","f"])
mySeries5
```

Out[15]
```
b    22
c    23
a    21
d    24
e    25
g    27
f    26
dtype: int64
```

Tricks

The *series.reindex()* method changes the the index labels of a series, but the correspondence between key and value is not be destroyed.

Notes

Regardless of the results order, the index and values of mySeries4 itself has not changed.

In[16] | `mySeries5=mySeries4.reindex(index=["b","c","a","d","e","g","f"])`
        | `mySeries4`

Out[16] | a   21
        | b   22
        | c   23
        | d   24
        | e   25
        | f   26
        | g   27
        | dtype: int64

Notes

The *series.reindex( )* method is used to create a new index and reindex the DataFrame. By default, holes in the new index that do not have corresponding records in the DataFrame are assigned NaN.

In[17] | `mySeries5=mySeries4.reindex(index=["new1","c","a","new2","e","g","new3"])`
        | `mySeries5`

Out[17] | new1   NaN
        | c   23.0
        | a   21.0
        | new2   NaN
        | e   25.0
        | g   27.0
        | new3   NaN
        | dtype: float64

Notes

The *Series.reindex( )* method does not modify the explicit index of the original Series object.

In[18] | `mySeries4`

Out[18] | a   21
        | b   22
        | c   23
        | d   24
        | e   25
        | f   26
        | g   27
        | dtype: int64

4.4 DataFrame

Q&A

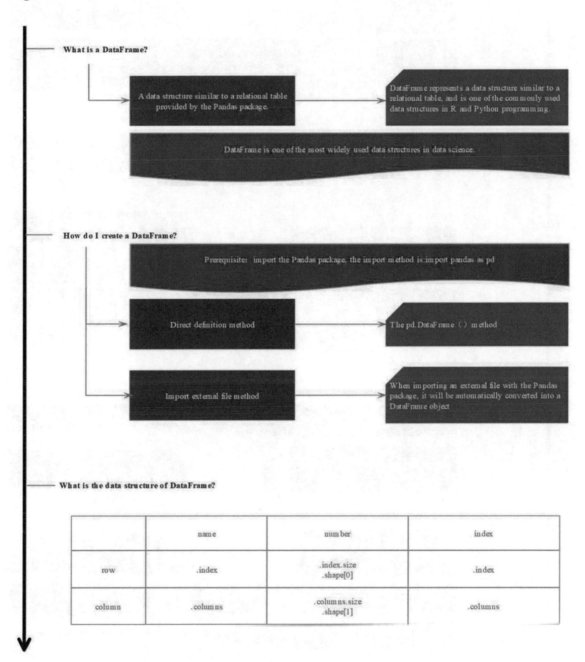

	name	number	index
row	.index	.index.size .shape[0]	.index
column	.columns	.columns.size .shape[1]	.columns

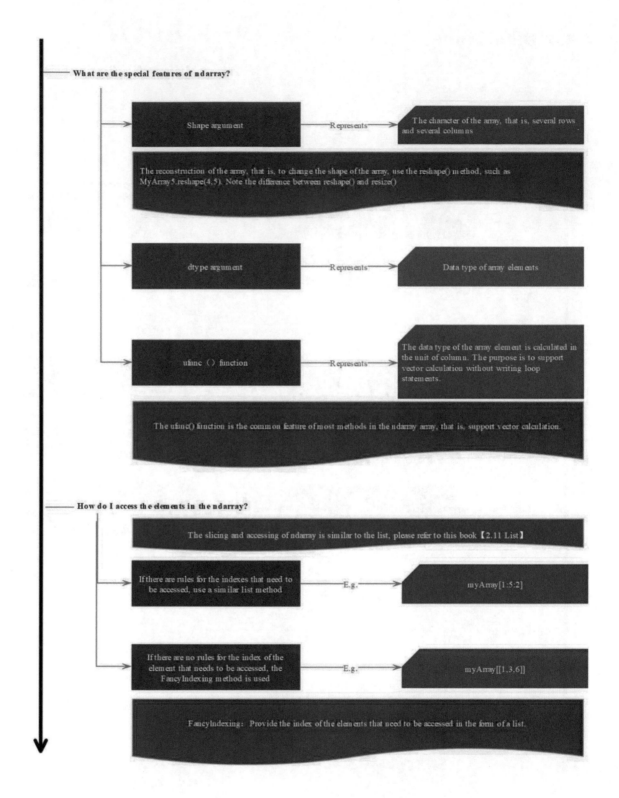

What are the special features of ndarray?

Shape argument —Represents→ The character of the array, that is, several rows and several columns

The reconstruction of the array, that is, to change the shape of the array, use the reshape() method, such as MyArray5.reshape(4,5). Note the difference between reshape() and resize()

dtype argument —Represents→ Data type of array elements

ufunc ( ) function —Represents→ The data type of the array element is calculated in the unit of column. The purpose is to support vector calculation without writing loop statements.

The ufunc() function is the common feature of most methods in the ndarray array, that is, support vector calculation.

How do I access the elements in the ndarray?

The slicing and accessing of ndarray is similar to the list, please refer to this book 【2.11 List】

If there are rules for the indexes that need to be accessed, use a similar list method —E.g.→ myArray[1:5:2]

If there are no rules for the index of the element that needs to be accessed, the FancyIndexing method is used —E.g.→ myArray[[1,3,6]]

FancyIndexing: Provide the index of the elements that need to be accessed in the form of a list.

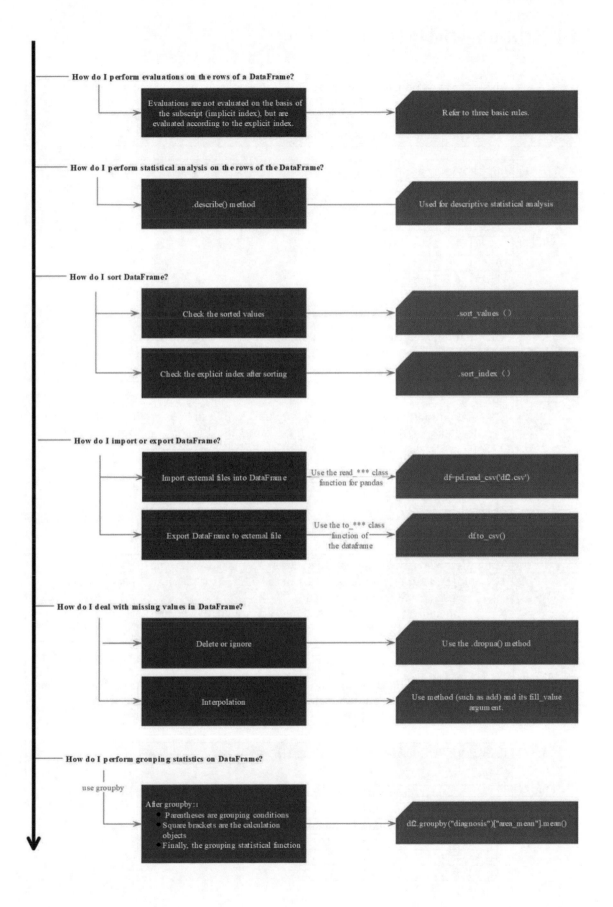

How do I perform evaluations on the rows of a DataFrame?

Evaluations are not evaluated on the basis of the subscript (implicit index), but are evaluated according to the explicit index.

Refer to three basic rules.

How do I perform statistical analysis on the rows of the DataFrame?

.describe() method

Used for descriptive statistical analysis

How do I sort DataFrame?

Check the sorted values

.sort_values ( )

Check the explicit index after sorting

.sort_index ( )

How do I import or export DataFrame?

Import external files into DataFrame

Use the read_*** class function for pandas

df=pd.read_csv('df2.csv')

Export DataFrame to external file

Use the to_*** class function of the dataframe

df.to_csv()

How do I deal with missing values in DataFrame?

Delete or ignore

Use the .dropna() method

Interpolation

Use method (such as add) and its fill_value argument.

How do I perform grouping statistics on DataFrame?

use groupby

After groupby::
- Parentheses are grouping conditions
- Square brackets are the calculation objects
- Finally, the grouping statistical function

df2.groupby("diagnosis")["area_mean"].mean()

4.4.1 Creating DataFrames

Notes

There are two common ways to create a DataFrame in data science projects.
The first way is to type values in Python pandas directly, and this way is rarely used.
The second commonly used way is to load the datasets from existing files.
(1) The *pd.DataFrame()* method is used to type values.

In[1]
```
import numpy as np
import pandas as pd
df1=pd.DataFrame(np.arange(10).reshape(2,5))
df1
```

Out[1]

	0	1	2	3	4
0	0	1	2	3	4
1	5	6	7	8	9

Tricks

The "data" parameter of pd.DataFrame() can be assigned ndarray, list, dictionary, tuple, Series, etc.

Notes

(2) When importing values from existing files into Python using the pandas package, the data stored on computer will be automatically converted into a DataFrame object

In[2]
```
df2 = pd.read_csv('bc_data.csv')
df2.shape
```

Out[2] (569, 32)

Tips

The difference between numpy.ndarrays and pandas.DataFrame are:
- numpy.ndarrays represents a matrix-like data whereas pandas.DataFrame represents a SQL-table-like data.
- numpy.ndarrays can be multi-dimensional whereas pandas.DataFrame can only be two-dimensional.

Notes

We use the Fancy Indexing method here to select the "id", "diagnosis", "area_mean" columns of the df2 object. Refers to this book [4.2 Multidimensional arrays].

In[3]
```
df2=df2[["id","diagnosis","area_mean"]]
df2.head()
```

Out[3]

	id	diagnosis	area_mean
0	842302	M	1001.0
1	842517	M	1326.0
2	84300903	M	1203.0
3	84348301	M	386.1
4	84358402	M	1297.0

Tips

The .head() function and the .tail() function are two functions commonly used in data science projects, which are used to return the first and last n (the default value is 5) rows. If we have a large amount of data, it is not possible or necessary to display all of the rows.

4.4.2 Index or columns of DataFrames

Notes

The .index attribute is used to retrieve the axis labels of a pandas object, such as a DataFrame or a Series.

In[4] `df2.index`

Out[4] RangeIndex(start=0, stop=569, step=1)

Notes

The .index.size attribute is used to get the number of elements in the underlying data.

In[5] `df2.index.size`

Out[5] 569

Notes

The .columns attribute is used to get the column labels of the DataFrame.

In[6] `df2.columns`

Out[6] Index(['id', 'diagnosis', 'area_mean'], dtype='object')

Notes

The .columns.size attribute is used to get the number of columns.

In[7] `df2.columns.size`

Out[7] 3

Notes

The .shape attribute is used to get the shape of the DataFrame at the same time, i.e. the number of rows and columns.

In[8] `df2.shape`

Out[8] (569, 3)

Notes | In this case. The tuple represents the dimensions of the DataFrame 'df2', with the first element indicating the number of rows and the second indicating the number of columns. Therefore, 'df2.shape[0]' accesses the 0th element of the tuple (the number of rows), and 'df2.shape[1]' accesses the 1st element (the number of columns).

In[9] |
```
print("the number of rows:", df2.shape[0])
print("the number of columns:", df2.shape[1])
```

Out[9]   the number of rows: 569
the number of columns: 3

4.4.3 Slicing DataFrames

Notes | The way of accessing elements in a Python DataFrame is unique and differs from other programming languages. For instance, you cannot use the same syntax as C and Java, i.e., 'df2[1][2]'. Similarly, you cannot use the syntax from R language, i.e., 'df2[1,2]'. Instead, in pandas, we access data through methods like .iloc, .loc, or by column labels.

Notes | (1) Reading values by column name:
One common method for accessing data in a DataFrame is using the column name within square brackets.

In[10] | `df2["id"].head()`

Out[10]
```
0          842302
1          842517
2        84300903
3        84348301
4        84358402
Name: id, dtype: int64
```

Notes | Method 2: Using the column name as an attribute of the DataFrame.

In[11] | `df2.id.head()`

Out[11]
```
0          842302
1          842517
2        84300903
3        84348301
4        84358402
Name: id, dtype: int64
```

Notes   Method 3: Using column name and row number together.

In[12]   `df2["id"][2]`

Out[12]   84300903

Tricks   In pandas, the 0th axis refers to the DataFrame's rows and the 1st axis refers to its columns. Hence, we first specify the column ('id') and then the row (2). This is why 'df2[2]["id"]' is not valid and will raise an exception - it incorrectly assumes row-first indexing.

Notes   Method 4: Using attribute name and row number together.

In[13]   `df2.id[2]`

Out[13]   84300903

Notes   Method 5——Using slices.

In[14]   `df2["id"][[2,4]]`

Out[14]   2   84300903
4   84358402
Name: id, dtype: int64

Notes   (1) Reading values by label(s) or a boolean array (explicit index).
The .loc indexer in pandas allows us to access a data point in the DataFrame using explicit labels for both rows and columns.

In[15]   `df2.loc[1,"id"]`

Out[15]   842517

Notes   (2) Reading values by integer-location (implicit index).
The .iloc indexer in pandas allows us to access a data point in the DataFrame using implicit integer-based indexing, which is similar to standard list indexing in Python.

In[16]   `df2.iloc[1,0]`

Out[16]   842517

240

| | The main difference between .loc and .iloc lies in how they handle indexing:
Tricks | (1). loc[ ] is label-based.
| (2). iloc[ ] is integer position-based.

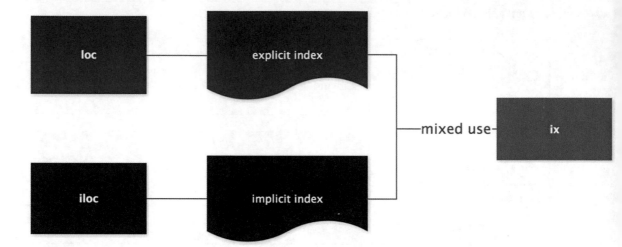

| | The .loc, .iloc, and .ix indexers in pandas are accessed using square brackets (e.g., 'df.loc[]', 'df.iloc[]'), not parentheses. It's worth noting that the .ix indexer was available in earlier versions of pandas, but it has been deprecated since version 0.20.0. Thus, for current versions of pandas, only .loc and .iloc should be used for label-based and
Tips | integer-based indexing, respectively.

| | (3) Accessing non-consecutive elements by Fancy Indexing.
Notes |

In[17] `df2[["area_mean","id"]].head()`

Out[17]

	area_mean	id
0	1001.0	842302
1	1326.0	842517
2	1203.0	84300903
3	386.1	84348301
4	1297.0	84358402

| | (4) Rows and columns of a DataFrame each have their unique explicit indices (or labels).
| The 'index' attribute of the DataFrame is used to get the labels of the rows.
Notes | The 'columns' attribute is used to get the labels of the columns.

In[18] `df2.index`

Out[18] RangeIndex(start=0, stop=569, step=1)

Tricks

The return value of 'df2.index' is a RangeIndex object, which is a kind of iterator used for lazy evaluation in pandas. To print all values of the index directly, we can use the '*' operator within a print function, like so: *'print(*df2.index)'*.

In[19] df2.columns

Out[19] Index(['id', 'diagnosis', 'area_mean'], dtype='object')

Notes

(5) Using explicit index and the *.head()* function together.

In[20] df2["id"].head()

Out[20]
```
0           842302
1           842517
2         84300903
3         84348301
4         84358402
Name: id, dtype: int64
```

Notes

(6) The *reset_index()* method is used to reset the index.

In[21] df2.reindex(index=["1","2","3"], columns=["1","2","3"])
        df2.head()

Out[21]

	id	diagnosis	area_mean
0	842302	M	1001.0
1	842517	M	1326.0
2	84300903	M	1203.0
3	84348301	M	386.1
4	84358402	M	1297.0

Tricks

Just like with Series, the reindex() method in a DataFrame can be used to create a new object with the data conformed to a new index. This function does not modify the explicit index of the original DataFrame.

In[22] df2.reindex(index=[2,3,1], columns=["diagnosis","id","area_mean"])

Out[22]

	diagnosis	id	area_mean
2	M	84300903	1203.0
3	M	84348301	386.1
1	M	842517	1326.0

Notes | In pandas, we can add a new column during the reindexing process, effectively creating an explicit index for that column. For instance, if we want to add a new column named 'MyNewColumn', we can include it in the list of columns when calling the reindex method:

In[23]
```
df3=df2.reindex(index=[2,3,1], columns=["diagnosis","id","area_mean",
"MyNewColumn"],fill_value=100)
df3
```

Out[23]

	diagnosis	id	area_mean	MyNewColumn
2	M	84300903	1203.0	100
3	M	84348301	386.1	100
1	M	842517	1326.0	100

4.4.4 Filtering DataFrames

Notes | The *pandas.read_csv()* function is used to read a CSV (Comma Separated Values) file and convert it into a pandas DataFrame.

In[24]
```
import pandas as pd
df2 = pd.read_csv('bc_data.csv')
df2=df2[["id","diagnosis","area_mean"]]
df2.head()
```

Out[24]

	id	diagnosis	area_mean
0	842302	M	1001.0
1	842517	M	1326.0
2	84300903	M	1203.0
3	84348301	M	386.1
4	84358402	M	1297.0

Notes | When used with an argument like 'df2.drop([2])', the '2' is interpreted as a label-based (or explicit) index, rather than a positional (or implicit) index.

In[25] | `df2.drop([2]).head()`

Out[25]

	id	diagnosis	area_mean
0	842302	M	1001.0
1	842517	M	1326.0
3	84348301	M	386.1
4	84358402	M	1297.0
5	843786	M	477.1

Notes

The *.drop()* method in pandas does not modify the original DataFrame unless the 'inplace' parameter is set to True.

In[26]   `df2.head()`

Out[26]

	id	diagnosis	area_mean
0	842302	M	1001.0
1	842517	M	1326.0
2	84300903	M	1203.0
3	84348301	M	386.1
4	84358402	M	1297.0

In[27]
```
import pandas as pd
df2 = pd.read_csv('bc_data.csv')
df2=df2[["id","diagnosis","area_mean"]]
df2.drop([3,4], axis=0, inplace=True)
df2.head()
```

Out[27]

	id	diagnosis	area_mean
0	842302	M	1001.0
1	842517	M	1326.0
2	84300903	M	1203.0
5	843786	M	477.1
6	844359	M	1040.0

Tricks

Running these lines of code may raise exceptions if the initial state of 'df2' isn't preserved. This could be due to previous operations that have modified 'df2'.

Tricks

The first parameter of the 'df2.drop()' function in pandas is 'labels', which refers to the labels of the rows or columns you want to drop. The 'labels' parameter can accept a single label or a list-like object containing multiple labels.

Tricks

If 'inplace=True' is specified, the operation is performed inplace, modifying the original DataFrame. No new DataFrame is returned, and the original DataFrame is changed.

If 'inplace=False' is specified (which is the default setting), a new DataFrame is returned with the changes, while the original DataFrame remains unchanged.

	Whether to modify the data itself (in-place modification)	whether to return a new value (return a new value)
inplace=True	Yes	No
inplace=False	No	Yes

In[28]
```
import pandas as pd
df2 = pd.read_csv('bc_data.csv')
df2=df2[["id","diagnosis","area_mean"]]
df2.drop([3,4], axis=0, inplace=False)

df2.head()
```

Out[28]

	id	diagnosis	area_mean
0	842302	M	1001.0
1	842517	M	1326.0
2	84300903	M	1203.0
3	84348301	M	386.1
4	84358402	M	1297.0

Notes

There are several ways to remove a column from a pandas DataFrame:

One method is to use the del statement.

In[29]
```
import pandas as pd
df2 = pd.read_csv('bc_data.csv')
df2=df2[["id","diagnosis","area_mean"]]
del df2["area_mean"]
df2.head()
```

Out[29]

	id	diagnosis
0	842302	M
1	842517	M
2	84300903	M
3	84348301	M
4	84358402	M

Notes

Another method is to use the *drop()* function with the 'columns' parameter.

In[30]
```
import pandas as pd
df2 = pd.read_csv('bc_data.csv')
df2=df2[["id","diagnosis","area_mean"]]
df2.drop(["id","diagnosis"], axis=1, inplace=True)

df2.head()
```

Out[30]

	area_mean
0	1001.0
1	1326.0
2	1203.0
3	386.1
4	1297.0

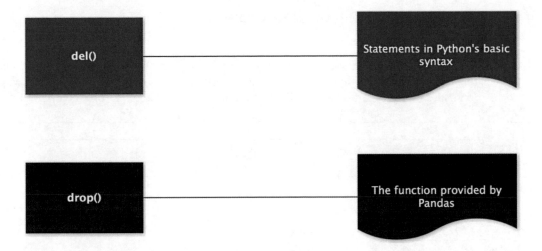

 Notes A common way to filter a DataFrame by certain column values is by using Boolean indexing, or creating a condition that returns a series of True and False value. For instance, to select all rows from the DataFrame 'df2' where the value in the 'area_mean' column is greater than 1000, you would write:

In[31]
```
import pandas as pd
df2 =pd.read_csv('bc_data.csv')

df2=df2[["id","diagnosis","area_mean"]]
df2[df2.area_mean> 1000].head()
```

Out[31]

	id	diagnosis	area_mean
0	842302	M	1001.0
1	842517	M	1326.0
2	84300903	M	1203.0
4	84358402	M	1297.0
6	844359	M	1040.0

 Notes To select and display only the 'id' and 'diagnosis' columns for the first five rows where 'area_mean' is greater than 1000 in the DataFrame 'df2', you can use the following command.

In[32]
```
df2[df2.area_mean> 1000][["id","diagnosis"]].head()
```

Out[32]

	id	diagnosis
0	842302	M
1	842517	M
2	84300903	M
4	84358402	M
6	844359	M

4.4.5 Arithmetic operating on DataFrames

Notes When performing arithmetic operations between two DataFrames, it's important that they have the same structure or the operation might not behave as expected. One way to ensure this is to align the DataFrames on their explicit index before the operation.

In[33]
```
df4=pd.DataFrame(np.arange(6).reshape(2,3))
df4
```

Out[33]

	0	1	2
0	0	1	2
1	3	4	5

Tricks In languages like C and Java, calculations involving arrays or lists are commonly performed based on position indices (implicit indices). However, in Python, particularly when using the pandas library, operations can be performed based on explicit indices as well as position indices.

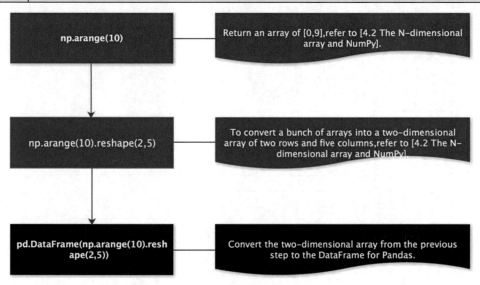

In[34]
```
df5=pd.DataFrame(np.arange(10).reshape(2,5))
df5
```

Out[34]

	0	1	2	3	4
0	0	1	2	3	4
1	5	6	7	8	9

In[35]
```
df4+df5
```

Out[35]

	0	1	2	3	4
0	0	2	4	NaN	NaN
1	8	10	12	NaN	NaN

Notes

When performing arithmetic operations using operators like +, -, *, etc., the resulting DataFrame may include NaN values if the operation involves NaN. To handle these cases, pandas provides specific methods such as add(), sub(), mul(), and div(), which can be more effective.

In[36]
```
df6=df4.add(df5,fill_value=10)
df6
```

Out[36]

	0	1	2	3	4
0	0	2	4	13.0	14.0
1	8	10	12	18.0	19.0

Tips

Though basic arithmetic operators like '+', '-', '*', and '/' can be used in data science tasks with pandas, it's generally recommended to use corresponding pandas DataFrame methods such as add(), sub(), mul(), and div() instead. This is because these methods are more flexible and allow for additional parameters to be set.

Notes

When performing arithmetic operations with broadcasting rules, we need to ensure the DataFrames involved have compatible shapes. This is so that the smaller DataFrame can be 'broadcast' across the larger DataFrame, meaning its values are reused to match the shape of the larger DataFrame.

In[37]
```
s1=pd.Series(np.arange(3))
s1
```

Out[37]
```
0    0
1    1
2    2
dtype: int32
```

In[38]
```
df6-s1
```

Out[38]

	0	1	2	3	4
0	0.0	1.0	2.0	NaN	NaN
1	8.0	9.0	10.0	NaN	NaN

Notes

We can perform arithmetic operations between a pandas Series and a DataFrame. These operations are executed based on the explicit index (labels) of the Series and DataFrame.

In[39]
```
df5=pd.DataFrame(np.arange(10).reshape(2,5))
s1=pd.Series(np.arange(3))
df5-s1
```

Out[39]

	0	1	2	3	4
0	0.0	0.0	0.0	NaN	NaN
1	5.0	5.0	5.0	NaN	NaN

Notes

We can also apply the *sub()* function in pandas, setting the axis parameter to 1 to perform subtraction between DataFrames across columns. The *add()*, *sub()*, *mul()*, and *div()* functions in pandas correspond to the arithmetic operators +, -, *, and /, respectively.

In[40]
```
df5=pd.DataFrame(np.arange(10).reshape(2,5))
s1=pd.Series(np.arange(3))
df5.sub(s1,axis=1)
```

Out[40]

	0	1	2	3	4
0	0.0	0.0	0.0	NaN	NaN
1	5.0	5.0	5.0	NaN	NaN

Notes

In pandas, setting the parameter axis=1 during an operation signifies the following:

1. The number of rows remains the same before and after the operation.
2. The operation is performed across all columns in each row.
3. Each column is considered as a whole during the operation.

Notes

When performing arithmetic operations along the vertical axis (axis=0) in pandas, we are applying these operations across all rows for each column. Before we can do this, we must first ensure that the DataFrames involved have the same number of columns.

In[41]
```
df5=pd.DataFrame(np.arange(10).reshape(2,5))
s1=pd.Series(np.arange(3))
df5.sub(s1,axis=0)
```

Out[41]

	0	1	2	3	4
0	0.0	1.0	2.0	3.0	4.0
1	4.0	5.0	6.0	7.0	8.0
2	NaN	NaN	NaN	NaN	NaN

In[42]
```
df7=pd.DataFrame(np.arange(20).reshape(4,5))
df7
```

Out[42]

	0	1	2	3	4
0	0	1	2	3	4
1	5	6	7	8	9
2	10	11	12	13	14
3	15	16	17	18	19

In[43]
```
df7+2
```

Out[43]

	0	1	2	3	4
0	2	3	4	5	6
1	7	8	9	10	11
2	12	13	14	15	16
3	17	18	19	20	21

Notes

Additionally, pandas provides many more functions to support a wide variety of data processing needs. For operations that need to be performed on a column-by-column basis without crossing between columns, pandas allows you to set axis=0. This ensures that the operation is applied individually to each column, treating each one as a separate entity.

In[44]
```
print(df7)
print("df7.cumsum=",df7.cumsum())
```

Out[44]
```
   0   1   2   3   4
0  0   1   2   3   4
1  5   6   7   8   9
2  10 11  12  13  14
3  15 16  17  18  19
df7.cumsum=    0  1  2  3  4
0  0   1   2   3   4
1  5   7   9  11  13
2  15 18  21  24  27
3  30 34  38  42  46
```

In[45]
```
df7
```

Out[45]

	0	1	2	3	4
0	0	1	2	3	4
1	5	6	7	8	9
2	10	11	12	13	14
3	15	16	17	18	19

Notes

In the line df7.rolling(2).sum(), we are performing a rolling sum operation on the DataFrame df7. This calculates the sum of every two adjacent elements in the DataFrame, indicating that the size of the rolling window for calculations is 2.

In[46]
```
df7.rolling(2).sum()
```

Out[46]

	0	1	2	3	4
0	NaN	NaN	NaN	NaN	NaN
1	5.0	7.0	9.0	11.0	13.0
2	15.0	17.0	19.0	21.0	23.0
3	25.0	27.0	29.0	31.0	33.0

In[47]
```
df7.rolling(2,axis=1).sum()
```

Out[47]

	0	1	2	3	4
0	NaN	1.0	3.0	5.0	7.0
1	NaN	11.0	13.0	15.0	17.0
2	NaN	21.0	23.0	25.0	27.0
3	NaN	31.0	33.0	35.0	37.0

Notes

The *DataFrame.cov()* function is used to compute pairwise covariance of columns, excluding NA/null values.

In[48] `df7.cov()`

Out[48]

	0	1	2	3	4
0	41.666667	41.666667	41.666667	41.666667	41.666667
1	41.666667	41.666667	41.666667	41.666667	41.666667
2	41.666667	41.666667	41.666667	41.666667	41.666667
3	41.666667	41.666667	41.666667	41.666667	41.666667
4	41.666667	41.666667	41.666667	41.666667	41.666667

Notes

The *DataFrame.corr()* function is used to compute pairwise correlation of columns, excluding NA/null values.

In49] `df7.corr()`

Out[49]

	0	1	2	3	4
0	1.0	1.0	1.0	1.0	1.0
1	1.0	1.0	1.0	1.0	1.0
2	1.0	1.0	1.0	1.0	1.0
3	1.0	1.0	1.0	1.0	1.0
4	1.0	1.0	1.0	1.0	1.0

Notes

The *.T* attribute is used to transpose index and columns.

In[50]
```
import pandas as pd
df2 = pd.read_csv('bc_data.csv')

df2=df2[["id","diagnosis","area_mean"]][2:5]
df2.T
```

Out[50]

	2	3	4
id	84300903	84348301	84358402
diagnosis	M	M	M
area_mean	1203	386.1	1297

In[51] `print(df6)`

Out[51]
```
     0   1   2    3    4
0 0  2   4  13.0 14.0
1 8  10  12  18.0 19.0
```

In[52] `df6>5`

Out[52]

	0	1	2	3	4
0	False	False	False	True	True
1	True	True	True	True	True

In[53] `print(s1)`

Out[53]
```
0    0
1    1
2    2
dtype: int32
```

In[54] `df6>s1`

Out[54]

	0	1	2	3	4
0	Falsc	True	True	False	False
1	True	True	True	False	False

4.4.6 Descriptive analysis of DataFrames

Notes

pandas.DataFrame.describe() generates descriptive statistics include those that summarize the central tendency, dispersion and shape of a dataset's distribution, excluding NaN values.

In[55]
```
import numpy as np
import pandas as pd

df2 = pd.read_csv('bc_data.csv')

df2=df2[["id","diagnosis","area_mean"]]

df2.describe()
```

Out[55]

	id	area_mean
count	5.690000e+02	569.000000
mean	3.037183e+07	654.889104
std	1.250206e+08	351.914129
min	8.670000e+03	143.500000
25%	8.692180e+05	420.300000
50%	9.060240e+05	551.100000
75%	8.813129e+06	782.700000
max	9.113205e+08	2501.000000

Tricks

The pandas.DataFrame.info() method prints comprehensive information about a DataFrame. This includes details about the index data type, columns, the count of non-null values in each column, and memory usage.

A commonly used method to filter a DataFrame by column value is to apply the filtering condition directly to the DataFrame object. When using the syntax df2[df2.diagnosis == 'M'], the expression df2.diagnosis == 'M' evaluates to a Boolean Series where each element is either True or False, indicating whether the corresponding row satisfies the condition.

Notes

In[56]   `dt = df2[df2.diagnosis=='M']`

In data science projects, the amount of data can be large, and it's often unnecessary to access all rows of the data at once. Instead, it's common to only need the first or last few rows for analysis or inspection purposes. This is particularly applicable when the data has a consistent structure, with each row having the same set of columns.

Notes

In[57]   `dt.head()`

Out[57]

	id	diagnosis	area_mean
0	842302	M	1001.0
1	842517	M	1326.0
2	84300903	M	1203.0
3	84348301	M	386.1
4	84358402	M	1297.0

By using functions like .head() or .tail(), you can easily access a specified number of rows from the beginning or end of the DataFrame, respectively. These functions are efficient ways to quickly examine a subset of the data without loading the entire dataset, which can be time-consuming and resource-intensive.

Notes

In[58]   `dt.tail()`

Out[58]

	id	diagnosis	area_mean
563	926125	M	1347.0
564	926424	M	1479.0
565	926682	M	1261.0
566	926954	M	858.1
567	927241	M	1265.0

The function DataFrame.tail(n=5) in pandas returns the last 'n' rows from the DataFrame based on their position. This function is particularly useful for quickly verifying data, such as after performing sorting or appending rows to the DataFrame.

Tricks

The *count()* method counts the number of non-null (non-empty) values for each column by default.

Notes

In[59]   `df2[df2.diagnosis=='M'].count()`

Out[59]   id   212
          diagnosis   212
          area_mean   212
          dtype: int64

Notes

In pandas DataFrame, fancy indexing refers to accessing non-consecutive rows or columns using specific indices or boolean conditions.

In[60]   `df2[["area_mean","id"]].head()`

Out[60]

	area_mean	id
0	1001.0	842302
1	1326.0	842517
2	1203.0	84300903
3	386.1	84348301
4	1297.0	84358402

4.4.7 Sorting DataFrames

Notes

Firstly we check the first 8 rows of the df2 object.

In[61]   `df2.head(8)`

Out[61]

	id	diagnosis	area_mean
0	842302	M	1001.0
1	842517	M	1326.0
2	84300903	M	1203.0
3	84348301	M	386.1
4	84358402	M	1297.0
5	843786	M	477.1
6	844359	M	1040.0
7	84458202	M	577.9

Notes

The *sort_values()* method in pandas can be used to sort the DataFrame by the values along either axis, which can be the rows (axis=0) or the columns (axis=1)."

In[62]   `df2.sort_values(by="area_mean",axis=0,ascending=True).head()`

Out[62]

	id	diagnosis	area_mean
101	862722	B	143.5
539	921362	B	170.4
538	921092	B	178.8
568	92751	B	181.0
46	85713702	B	201.9

Notes

The *sort_index()* method in pandas is used to sort an object (e.g., DataFrame or Series) by its labels along a specified axis. By default, it sorts the object based on the index labels, but you can also specify axis=1 to sort along the columns.

In[63]   df2.sort_index(axis=1).head(3)

Out[63]

	area_mean	diagnosis	id
0	1001.0	M	842302
1	1326.0	M	842517
2	1203.0	M	84300903

Notes

Setting axis=0 in pandas implies that the operation is applied vertically to all rows in each column, while maintaining the same number of columns. Each row is treated as a collective entity during the operation.

In[64]   df2.sort_index(axis=0,ascending=False).head(3)

Out[64]

	id	diagnosis	area_mean
568	92751	B	181.0
567	927241	M	1265.0
566	926954	M	858.1

4.4.8 Importing/Exporting DataFrames

Notes

The prerequisite for importing and exporting a DataFrame is to know the current working directory, as described in [3.8 Current working directory]. To retrieve the current working directory of a process, you can use the *getcwd()* method from the *os* package.

In[65]
```
import os
print(os.getcwd())
```

Out[65]   C:\Users\soloman\clm

Notes

The *to_***()* method :writes a DataFrame object to a file, including:
- pandas.DataFrame.to_csv(): Write object to a comma-separated values (csv) file.
- pandas.DataFrame.to_excel(): Write object to an Excel sheet.
- pandas.DataFrame.to_json(): Convert the object to a JSON string.
- pandas.DataFrame.to_html(): Render a DataFrame as an HTML table.
- pandas.DataFrame.to_xml(): Render a DataFrame to an XML document.
- pandas.DataFrame.to_sql(): Write records stored in a DataFrame to a SQL database.

In[66]   df2.head(3).to_csv("df2.csv")

Notes

The *read_***()* method reads a file into DataFrame, including:
- pandas.read_csv(): Read a comma-separated values (csv) file into DataFrame.
- pandas.read_excel(): Read an Excel file into a pandas DataFrame.
- pandas.read_json() : Convert a JSON string to pandas object.
- pandas.read_html(): Read HTML tables into a list of DataFrame objects.
- pandas.read_xml(): Read XML document into a DataFrame object.
- pandas.read_sql(): Read SQL query or database table into a DataFrame.

In[67]
```
import pandas as pd
df3 = pd.read_csv('df2.csv')
df3
```

Out[67]

	Unnamed: 0	id	diagnosis	area_mean
0	0	842302	M	1001.0
1	1	842517	M	1326.0
2	2	84300903	M	1203.0

Notes

One more example is calling the *to_excel()* method to write the first 3 rows of DataFrame df2 to an Excel sheet named "df3.xls".

In[68]
```
df2.head(3).to_excel("df3.xls")
```

Notes

Next, we can use the *read_excel()* method to read the Excel file 'df3.xls' into a pandas DataFrame and save it as 'df3'.

In[69]
```
df3 = pd.read_excel("df3.xls")
df3
```

Out[69]

	id	diagnosis	area_mean
0	842302	M	1001
1	842517	M	1326
2	84300903	M	1203

4.4.9 Handling missing values with Pandas

Notes

When accessing the *.empty* attribute of a DataFrame, if the DataFrame is empty (i.e., it has no rows or columns), it will return True. On the other hand, if the DataFrame has any data (at least one row or column), it will return False.

In[70]
```
df3.empty
```
Out[70]   False

Notes

np.nan is a numeric value and None is an object in Python. As a result, np.nan can be used in mathematical operations, while None cannot.

In[71]
```
np.nan-np.nan +1
```
Out[71]   nan

In[72]
```
np.nan-np.nan
```
Out[72]   nan

Notes

The exception TypeError: unsupported operand type(s) for +: 'NoneType' and 'int' is raised because None cannot be used as a numerical value in mathematical operations.

In[73] | None+1

```
TypeError                    Traceback (most recent call last)
<ipython-input-83-6e170940e108> in <module>()
----> 1 None+1

TypeError: unsupported operand type(s) for +: 'NoneType' and 'int'
```

In[74] | import pandas as pd
import numpy as np
A=pd.DataFrame(np.array([10,10,20,20]).reshape(2,2),columns=list("ab"),
index=list("SW"))
A

Out[74]

	a	b
S	10	10
W	20	20

Notes

Here, the *list("ab")* method is used to convert a string, such as "ab", into a list of individual strings, ['a', 'b'], in Python. For more details, please refer to [2.17 Built-in Functions].

In[75] | list("ab")
Out[75] | ['a', 'b']

In[76] | B=pd.DataFrame(np.array([1,1,1,2,2,2,3,3,3]).reshape(3,3),
columns=list("abc"),index=list("SWT"))
B

Out[76]

	a	b	c
S	1	1	1
W	2	2	2
T	3	3	3

Notes

Here are the revised tips for Python beginners:

1. Arithmetic operations in pandas DataFrames are performed based on the explicit index of rows and columns.
2. Missing values in pandas DataFrames can be filled with NaN (Not a Number) to ensure that arithmetic operations do not raise exceptions.
3. The basic process for performing arithmetic operations on DataFrames is as follows: First, ensure that the DataFrames have compatible shapes by aligning their indices. Then, fill any missing values with NaN in the resulting DataFrame. Finally, perform the desired arithmetic operations.

In[77]

```
C=A+B
C
```

Out[77]

	a	b	c
S	11.0	11.0	NaN
T	NaN	NaN	NaN
W	22.0	22.0	NaN

Notes

In the expression A.add(B, fill_value=0), the *fill_value=0* parameter specifies that any missing values in A should be filled with 0 before adding B to A.

In[78]

```
A.add(B,fill_value=0)
```

Out[78]

	a	b	c
S	11.0	11.0	1.0
T	3.0	3.0	3.0
W	22.0	22.0	2.0

Notes

The parameter "*fill_value = A.stack().mean()*" in the expression A.add(B, fill_value=A. stack().mean()) means that existing missing values in A should be filled with the mean of all the values in A.

In[79]

```
A.add(B,fill_value=A.stack().mean())
```

Out[79]

	a	b	c
S	11.0	11.0	16.0
T	18.0	18.0	18.0
W	22.0	22.0	17.0

Notes

A.mean(axis=1) calculates the mean of all rows in each column of DataFrame A. By specifying axis=1, the mean() function calculates the mean value for each row in every column of A.

In[80]

```
A.mean()
```

Out[80]

```
a    15.0
b    15.0
dtype: float64
```

Notes

In pandas, the *stack()* method is used to pivot a DataFrame from a wide format to a long format by creating a multi-level index. It essentially "stacks" or compresses the columns of the DataFrame into a single column, resulting in a reshaped DataFrame or Series with a multi-level index.

In[81]   `A.stack()`

Out[81]
```
S    a    10
     b    10
W    a    20
     b    20
dtype: int32
```

In[82]   `A.stack().mean()`

Out[82]   15.0

In[83]   `C`

Out[83]

	a	b	c
S	11.0	11.0	NaN
T	NaN	NaN	NaN
W	22.0	22.0	NaN

There are four important functions in pandas to handle missing values in a DataFrame: *isnull( )*, *notnull( )*, *dropna( )*, and *fillna( )*.

(1) *isnull( )*: This function returns a Boolean mask that identifies missing values in the DataFrame.

In[84]   `C.isnull()`

Out[84]

	a	b	c
S	False	False	True
T	True	True	True
W	False	False	True

(2) *notnull( )*: This function is the opposite of isnull().

In[85]   `C.notnull()`

Out[85]

	a	b	c
S	True	True	False
T	False	False	False
W	True	True	False

(3) *dropna()*: This function is used to remove or drop rows or columns that contain missing values.

In[86] `C.dropna(axis='index')`

Out[86]

	a	b	c

(4) *fillna()*: This function is used to fill missing values in the DataFrame with a specified value or a calculated value.

In[87] `C.fillna(0)`

Out[87]

	a	b	c
S	11.0	11.0	0.0
T	0.0	0.0	0.0
W	22.0	22.0	0.0

By specifying method="ffill", missing values in the DataFrame are filled with the last known non-null value.

In[88] `C.fillna(method="ffill")`

Out[88]

	a	b	c
S	11.0	11.0	NaN
T	11.0	11.0	NaN
W	22.0	22.0	NaN

By specifying method="bfill", missing values in the DataFrame are filled with the next non-null value.

In[89] `C.fillna(method="bfill",axis=1)`

Out[89]

	a	b	c
S	11.0	11.0	NaN
T	NaN	NaN	NaN
W	22.0	22.0	NaN

4.4.10 Grouping DataFrames

In[90]
```
import pandas as pd
df2 = pd.read_csv('bc_data.csv')
df2=df2[["id","diagnosis","area_mean"]]
df2.head()
```

Out[90]

	id	diagnosis	area_mean
0	842302	M	1001.0
1	842517	M	1326.0
2	84300903	M	1203.0
3	84348301	M	386.1
4	84358402	M	1297.0

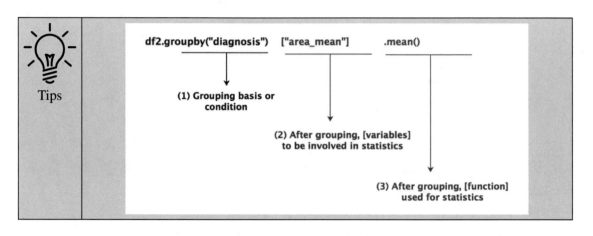

Tips

df2.groupby("diagnosis")   ["area_mean"]   .mean()

(1) Grouping basis or condition

(2) After grouping, [variables] to be involved in statistics

(3) After grouping, [function] used for statistics

In[91]
```
df2.groupby("diagnosis")["area_mean"].mean()
```

Out[91]
```
diagnosis
B        462.790196
M        978.376415
Name: area_mean, dtype: float64
```

Notes

To aggregate using one or more operations over the specified axis, we can call the method the *aggregate()*.

In[92]
```
df2.groupby("diagnosis")["area_mean"].aggregate(["mean","sum","max",
np.median])
```

Out[92]

	mean	sum	max	median
diagnosis				
B	462.790196	165216.1	992.1	458.4
M	978.376415	207415.8	2501.0	932.0

Tricks

The DataFrame.aggregate() method provides us with the flexibility to apply multiple functions at once or pass a list of functions to each group. In this example, we aggregate a list of operation names such as 'mean', 'sum', 'max', and 'np.median'.

Notes

The pandas.DataFrame.unstack() method performs the following actions:

It returns a DataFrame with a new level of column labels, where the innermost level consists of the pivoted index labels.

If the index of the DataFrame is not a MultiIndex (hierarchical index), the output will be a Series. This is analogous to the stack() operation when the columns are not a MultiIndex.

In[93] df2.groupby("diagnosis")["area_mean"].aggregate(["mean","sum"]).
        unstack()

Out[93]
```
        diagnosis
mean    B               462.790196
        M               978.376415
sum     B            165216.100000
        M            207415.800000
dtype: float64
```

Tricks

The *stack()*, *unstack()*, *pivot()*, and *melt()* methods are commonly used in data science to convert data formats:

1. pandas.DataFrame.stack(): This method returns a reshaped DataFrame or Series with a multi-level index. It adds one or more new inner-most levels compared to the current DataFrame, creating a hierarchical structure.

2. pandas.DataFrame.unstack(): The unstack() method returns a DataFrame with a new level of column labels. The inner-most level of the resulting DataFrame consists of the pivoted index labels. This operation is useful for reshaping data from long to wide format.

3. pandas.DataFrame.pivot(): The pivot() method reshapes data, essentially producing a "pivot" table. It uses unique values from specified index/columns to form axes of the resulting DataFrame, allowing for easy restructuring of data based on column values.

4. pandas.DataFrame.melt(): The melt() method is used to transform a DataFrame into a specific format.

Notes

By utilizing the *apply()* method in pandas, you can apply a user-defined function to groups within a DataFrame.

In[94]
```
def myfunc(x):
    x["area_mean"]/=x["area_mean"].sum()
    return x

df2.groupby("diagnosis").apply(myfunc).head()
```

Out[94]

	id	diagnosis	area_mean
0	842302	M	0.004826
1	842517	M	0.006393
2	84300903	M	0.005800
3	84348301	M	0.001861
4	84358402	M	0.006253

4.5 Date and time

Q&A

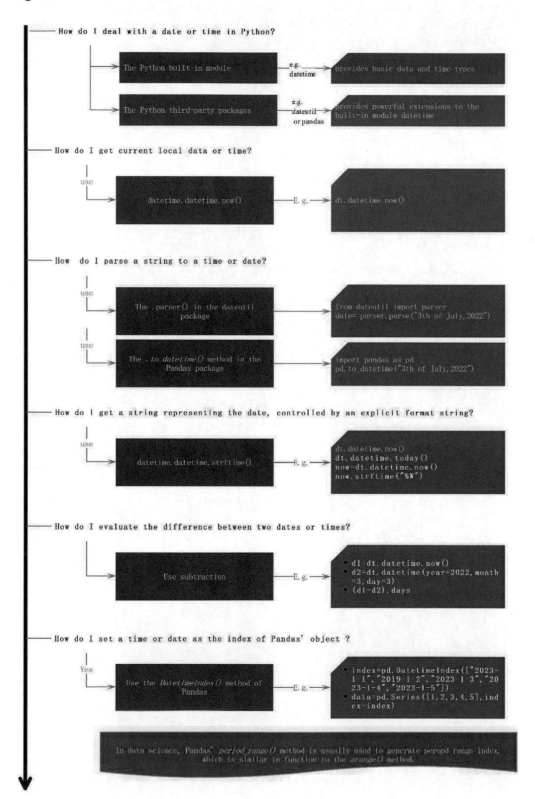

How do I deal with a date or time in Python?

The Python built-in module — e.g. datetime → provides basic data and time types

The Python third-party packages — e.g. dateutil or pandas → provides powerful extensions to the built-in module datetime

How do I get current local data or time?

use → datetime.datetime.now() — E.g. → dt.datetime.now()

How do I parse a string to a time or date?

use → The .parser() in the dateutil package →
```
from dateutil import parser
date= parser.parse("3th of July, 2022")
```

use → The .to_datetime() method in the Pandas package →
```
import pandas as pd
pd.to_datetime("3th of July, 2022")
```

How do I get a string representing the date, controlled by an explicit format string?

use → datetime.datetime.strftime() — E.g. →
```
dt.datetime.now()
dt.datetime.today()
now=dt.datetime.now()
now.strftime("%W")
```

How do I evaluate the difference between two dates or times?

Use subtraction — E.g. →
- d1=dt.datetime.now()
- d2=dt.datetime(year=2022, month=3, day=3)
- (d1-d2).days

How do I set a time or date as the index of Pandas' object ?

Yes → Use the DatetimeIndex() method of Pandas — E.g. →
- index=pd.DatetimeIndex(["2023-1-1","2019-1-2","2023-1-3","2023-1-4","2023-1-5"])
- data=pd.Series([1,2,3,4,5], index=index)

In data science, Pandas' period_range() method is usually used to generate peropd range index, which is similar in function to the arange() method.

By utilizing the combination of the built-in datetime module and third-party packages such as dateutil or pandas, Python developers can effectively manage and manipulate dates and times in a wide range of scenarios, from basic operations to sophisticated time series analysis.

Tips

4.5.1 Creating a time or date object

Notes

(1) to create a time object: *datetime.time()*

In[1]
```
import datetime as dt
myTime = dt.time(12,34,59)
print("myTime:",myTime)
print("myTime.hour:",myTime.hour)
print("myTime.minute:",myTime.minute)
print("myTime.second:",myTime.second)
```
Out[1]
```
myTime: 12:34:59
myTime.hour: 12
myTime.minute: 34
myTime.second: 59
```

Tricks

The python built-in module *datetime* provides three different classes for creating dates or times:
- datetime.time() returns an idealized time, independent of any particular day, including attributes: hour, minute, second, microsecond.
- datetime.date( ) returns an idealized naïve date with attributes: year, month, and day.
- datetime.datetime() returns a combination of a date and a time, including attributes: year, month, day, hour, minute, second, microsecond, and tzinfo.

Notes

(2) to create a combination of a date and a time

In[2] `dt.datetime(year = 2018,month = 3,day = 3)`
Out[2] `datetime.datetime(2018, 3, 3, 0, 0)`

Tricks

Here, you can access the documentation of datetime.datetime by typing 'dt.datetime?'.

In[3] | dt.datetime?

Out[3]   Init signature: dt.datetime(self, /, *args, **kwargs)
Docstring:
datetime(year, month, day[, hour[, minute[, second[, microsecond[,tzinfo]]]]])

The year, month and day arguments are required. tzinfo may be None,
or an instance of a tzinfo subclass. The remaining arguments may be ints.
File:
c:\users\administrator\appdata\local\programs\python\python36\lib\datetime.py
Type: type

Notes

In the *dt.datetime()* function, the year, month, and day arguments are required. The tzinfo argument may be set to None or an instance of a tzinfo subclass. The remaining arguments are optional but must be integers.

In[4] | dt.datetime(month=3,day=3,second=59)

TypeError   Traceback (most recent call last)
<ipython-input-5-6fbb4e101d77> in <module>()
----> 1 dt.datetime(month=3,day=3,second=59)

TypeError: Required argument 'year' (pos 1) not found

Notes

However, the *second, minute, and hour* arguments are optional for the datetime. datetime() function.

In[5] | dt.datetime(year = 2018,month = 3,day = 3)

Out[5]   datetime.datetime(2018, 3, 3, 0, 0)

4.5.2 Parsing a string to a time or date object

Tips

There are many formats used to represent time or date, such as '3rd of July, 2022', '2022-1-3', and '2022-07-03 00:00:00'. However, most of these formats are not represented in the standard format of the Python built-in module datetime. Attempting to parse these formats using the standard datetime module can raise an exception.

In[6] | dt.datetime("3th of July,2022")

TypeError   Traceback (most recent call last)
<ipython-input-8-c7659db11b43> in <module>()
----> 1 dt.datetime("3th of July,2022")

TypeError: an integer is required (got type str)

In[7]
```
dt.datetime("2022-1-3")
```

TypeError   Traceback (most recent call last)
<ipython-input-9-c1b53c571977> in <module>()
----> 1 dt.datetime("2022-1-3")

TypeError: an integer is required (got type str)

Tricks

In data science, there are common methods used for parsing a string into a standard date or time format:
1. The *parser.parse()* method in the dateutil package
2. The *to_datetime()* method in the pandas package

Notes

(1) *parser.parse()*

In[8]
```
# to parse the string "3th of July,2022" to a datetime

from dateutil import parser
date= parser.parse("3th of July,2022")
print(date)
```
Out[8] 2022-07-03 00:00:00

In[9]
```
# to parse the string "2022-1-3" to a datetime

date= parser.parse("2022-1-3")
print(date)
```
Out[9] 2022-01-03 00:00:00

Notes

(2) panadas. *to_datetime()*

In[10]
```
# to parse the string "3th of July,2022" to a datetime

import pandas as pd
pd.to_datetime("3th of July,2018")
```
Out[10] Timestamp('2022-07-03 00:00:00')

In[11]
```
# to parse the string "2022-1-3" to a datetime

import pandas as pd
pd.to_datetime("2022-1-3")
```
Out[11] Timestamp('2022-01-03 00:00:00')

4.5.3 Getting current local data or time object

(1) To obtain the current local date and time, you can use the datetime.datetime.now() function.

In[12]
```
dt.datetime.now()
```

Out[12]   datetime.datetime(2022, 5, 24, 21, 39, 50, 155634)

(2) To obtain the current local date, you can use the datetime.*datetime.today()* function.

In[13]
```
dt.datetime.today()
```

Out[13]   datetime.datetime(2022, 5, 24, 21, 39, 50, 913872)

(3) To obtain a string representation of a date, controlled by an explicit format string, you can use the datetime.datetime.strftime() method.

In[14]
```
now=dt.datetime.now()
now.strftime("%W"),now.strftime("%a"),now.strftime("%A"),
now.strftime("%B"),now.strftime("%C"),now.strftime("%D")
```

Out[14]   ('51', 'Sun', 'Sunday', 'December', '20', '12/23/18')

Tricks

The format codes in datetime.strftime():
- %I   Hour (12-hour clock) as a zero-padded decimal number.
- %p   Locale's equivalent of either AM or PM.
- %M   Minute as a zero-padded decimal number.
- %S   Second as a zero-padded decimal number.
- %f   Microsecond as a decimal number, zero-padded to 6 digits.
- %z   UTC offset in the form ±HHMM[SS[.ffffff]] (empty string if the object is naive).
- %Z   Time zone name (empty string if the object is naive).
- %j   Day of the year as a zero-padded decimal number.
- %U   Week number of the year (Sunday as the first day of the week) as a zero-padded decimal number. All days in a new year preceding the first Sunday are considered to be in week 0.
- %W   Week number of the year (Monday as the first day of the week) as a zero-padded decimal number. All days in a new year preceding the first Monday are considered to be in week 0.
- %c   Locale's appropriate date and time representation.
- %x   Locale's appropriate date representation.
- %X   Locale's appropriate time representation.
- %%   A literal '%' character.

4.5.4 Evaluating the difference between two date or time objects

Notes

You can evaluate the duration, or the difference between two date or time objects, by subtracting one object from another.

In[15]
```
d1=dt.datetime.now()
d2=dt.datetime(year=2017,month=3,day=3)
(d1-d2).days
```
Out[15]   447

Tricks

Here, the .days attribute means the unit of evaluation.

4.5.5 Setting a time or date object as the index of Pandas

Notes

(1) Create a datetime index: pandas. *DatetimeIndex( )*

In[16]
```
myindex=pd.DatetimeIndex(["2023-1-1","2024-1-2","2023-1-3","2023-1-4",
"2023-1-5"])
```

Notes

(2) Set the datetime index: pandas.DataFrame() or pandas.Series()

In[16]
```
data=pd.Series([1,2,3,4,5],index=myindex)
data
```
Out[16]
```
2023-01-01    1
2024-01-02    2
2023-01-03    3
2023-01-04    4
2023-01-05    5
dtype: int64
```

Notes

(3) Access a data item by slicing a DataFrame or Series

In[17]   `data["2023-1-2"]`

Out[17]   Series([], dtype: int64)

In[18] `data["2023"]`

Out[18]
```
2023-01-01   1
2023-01-03   3
2023-01-04   4
2023-01-05   5
dtype: int64
```

In[19] `data- data["2023-1-4"]`

Out[19]
```
2023-01-01   NaN
2023-01-03   NaN
2023-01-04   0.0
2023-01-05   NaN
2024-01-02   NaN
dtype: float64
```

In[20]
```
# to show the current value of the data object
data
```

Out[20]
```
2023-01-01   1
2024-01-02   2
2023-01-03   3
2023-01-04   4
2023-01-05   5
dtype: int64
```

Notes

(4) To cast data to a PeriodArray or PeriodIndex at a specific frequency: .to_period()

In[21] `data.to_period(freq="D")`

Out[21]
```
2023-01-01   1
2024-01-02   2
2023-01-03   3
2023-01-04   4
2023-01-05   5
Freq: D, dtype: int64
```

Notes

Here, "freq = "M"" means the time unit is Month.
- A, Y: year end frequency
- M : month end frequency
- W : weekly frequency
- D : calendar day frequency
- B : business day frequency
- C : custom business day frequency
- Q : quarter end frequency
- H : hourly frequency
- T, min: minutely frequency
- S : secondly frequency

In[22] `data.to_period(freq="M")`

Out[22]
```
2023-01    1
2024-01    2
2023-01    3
2023-01    4
2023-01    5
Freq: M, dtype: int64
```

Notes

(5) evaluate the result of an expression by datetime index

In[23] `data- data[3]`

Out[23]
```
2023-01-01    -3
2024-01-02    -2
2023-01-03    -1
2023-01-04     0
2023-01-05     1
dtype: int64
```

In[24] `data- data["20230104"]`

Out[24]
```
2023-01-01    NaN
2023-01-03    NaN
2023-01-04    0.0
2023-01-05    NaN
2024-01-02    NaN
dtype: float64
```

4.5.6 The pandas.period_range() method

Notes

To get a fixed freqeuency PeriodIndex: pandas. period_range()

In[25] `pd.period_range("2024-1",periods=10, freq="D")`

Out[25]
```
PeriodIndex(['2024-01-01', '2024-01-02', '2024-01-03', '2024-01-04',
             '2024-01-05', '2024-01-06', '2024-01-07', '2024-01-08',
             '2024-01-09', '2024-01-10'],
            dtype='period[D]', freq='D')
```

In[26] `pd.period_range("2024-1",periods=10, freq="M")`

Out[26]
```
PeriodIndex(['2024-01', '2024-02', '2024-03', '2024-04', '2024-05', '2024-06',
             '2024-07', '2024-08', '2024-09', '2024-10'],
            dtype='period[M]', freq='M')
```

Tricks

pandas.period_range(start=None, end=None, periods=None, freq=None, name= None)
- start : Left bound for generating periods.
- end : Right bound for generating periods.
- periods : Number of periods to generate.
- freq : frequency, e.g. "D" for daily frequency.
- name : Name of the resulting PeriodIndex

4.6 Data visualization

Q&A

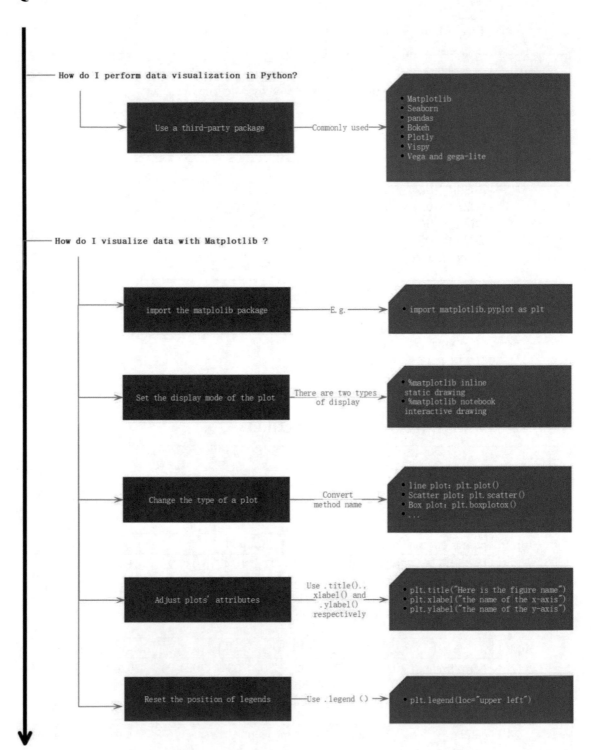

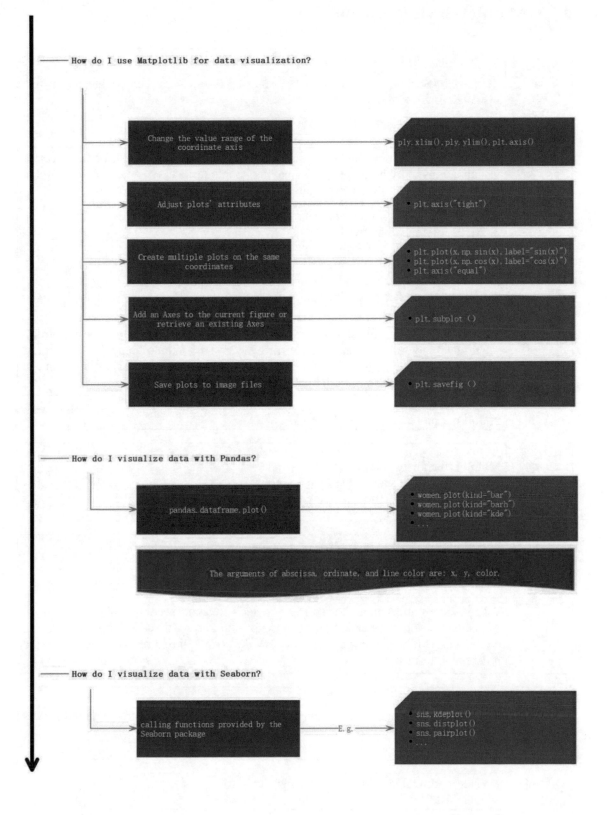

How do I use Matplotlib for data visualization?

Change the value range of the coordinate axis	ply.xlim(), ply.ylim(), plt.axis()
Adjust plots' attributes	• plt.axis("tight")
Create multiple plots on the same coordinates	• plt.plot(x, np.sin(x), label="sin(x)") • plt.plot(x, np.cos(x), label="cos(x)") • plt.axis("equal")
Add an Axes to the current figure or retrieve an existing Axes	• plt.subplot()
Save plots to image files	• plt.savefig()

How do I visualize data with Pandas?

pandas.dataframe.plot()	• women.plot(kind="bar") • women.plot(kind="barh") • women.plot(kind="kde") • ...

The arguments of abscissa, ordinate, and line color are: x, y, color.

How do I visualize data with Seaborn?

calling functions provided by the Seaborn package	E.g.	• sns.kdeplot() • sns.distplot() • sns.pairplot() • ...

4.6.1 Matplotlib visualization

Tips

Matplotlib, Seaborn, and Pandas are widely used and important packages for data visualization in Python.

Notes

Matplotlib is a comprehensive library for creating static, animated, and interactive visualizations in Python. It excels at making simple tasks easy and enabling complex tasks to be achieved. Some key features of Matplotlib include:

1. Create publication-quality plots
2. Make interactive figures3.
3. Customize visual style and layout
4. Export to various file formats
5. Embed in JupyterLab and Graphical User Interfaces
6. Extensive ecosystem of third-party packages

Notes

The matplotlib is organized in a hierarchy. At the top of the hierarchy is the matplotlib "state-machine environment" which is provided by the matplotlib.pyplot module. At this level, simple functions are used to add plot elements (lines, images, text, etc.) to the current axes in the current figure.

In[1] `import matplotlib.pyplot as plt`

Tricks

Matplotlib is the whole package;
matplotlib.pyplot is a module in matplotlib;
matplotlib.pylab is a module that gets installed alongside matplotlib.

In[2]
```
import matplotlib.pyplot as plt

%matplotlib inline
```

Tricks

When %matplotlib inline is used in a Jupyter notebook or compatible environment, it enables the inline backend for Matplotlib. This means that the output of plotting commands will be displayed directly below the code cell that produced it, within the notebook interface.

Notes

You can also use the magic command "%matplotlib notebook" to create interactive figures if your environment allows it.

In[3]
```
women = pd.read_csv('women.csv',index_col =0)
women.head()
```

Out[3]

	height	weight
1	58	115
2	59	117
3	60	120
4	61	123
5	62	126

Notes | To plot y versus x as lines and/or markers : matplotlib.pyplot.plot().

In[4]
```
plt.plot(women["height"], women["weight"])
plt.show()
```

Out[4]

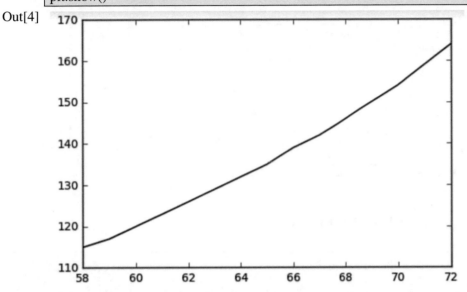

Tricks | If you don't write plt.show(), it will display [<matplotlib.lines.Line2D at 0x2064770b550>]

Notes | To generate a dataset t for visualization purposes, you can use the np.arange function with the specified parameters:

In[5]
```
import numpy as np
t=np.arange(0.,4.,0.1)
t
```

Out[5]
```
array([ 0. , 0.1, 0.2, 0.3, 0.4, 0.5, 0.6, 0.7, 0.8, 0.9, 1. ,
        1.1, 1.2, 1.3, 1.4, 1.5, 1.6, 1.7, 1.8, 1.9, 2. , 2.1,
        2.2, 2.3, 2.4, 2.5, 2.6, 2.7, 2.8, 2.9, 3. , 3.1, 3.2,
        3.3, 3.4, 3.5, 3.6, 3.7, 3.8, 3.9])
```

Notes | The method to display multiple lines in a figure using Matplotlib is to pass multiple arguments to the plt.plot() function. The argument format is as follows: "x1, y1, x2, y2, x3, y3, x4, y4, ...".

In[6] `plt.plot(t,t,t,t+2,t,t**2,t,t+8)`
`plt.show()`

Out[6]

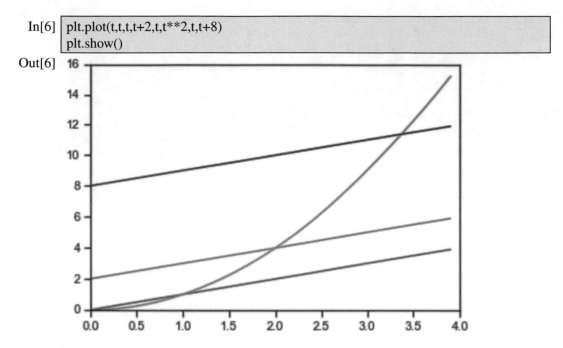

4.6.2 Adjusting plot attributes

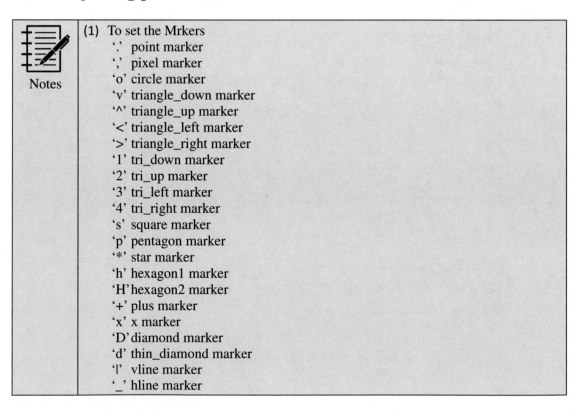

Notes

(1) To set the Mrkers
    '.' point marker
    ',' pixel marker
    'o' circle marker
    'v' triangle_down marker
    '^' triangle_up marker
    '<' triangle_left marker
    '>' triangle_right marker
    '1' tri_down marker
    '2' tri_up marker
    '3' tri_left marker
    '4' tri_right marker
    's' square marker
    'p' pentagon marker
    '*' star marker
    'h' hexagon1 marker
    'H' hexagon2 marker
    '+' plus marker
    'x' x marker
    'D' diamond marker
    'd' thin_diamond marker
    '|' vline marker
    '_' hline marker

In[7]
```
plt.plot(women["height"], women["weight"],"o")
plt.show()
```

Out[7]
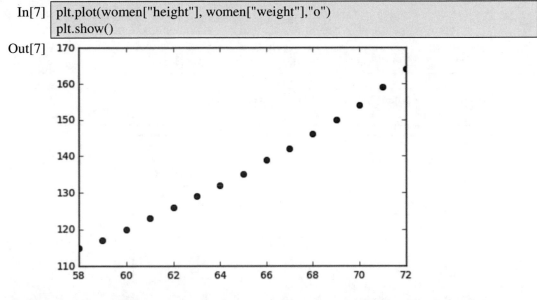

Notes

(2) to set line styles and colors , e.g. ' g--' for green dashed line style('--').
Line Styles:
   '-'   solid line style
   '--'   dashed line style
   '-.'   dash-dot line style
   ':'   dotted line style

Colors:
   'b'   blue
   'g'   green
   'r'   red
   'c'   cyan
   'm'   magenta
   'y'   yellow
   'k'   black
   'w'   white

In[8]
```
plt.plot(women["height"], women["weight"],"g--")
plt.show()
```

Out[8]
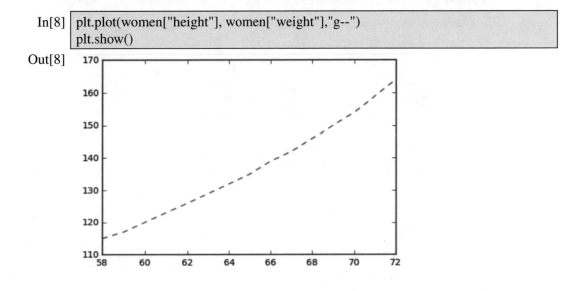

One more example of setting line styles and colors is "rD", which means "red+diamond". More arguments, please refer to Matplotlib's official website documentation.
You can learn more about the meaning of the third argument of plt.plot() through the help documentation. The specific command is: plt.plot?

In[9]
```python
plt.plot(women["height"], women["weight"],"rD")
plt.show()
```

Out[9]

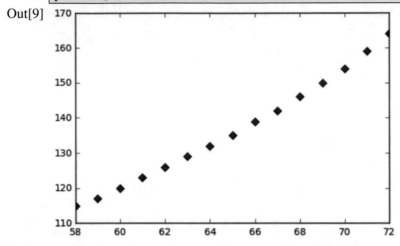

Notes   (3) To set the title of a plot and change axis labels:plt.title(), plt.xlabel() and plt.ylabel().

In[10]
```python
plt.plot(women["height"], women["weight"],"g--")
plt.title("plotting the dataset women")
plt.xlabel("height")
plt.ylabel("weight")

plt.show()
```

Out[10]

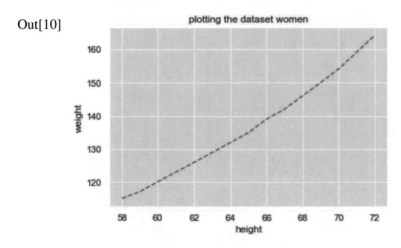

Tricks

plt.title(), plt.xlabel() and plt.ylabel() correspond to the title, X-axis label and X-axis label.

Tricks

The correct placement of plt.title(), plt.xlabel(), and plt.ylabel() within plt.plot() and between plt.show() ensures that the plot is configured with the desired title and axis labels before it is shown.

Notes

(4) to set the location of the legend: plt.legend(loc = "location").

In[11]
```
plt.plot(women["height"], women["weight"],"g--")
plt.title("plotting the dataset women")
plt.xlabel("height")
plt.ylabel("weight")

plt.legend(loc="upper left",labels=["Legend"])

plt.show()
```

Out[11]

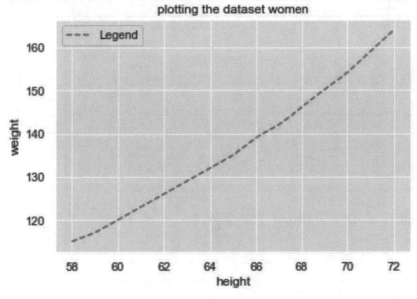

Tricks

The argument loc="upper left" in the context of plt.legend() specifies that the legend should be positioned in the upper left corner of the plot.

To gain more information about the available options for the loc argument, you can refer to the docstring of plt.legend().

4.6.3 Changing the type of a plot

Notes

To switch the plotting functions in Matplotlib, such as changing from plt.plot() to plt.scatter() to create a scatter plot, you can use the appropriate function based on the type of plot you want to generate.

In[12]
```
plt.scatter(women["height"], women["weight"])
plt.show()
```

Out[12]

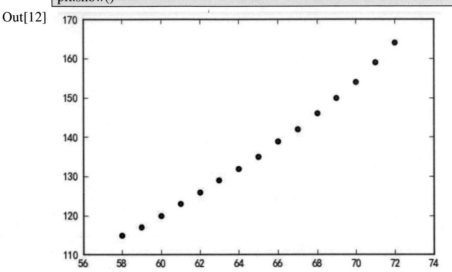

Tricks

I highly recommend accessing the example plots provided on the official Matplotlib website (https://matplotlib.org/stable/gallery/index.html). Each example not only showcases the visualization effects but also provides the corresponding source code.

4.6.4 Changing the value range of the axes of a plot

Notes

plt.xlim(11, –2) means "the value range of the x-axis is from 11 to –2". plt.ylim(2.2, –1.3) means "the value range of the y-axis is from 2.2 to -1.3".

In[13]
```
import matplotlib.pyplot as plt
import numpy as np
%matplotlib inline
x=np.linspace(0,10,100)

plt.plot(x,np.sin(x))
plt.xlim(11,-2)
plt.ylim(2.2,-1.3)
```

Out[13]   (2.2, -1.3)

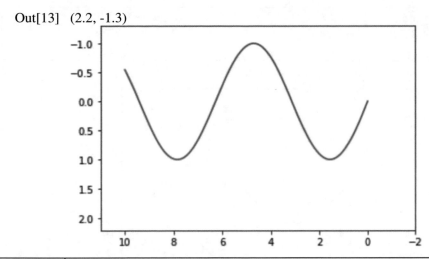

Notes

To get or set various axis properties in Matplotlib, you can use the matplotlib.pyplot.axis() function.

In[14]
```
plt.plot(x,np.sin(x))
plt.axis([-1,21,-1.6,1.6])
```

Out[14]   (-1.0, 21.0, -1.6, 1.6)

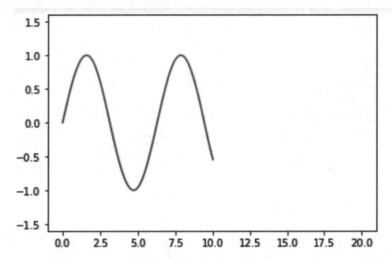

Notes

To set equal scaling for both the x-axis and y-axis by changing the axis limits: plt.axis("equal")

In[15]
```
plt.plot(x,np.sin(x))
plt.axis([-1,21,-1.6,1.6])
plt.axis("equal")
```

Out[15]   (-0.5, 10.5, -1.0993384025373631, 1.0996461858110391)

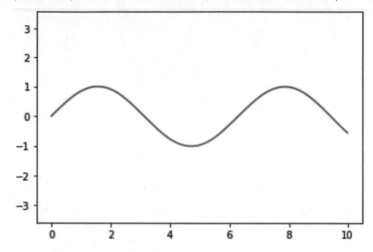

4.6.5 Adjusting the margins of a plot

Notes | To set limits just large enough to show all data and disable further autoscaling: plt.axis("tight")

In[16]
```
plt.plot(x,np.sin(x))
plt.axis([-1,21,-1.6,1.6])
plt.axis("tight")
```

Out[16]   (-0.5, 10.5, -1.0993384025373631, 1.0996461858110391)

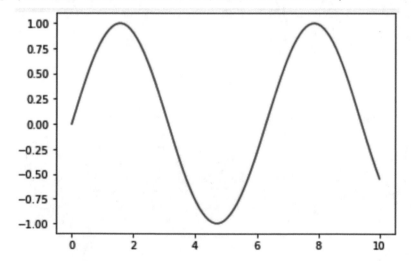

4.6.6 Creating multiple plots on the same coordinates

Notes

To create multiple plots on the same coordinates, you can write multiple functions in the same cell and call plt.legend() to display multiple labels for the plots.

In[17]
```python
plt.plot(x,np.sin(x),label="sin(x)")
plt.plot(x,np.cos(x),label="cos(x)")
plt.axis("equal")
plt.legend()
```

Out[17]   <matplotlib.legend.Legend at 0x124156820>

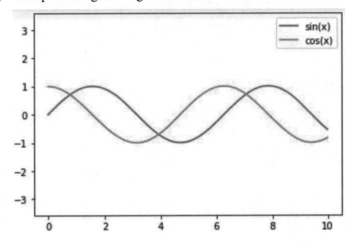

4.6.7 Adding an Axes to the current figure or retrieving an existing Axes

Notes

To add an Axes to the current figure or retrieve an existing Axes, you can call the plt.subplot(x, y, z) function before each code line of creating a plot.

In[18]
```python
plt.subplot(2,3,5)
plt.scatter(women["height"], women["weight"])

plt.subplot(2,3,1)
plt.scatter(women["height"], women["weight"])
plt.show()
```

Out[18]

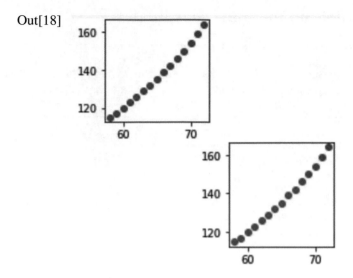

4.6.8 Saving plots to image files

Notes

To save the current plot : plt.savefig().

In[19]

```
women = pd.read_csv('women.csv')
plt.plot(women.height, women.weight)
plt.savefig("sagefig.png")
```

Out[19]

Tricks

The code plt.savefig("savefig.png") will save the current plot to the current working directory with the filename "savefig.png". However, you can customize the file name and path by providing the desired directory and filename in the plt.savefig() function.

4.6.9 Creating more complicate plots

Notes

First, generate the experimental datasets X and y that will be used for visualization. The make_blobs function is used to generate a random dataset that conforms to a normal distribution.

In[20]
```
from sklearn.datasets import make_blobs
X,y=make_blobs(n_samples=300,centers=4,random_state=0, cluster_std=1.0)
plt.scatter(X[:,0],X[:,1],c=y,s=50,cmap="rainbow")
```

Out[20]   <matplotlib.collections.PathCollection at 0x127316910>

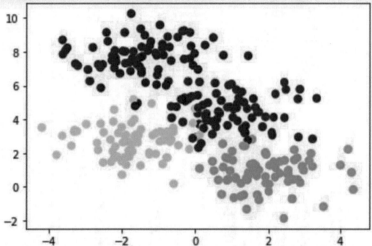

Tricks

The arguments of make_blobs(n_samples=300,centers=4,random_state=0, cluster_std=1.0) mean:
- n_samples: The number of samples, that is, the number of rows.
- n_features: The number of features of each sample, that is, the number of columns. #centers: The number of categories.
- random_state: how random numbers are generated.
- cluster_std: variance of each category.
- return value, there are two:
- X : Test set, type is array, shape is [n_samples, n_features].
- y : Label of each member, also an array, shape is [n_samples].

Tricks

The arguments of the *plt.scatter()* function are as follows.
- [:,0] and X[:,1] are the x-coordinate and y-coordinate respectively.
- c is the color.
- s is the size of the point.
- cmap is the color map which is a supplement to c.

The meaning of X[:,0] is to read the 0th column of the dataframe X, refer to [4.4 DataFrame].

4.6.10 Data visualization with Pandas

Notes

Pandas provides several different options for visualizing data with .plot() and their usage is similar to matplotlib.

In[21]

```
import pandas as pd
women = pd.read_csv('women.csv',index_col =0)
women.plot(kind="bar")
plt.show()
```

Out[21]

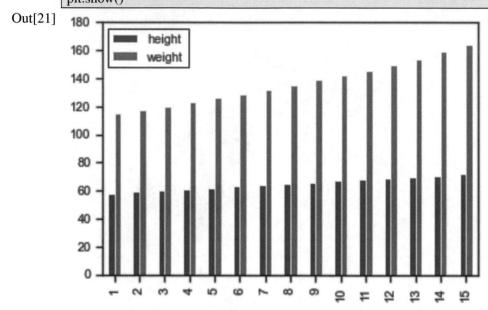

Tricks

The kind of plot to produce:
- 'line' : line plot (default)
- 'bar' : vertical bar plot
- 'barh' : horizontal bar plot
- 'hist' : histogram
- 'box' : boxplot
- 'kde' : Kernel Density Estimation plot
- 'density' : same as 'kde'
- 'area' : area plot
- 'pie' : pie plot
- 'scatter' : scatter plot (DataFrame only)
- 'hexbin' : hexbin plot (DataFrame only)

In[22]

```
women.plot(kind="barh")
plt.show()
```

Out[22]

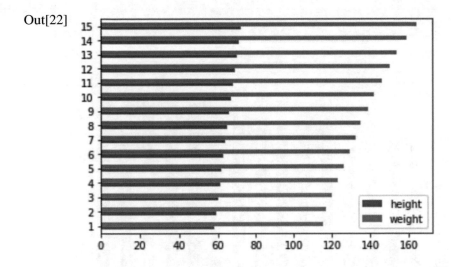

In[23]
```
women.plot(kind="bar",x="height",y="weight",color="g")
plt.show()
```

Out[23]

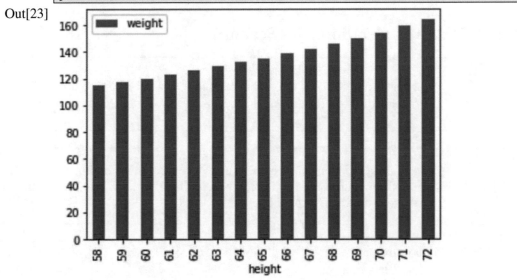

In[24]
```
women.plot(kind="kde")
plt.show()
```

Out[24]

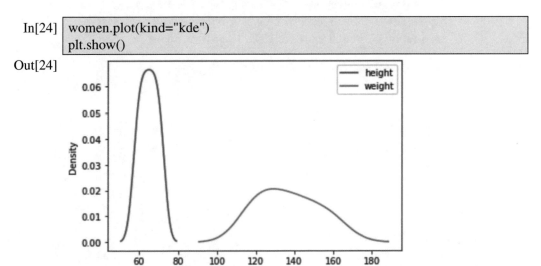

In[25]
```
women.plot(kind="bar",x="height",y="weight",color="g")
plt.legend(loc="best")
plt.show()
```

Out[25]

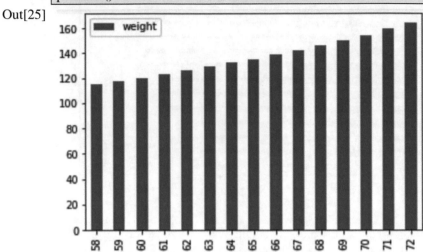

4.6.11 Data visualization with Seaborn

Notes

Seaborn is a Python data visualization library based on matplotlib. It provides a high-level interface for drawing attractive and informative statistical graphics.

Tricks

Note that the function name for drawing plots in Seaborn is lmplot, which is different from the function name in Matplotlib. Additionally, the arguments for lmplot also differ from those in Matplotlib.

In[26]
```
import pandas as pd
import seaborn as sns
sns.set(style="ticks")
df_women = pd.read_csv('women.csv', index_col=0,header=0)
sns.lmplot(x="height", y="weight", data=df_women)
```

Out[26]   <seaborn.axisgrid.FacetGrid at 0x13aa055b0>

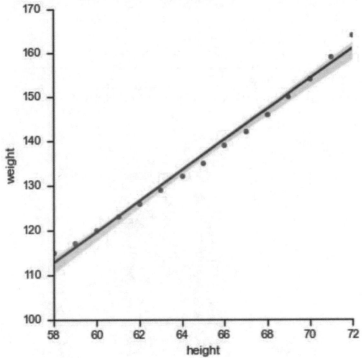

Notes

To create a Kernel Density Estimation (KDE) plot for visualizing the distribution of observations in a dataset : sns.kdeplot().

In[27]   `sns.kdeplot(women.height, shade=True)`

Out[27]   <matplotlib.axes._subplots.AxesSubplot at 0x135acc9a0>

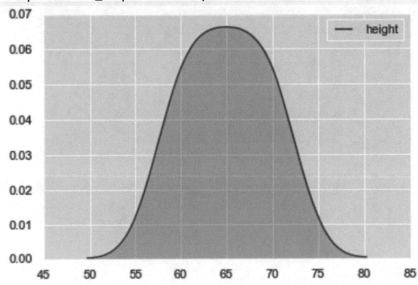

Notes To visualize the univariate or bivariate distribution of data : sns.distplot().

In[28]   sns.distplot(women.height)

Out[28]   <matplotlib.axes._subplots.AxesSubplot at 0x135b8c6a0>

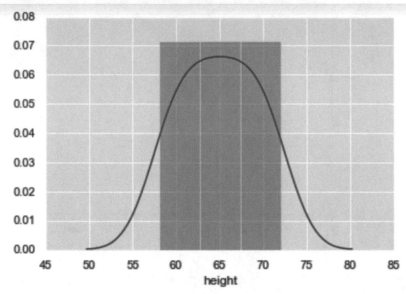

Notes To plot pairwise relationships in a dataset : sns.pairplot().

In[29]   sns.pairplot(women)

Out[29]   <seaborn.axisgrid.PairGrid at 0x135c44eb0>

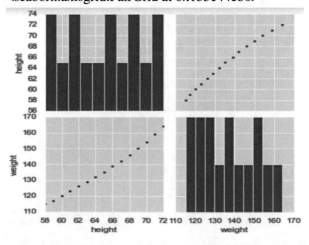

Notes To create a plot of two variables with bivariate and univariate graphs : *sns.jointplot( )*

In[30]   `sns.jointplot(women.height,women.weight,kind="reg")`

Out[30]   `<seaborn.axisgrid.JointGrid.at.0x22d35c20280>`

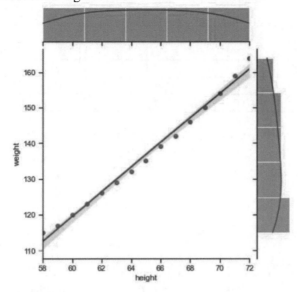

4.6.12 Data visualization cases projects

Notes

(1) Read data
Check the current working directory and ensure that the data file "salaries.csv" is located in the current working directory.

In[31]
```
# to show the current working directory
import os
os.getcwd()
```

Out[31]   `'C:\\Users\\Administrator\\Desktop'`

Tricks

The data file salaries.csv is available in the electronic resources of this book.

Notes

Calling the pandas.read_csv() method to read the file "salaries.csv" and store the data in a DataFrame object called df_salaries.

In[32]
```
import pandas as pd
df_salaries = pd.read_csv('salaries.csv', index_col=0)
```

Notes

Calling the df_salaries.head() method to display the first 6 rows of the DataFrame object df_salaries. For detailed descriptions, please refer to [4.4 DataFrame].

In[33] | df_salaries.head(6)

Out[33]

	rank	discipline	yrs.since.phd	yrs.service	sex	salary
1	Prof	B	19	18	Male	139750
2	Prof	B	20	16	Male	173200
3	AsstProf	B	4	3	Male	79750
4	Prof	B	45	39	Male	115000
5	Prof	B	40	41	Male	141500
6	AssocProf	B	6	6	Male	97000

Notes

(2) Import the seaborn package

In[34] | import seaborn as sns

Notes

(3) Visualize the data with the seaborn package
- To set the parameters that control the general style of the plots with sns.set_style()
- To create a scatter plot with sns.stripplot().
- To create a box plot with sns.boxplot()

In[35] | sns.set_style('darkgrid')

sns.stripplot(data=df_salaries, x='rank', y='salary', jitter=True, alpha=0.5)

sns.boxplot(data=df_salaries, x='rank', y='salary')

Out[35] | <matplotlib.axes._subplots.AxesSubplot at 0xd770b38>

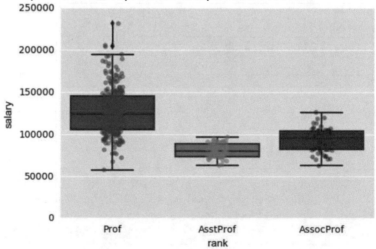

Tricks

Here, the argument "jitter=True" is used to add a small random noise to the data points in order to prevent them from overlapping and make the distribution more visible. The argument "alpha=0.5" is used to adjust the transparency of the data points, where 0.5 represents a medium level of opacity.

Exercises

[1] What will the following program print out?
import random
random.random()

A. 1
B. 4.063647000164759
C. 0.09656393185717627
D. -0.885155622826353

[2] What will the following program print out?
import random
random.randrange(0, 100, 2)

A. 69
B. 70
C. 100
D. 200

[3] What will the following program print out?
import random
round(random.uniform(-101,101),3)

A. 0
B. 101
C. -6.007
D. 11.070

[4] What will the following program print out?
import random
print(random.randint(0,9))

A. 1
B. 4.063647000164759
C. 0.09656393185717627
D. -0.885155622826353

[5] What will the following program print out?
import numpy as np
np.arange(1,20,4)

A. array([2, 6, 10, 14, 18])
B. array([1, 5, 9, 13, 17])
C. array([1, 4, 8, 12, 16])

[6] Which of the following is true of Python arrays?
A. When execute *array1 + array2,* if the number of rows or columns of this two arrays is different, the interpreter will raise ValueError.
B. Array is a special variable that can contain multiple values at a time.
C. When viewing the shape of an array or refactoring an array, the *reshape* method will modify the its elements.
D. Elements in an array cannot be modified.

[7]   Which of the following is true of Python arrays?
   A. The length of an array is fixed, and the data structures of the elements can be different.
   B. The length of an array is fixed, and the data structures of the elements always be the same.
   C. The length of an array is variable, and the data structures of the elements can be different.
   D. The length of an array is variable, and the data structures of the elements always be the same.

[8]   Which of these data structures in Python is mutable?
   A. list only
   B. tuple
   C. string
   D. list and array

[9]   What will the following program print out?
```
import pandas as pd
mySeries2=pd.Series([10,10], index=["a","b","c","d"])
mySeries2
```

   A. NameError
   B. ValueError
   C.

```
a    10
b    10
c    10
d    10
dtype: int64
```
   D.
```
a    10
b    10
dtype: int64
```

10.   What will the following program print out?
```
import pandas as pd
mySeries=pd.Series([10,9,8,7,6,5,4,3,2,1], index=["a","b","c","d","e","f","g","h","i","j"])
mySeries[3:9:3]
```
   A. ValueError
   B.
```
d    7
g    4
dtype: int64
```
   C.
```
c    8
f    5
dtype: int64
```

[11]   What will the following program print out?
```
import pandas as pd
mySeries=pd.Series([1,2,3,4,5], index=["a","b","c","a","b"])
mySeries[["a","b"]]
```

   A. NameError
   B.
```
a    1
b    2
c    4
d    5
dtype: int64
```

C.

```
a   1
a   4
b   2
b   5
dtype: int64
```

[12] What will the following program print out?

```
import numpy as np
import pandas as pd
mySeries1=pd.Series([1,2,3,4,5], index=["a","b","c","d","e"])
mySeries2=mySeries1.reindex(index=["b","c","a","d","e"])
np.all(mySeries2.values==mySeries1.values)
```

A. False
B. True
C. ValueError

[13] What will the following program print out?

```
import pandas as pd
mySeries4=pd.Series([21,22,23,24,25,26,27], index=["a","b","c","d","e","f","g"])
"c" in mySeries4
```

A. False
B. True
C. ValueError

[14] What will the following program print out?

```
import numpy as np
import pandas as pd
df=pd.DataFrame(np.arange(1,21).reshape(5,4))
df.iloc[3,2]
```

A. 18
B. 10
C. 15

[15] Which of the following is wrong of dataframe?
   A. The dataframe with only one-dimensional data is series, both of which are under the Pandas package.
   B. The row name of the dataframe can be accessed with the rows attributes.
   C. The column name of the dataframe can be accessed with the columns attributes.

[16] For the following code:
   {import datetime as dt}
   Which of the following time and date definitions is wrong?

   A. dt.datetime(2019,12,12,23,23,23)
   B. dt.datetime(2019,0,0,23,23,23)
   C. dt.datetime(2019,12,12,0)
   D. dt.time(23,23,23)

[17] When calculating the time difference, the calculating unit can be( )
   A. days
   B. seconds
   C. microseconds
   D. All of the above

[18] Which of the following is false of the *period_range* method?
    A. start: the lefthand side is the generation period
    B. end: the righthand side limits generation period
    C. periods: frequency of generation
    D. freq: frequency alias

[19] Which of the following is not a visual drawing tool?
    A. matplotlib
    B. seaborn
    C. plotnine
    D. Pandas

[20] Which of the following statements is false about matplotlib and seaborn?
    A. Both are drawing libraries.
    B. matplotlib is more encapsulated than seaborn.
    C. matplotlib has high flexibility in parameter setting details.
    D. seaborn can color by itself, which is beautiful and generous.

5. Data analysis with Python

Data analysis is one of the most critical stages in data science life cycle. This chapter will introduce various data analysis skills including:

- Statistical modelling with statsmodels
- Machine learning with sci-kit learn
- Natural language understanding with NLTK
- Image processing with OpenCV

© The Author(s), under exclusive license to Springer Nature Singapore Pte Ltd. 2023
C. Borjigin, *Python Data Science,* https://doi.org/10.1007/978-981-19-7702-2_5

5.1 Statistical modelling with statsmodels

Q&A

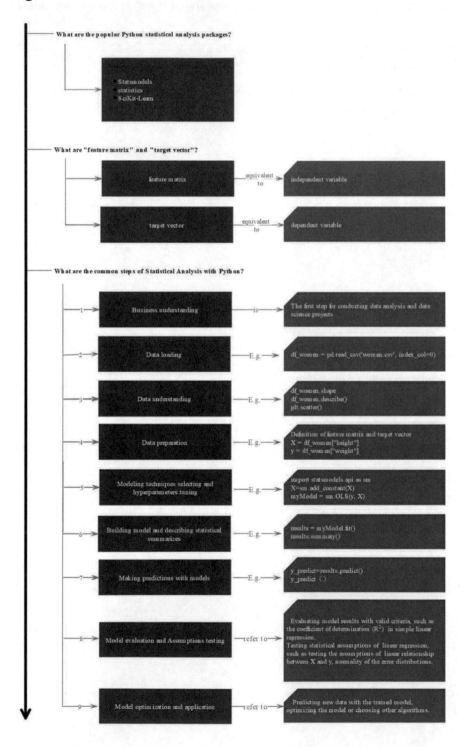

What are the popular Python statistical analysis packages?

- Statsmodels
- statistics
- SciKit-Learn

What are "feature matrix" and "target vector"?

| feature matrix | equivalent to | independent variable |
| target vector | equivalent to | dependent variable |

What are the common steps of Statistical Analysis with Python?

1. Business understanding — is — The first step for conducting data analysis and data science projects

2. Data loading — E.g. — df_women = pd.read_csv('women.csv', index_col=0)

3. Data understanding — E.g. — df_women.shape
df_women.describe()
plt.scatter()

4. Data preparation — E.g. — Definition of feature matrix and target vector
X = df_women["height"]
y = df_women["weight"]

5. Modeling techniques selecting and hyperparameters tuning — E.g. — import statsmodels.api as sm
X=sm.add_constant(X)
myModel = sm.OLS(y, X)

6. Building model and describing statistical summarizes — E.g. — results = myModel.fit()
results.summary()

7. Making predictions with models — E.g. — y_predict=results.predict()
y_predict（）

8. Model evaluation and Assumptions testing — refer to — Evaluating model results with valid criteria, such as the coefficient of determination (R^2) in simple linear regression.
Testing statistical assumptions of linear regression, such as testing the assumptions of linear relationship between X and y, normality of the error distributions.

9. Model optimization and application — refer to — Predicting new data with the trained model, optimizing the model or choosing other algorithms.

There are two main concepts in statistical analysis: the feature matrix and the target vector.

Taking y = F(X) as an example, X represents the feature matrix. The feature matrix is assumed to be two-dimensional, with a shape of [n_samples, n_features]. It is typically stored in a NumPy array or a Pandas DataFrame, although some Scikit-Learn models also accept SciPy sparse matrices. Each sample in the feature matrix is stored in a separate row.

Notes

y is the dependent variable and also termed "target vector" or "target array".

The target vector is usually one dimensional, with length n_samples. It is commonly stored in a NumPy array or Pandas Series.

Notes

X (Feature_Matrix)

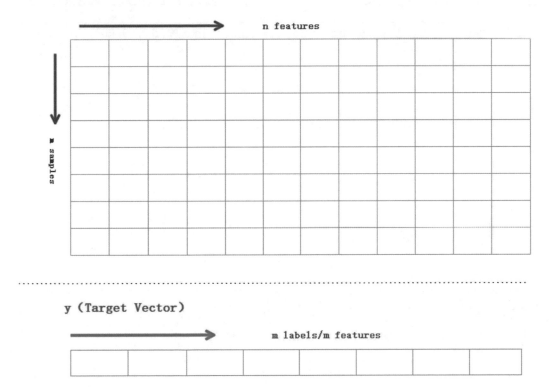

y (Target Vector)

5.1.1 Business understanding

Business understanding serves as the initial step in a data science project.
In this chapter, the business objective is to analyze the relationship between women's height and women's weight, in other words, predict a woman's weight by her height. The original data are obtained from The World Almanac and Book of Facts (1975). This data set gives the average heights and weights for American women aged 30–39. It is a data frame with 15 observations on 2 variables. It is structured as a data frame with 15 observations on 2 variables.
- women[,1]:height(in):numeric
- women[,2]:weight (lbs):numeric

Notes

5.1.2 Data loading

In[1]
```
# To obtain the current working directory in Python, you can use the os.getcwd()
method.

import os
print(os.getcwd())
```

Out[1]   C:\Users\soloman\clm

To get the current working directory in Python, you can use the os.getcwd() method. And if you want to change the current working directory, you can use the os.chdir(path) method.

Tips

In[2]
```
# to load data from the current working directory into Panda's DataFrame

import pandas as pd

df_women = pd.read_csv('women.csv', index_col=0)

print(df_women.head())
```

Out[2]

	height	weight
1	58	115
2	59	117
3	60	120
4	61	123
5	62	126

pd.read_csv() : Read a comma-separated values (csv) file into DataFrame.

Tips

The women.csv file is available in the learning resources for this textbook.

Tips

5.1.3 Data understanding

In[3]
```
# to get shape or dimensions of the df_women DataFrame

df_women.shape
```

Out[3]   (15, 2)

(1) pandas.DataFrame.shape: Returns a tuple representing the dimensionality of the DataFrame. For further details, please refer to [4.4 DataFrame].

Tips

In[4]   # to show column names (properties) of the df_women DataFrame

print(df_women.columns)

Out[4]   Index(['height', 'weight'], dtype='object')

(2) pandas.DataFrame.columns: Shows the column labels of the DataFrame. For further details, please refer to [4.4 DataFrame].

Tips

In[5]   # to generate descriptive statistics for the df_women DataFrame

df_women.describe()

Out[5]

	height	weight
count	15.000000	15.000000
mean	65.000000	136.733333
std	4.472136	15.498694
min	58.000000	115.000000
25%	61.500000	124.500000
50%	65.000000	135.000000
75%	68.500000	148.000000
max	72.000000	164.000000

(3) pandas.DataFrame.describe:Generates descriptive statistics. For further details, please refer to [4.4 DataFrame].

Tips

In[6]   # to plot the df_women DataFrame

```python
import matplotlib.pyplot as plt
%matplotlib inline
plt.scatter(df_women["height"], df_women["weight"])
plt.show()
```

Out[6]

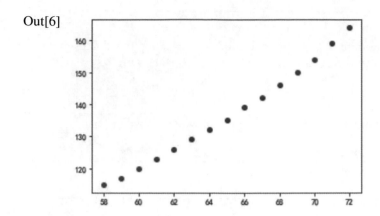

Tips

(4) For further details, please refer to [4.6 Data visualization].

5.1.4 Data wrangling

Tips

(4) The data visualization chart indicates that the relationship between dependent variable and independent variable is linear. So we can conduct a linear regression analysis. Firstly, we need to arrange data into a feature matrix and target vector.

In[7]
```
X = df_women["height"]
y = df_women["weight"]
```

Out[7]   (15, 2)

In[8] X

Out[8] 1   58
        2   59
        3   60
        4   61
        5   62
        6   63
        7   64
        8   65
        9   66
        10   67
        11   68
        12   69
        13   70
        14   71
        15   72
        Name: height, dtype: int64

In[9] | `y`

Out[9]

```
1    115
2    117
3    120
4    123
5    126
6    129
7    132
8    135
9    139
10   142
11   146
12   150
13   154
14   159
15   164
Name: weight, dtype: int64
```

Tips

"In fact, the data type of 'y' here is not the correct one for the target vector we require. We can check its data type using the *'type(y)'* function. Subsequent lines of code won't raise exceptions, as the 'statsmodels' package automatically handles data type conversions. However, if other packages, such as 'Scikit-Learn', are used, exceptions may occur. To prevent this, we can use the *'np.ravel()'* function to adjust the data type as needed."

5.1.5 Model selection and hyperparameter tuning

In[10]

```
# to import the statsmodels package

import statsmodels.api as sm
```

Tips

Statsmodels, statistics, and scikit-learn are three popular packages used for statistical analysis and machine learning in Python.

In[11] | `X`

Out[11]

```
1    58
2    59
3    60
4    61
5    62
6    63
7    64
8    65
9    66
10   67
11   68
12   69
13   70
14   71
15   72
Name: height, dtype: int64
```

By default, an intercept is included when we execute an OLS model using the *sm.add_constant( )* method.

Notes

Please do not write "X_add_const=sm.add_constant(X)" as "X=sm.add_constant(X)", otherwise the value of X will change when "X=sm.add_constant(X)" is run multiple times.

Notes

In[12]

```
X_add_const=sm.add_constant(X)
X_add_const
```

Out[12]

	const	height
1	1.0	58
2	1.0	59
3	1.0	60
4	1.0	61
5	1.0	62
6	1.0	63
7	1.0	64
8	1.0	65
9	1.0	66
10	1.0	67
11	1.0	68
12	1.0	69
13	1.0	70
14	1.0	71
15	1.0	72

statsmodels.tools.tools.add_constant(): Add a column of ones to an array

Tips

In[13]

```
# to describe a model

myModel = sm.OLS(y, X_add_const)
```

statsmodels is using endog and exog as names for the data, the observed variables that are used in an estimation problem. For further details, please refer to https://www.statsmodels.org/stable/endog_exog.html.

The first two arguments of the *sm.OLS( )* function are endog(y) and exog(X_add_const).

Tips

5.1.6 Fitting model and summarizing the Regression Results

In[14]
```
# to fit the model
results = myModel.fit()

# to summarize the model
print(results.summary())
```

Out[14]

OLS Regression Results

Dep. Variable:	weight	R-squared:	0.991
Model:	OLS	Adj. R-squared:	0.990
Method:	Least Squares	F-statistic:	1433.
Date:	Sat, 09 Apr 2022	Prob (F-statistic):	1.09e-14
Time:	09:32:10	Log-Likelihood:	-26.541
No. Observations:	15	AIC:	57.08
Df Residuals:	13	BIC:	58.50
Df Model:	1		
Covariance Type:	nonrobust		

	coef	std err	t	P>|t|	[0.025	0.975]
const	-87.5167	5.937	-14.741	0.000	-100.343	-74.691
height	3.4500	0.091	37.855	0.000	3.253	3.647

Omnibus:	2.396	Durbin-Watson:	0.315
Prob(Omnibus):	0.302	Jarque-Bera (JB):	1.660
Skew:	0.789	Prob(JB):	0.436
Kurtosis:	2.596	Cond. No.	982.

Notes:
[1] Standard Errors assume that the covariance matrix of the errors is correctly specified.
C:\Users\zc\Anaconda3\lib\site-packages\scipy\stats\stats.py:1604: UserWarning: kurtosistest
only valid for n>=20 ... continuing anyway, n=15
  "anyway, n=%i" % int(n))

In[15]
```
# to show the coefficients of the linear regression model
results.params
```

Out[15]
```
const    -87.516667
height    3.450000
dtype: float64
```

Here, the results object has many useful attributes. For further details, please refer to the official website of the statsmodels package.

Tips

5.1.7 Model evaluation

R-squared (the coefficient of determination) is a goodness-of-fit measure in linear regression models to show how well the data fit the regression model.

Notes

In[16]   # to show R-squared
          results.rsquared

Out[16]   0.9910098326857506

R-squared values range from 0 to 1. The closer its value is to 1, the better the regression line fits the data.

Tips

5.1.8 Assumptions testing

When conducting data science projects with statistical methods, it is not only necessary to evaluate the model results, but also to test the underlying statistical assumptions.

Notes

In statistical analysis, all parametric tests make certain assumptions about the data. It's important to test these assumptions to ensure valid results. Taking linear regression as an example, these assumptions include:

The first assumption is that a linear relationship exists between the dependent and independent variables. This can be tested by calculating the F-statistic.

The second assumption is that there's no autocorrelation in the residuals. This can be tested using the Durbin-Watson statistic.

The third assumption is that the underlying residuals are normally distributed, or approximately so. The Jarque–Bera test is a goodness-of-fit test of normality.

Notes

In[17]   # to show(extract) the p-value in F test

          results.f_pvalue

Out[17]   1.0909729585997406e-14

The F-test of overall significance indicates whether the regression model provides a better fit to the data than a model that contains no independent variables.

Notes

Tricks

A p-value less than some significance level (e.g. $\alpha = .05$) is statistically significant. It indicates strong evidence against the null hypothesis, as there is less than a 5% probability the null is correct. Hence, we reject the null hypothesis and accept the alternative hypothesis.

In[18]
```
# to show the Durbin Watson statistic

sm.stats.stattools.durbin_watson(results.resid)
```

Out[18]   0.31538037486218456

Notes

The Durbin Watson statistic is a test for autocorrelation in the residuals from regression models. The Durbin-Watson statistic will always have a value ranging between 0 and 4. A value of 2 indicates there is no autocorrelation detected in the samples.

In[19]
```
# to show the Jarque–Bera statistic and its p-value

sm.stats.stattools.jarque_bera(results.resid)
```

Out[19]   (1.6595730644310005,
            0.43614237873238126,
            0.7893583826332368,
            2.5963042257390314)

Tips

The *sm.stats.stattools.jarque_bera()* function returns four values -- JB, JBpv, skew, kurtosis, respectively.

Notes

In statistics, the Jarque–Bera test serves as a goodness-of-fit test of whether sample data have the skewness and kurtosis matching a normal distribution. The normal distribution of residuals is one of the assumptions of linear regression analysis.

In[20]
```
# to make a prediction with the model

y_predict=results.predict()
y_predict
```

Out[20]   array([112.58333333, 116.03333333, 119.48333333, 122.93333333,
            126.38333333, 129.83333333, 133.28333333, 136.73333333,
            140.18333333, 143.63333333, 147.08333333, 150.53333333,
            153.98333333, 157.43333333, 160.88333333])

Tips

In the statasmodels package, after a model has been fit predict returns the fitted values

5.1.9 Model optimization and re-selection

In[21]
```
# to visualize the predictions and compare against observations

plt.rcParams['font.family']="simHei"
plt.plot(df_women["height"], df_women["weight"],"o")  # the observations
plt.plot(df_women["height"], y_predict)   # the predictions
plt.title('Linear regression analysis of women's weight and height')
plt.xlabel('height')
plt.ylabel('weight')
```

Out[21] Text(0, 0.5, 'weight')

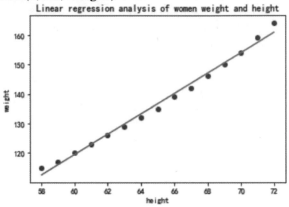

In addition to the statistics (e.g. R-squared), we can also display the goodness-of-fit by data visualization.

Tips

As can be seen from the above figure, the effect of simple linear regression in this case may be further optimized. Hence, we replace simple linear regression with polynomial regression.

Notes

In[22]
```
# to conduct data wrangling

import pandas as pd
import numpy as np
df_women = pd.read_csv('women.csv', index_col=0)
X = df_women["height"]
y = df_women["weight"]

X=np.column_stack((X, np.power(X,2), np.power(X,3)))
```

Tips

In the polynomial regression analysis, the feature matrix X consists of 3 parts ---X, the square of X, and the cube of X.

In[23]

```
X_add_const=sm.add_constant(X)

X_add_const
```

Out[23] array([[1.00000e+00, 5.80000e+01, 3.36400e+03, 1.95112e+05],
　　　　　　 [1.00000e+00, 5.90000e+01, 3.48100e+03, 2.05379e+05],
　　　　　　 [1.00000e+00, 6.00000e+01, 3.60000e+03, 2.16000e+05],
　　　　　　 [1.00000e+00, 6.10000e+01, 3.72100e+03, 2.26981e+05],
　　　　　　 [1.00000e+00, 6.20000e+01, 3.84400e+03, 2.38328e+05],
　　　　　　 [1.00000e+00, 6.30000e+01, 3.96900e+03, 2.50047e+05],
　　　　　　 [1.00000e+00, 6.40000e+01, 4.09600e+03, 2.62144e+05],
　　　　　　 [1.00000e+00, 6.50000e+01, 4.22500e+03, 2.74625e+05],
　　　　　　 [1.00000e+00, 6.60000e+01, 4.35600e+03, 2.87496e+05],
　　　　　　 [1.00000e+00, 6.70000e+01, 4.48900e+03, 3.00763e+05],
　　　　　　 [1.00000e+00, 6.80000e+01, 4.62400e+03, 3.14432e+05],
　　　　　　 [1.00000e+00, 6.90000e+01, 4.76100e+03, 3.28509e+05],
　　　　　　 [1.00000e+00, 7.00000e+01, 4.90000e+03, 3.43000e+05],
　　　　　　 [1.00000e+00, 7.10000e+01, 5.04100e+03, 3.57911e+05],
　　　　　　 [1.00000c+00, 7.20000e+01, 5.18400e+03, 3.73248e+05]])

Tips

Here, the purpose of calling the *sm.add_constant( )* function is to add a column of ones to the feature matrix, which represents the intercept term in the regression model.

In[24]

```
# to describe a new model
myModel_updated = sm.OLS(y, X_add_const)
```

In[25]

```
# to fit the model
results_updated = myModel_updated.fit()

# to summarize the model
print(results_updated.summary())
```

Out[25]   OLS Regression Results
==

Dep. Variable:	weight	R-squared:	1.000
Model:	OLS	Adj. R-squared:	1.000
Method:	Least Squares	F-statistic:	1.679e+04
Date:	Sat, 09 Apr 2022	Prob (F-statistic):	2.07e-20
Time:	09:32:21	Log-Likelihood:	1.3441
No. Observations:	15	AIC:	5.312
Df Residuals:	11	BIC:	8.144
Df Model:	3		
Covariance Type:	nonrobust		

==

	coef	std err	t	P>|t|	[0.025	0.975]
const	-896.7476	294.575	-3.044	0.011	-1545.102	-248.393
x1	46.4108	13.655	3.399	0.006	16.356	76.466
x2	-0.7462	0.211	-3.544	0.005	-1.210	-0.283
x3	0.0043	0.001	3.940	0.002	0.002	0.007

==

Omnibus:	0.028	Durbin-Watson:	2.388
Prob(Omnibus):	0.986	Jarque-Bera (JB):	0.127
Skew:	0.049	Prob(JB):	0.939
Kurtosis:	2.561	Cond. No.	1.25e+09

==

Notes:

[1] Standard Errors assume that the covariance matrix of the errors is correctly specified.

[2] The condition number is large, 1.25e+09. This might indicate that there are strong multicollinearity or other numerical problems.

C:\Users\zc\Anaconda3\lib\site-packages\scipy\stats\stats.py:1604: UserWarning: kurtosistest only valid for n>=20 ... continuing anyway, n=15

"anyway, n=%i" % int(n))

In[26]
```
# to show(extract) the p-value in F test

print('Display const and intercept: ',results_updated.params)
```

Out[26] Display const and intercept: const   -896.747633
x1   46.410789
x2   -0.746184
x3   0.004253
dtype: float64

In[27]
```
# to make a prediction with the new model

y_predict_updated=results_updated.predict()
y_predict_updated
```

Out[27]   array([114.63856209, 117.40676937, 120.18801264, 123.00780722,
           125.89166846, 128.86511168, 131.95365223, 135.18280543,
           138.57808662, 142.16501113, 145.9690943,   150.01585147,
           154.33079796, 158.93944911, 163.86732026])

In[28]
```
# to visualize the predictions and compare against observations

plt.rcParams['font.family']="simHei"
plt.scatter(df_women["height"], df_women["weight"])
plt.plot(df_women["height"], y_predict_updated)
plt.title('Linear regression analysis of women weight and height')
plt.xlabel('height')
plt.ylabel('weight')
```

Out[28]   Text(0, 0.5, 'weight')

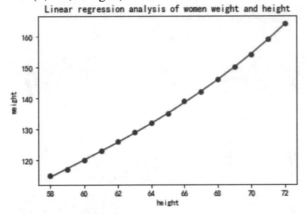

5.1.10 Model application

In[29]
```
h=63.5
results_updated.predict([1,h,np.power(h,2),np.power(h,3)])
```

Out[29]   array([130.39340008])

Tips

We can apply the fitted model to predict new data. For instance, it can be used to predict the weight of a woman who stands 63.5 inches tall.

Notes

The argument structure for the *'predict()'* method should match the form of the model 's independent variables. We can access the DocStrings by typing 'results.predict?'

5.2 Machine learning with scikit-learn

Q&A

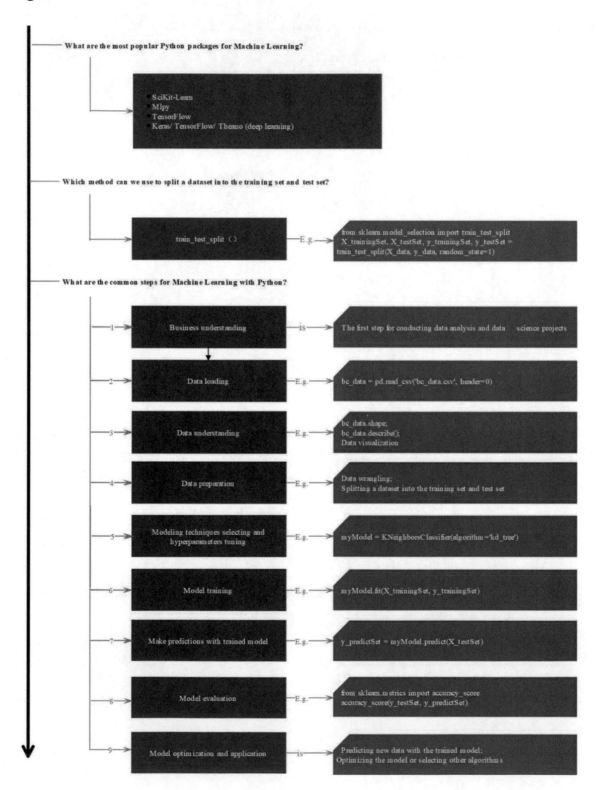

What are the most popular Python packages for Machine Learning?

- SciKit-Learn
- Mlpy
- TensorFlow
- Keras/ TensorFlow/ Theano (deep learning)

Which method can we use to split a dataset into the training set and test set?

train_test_split ( ) —E.g.→
```
from sklearn.model_selection import train_test_split
X_trainingSet, X_testSet, y_trainingSet, y_testSet =
train_test_split(X_data, y_data, random_state=1)
```

What are the common steps for Machine Learning with Python?

1	Business understanding	—is→	The first step for conducting data analysis and data science projects
2	Data loading	—E.g.→	bc_data = pd.read_csv('bc_data.csv', header=0)
3	Data understanding	—E.g.→	bc_data.shape; bc_data.describe(); Data visualization
4	Data preparation	—E.g.→	Data wrangling; Splitting a dataset into the training set and test set
5	Modeling techniques selecting and hyperparameters tuning	—E.g.→	myModel = KNeighborsClassifier(algorithm='kd_tree')
6	Model training	—E.g.→	myModel.fit(X_trainingSet, y_trainingSet)
7	Make predictions with trained model	—E.g.→	y_predictSet = myModel.predict(X_testSet)
8	Model evaluation	—E.g.→	from sklearn.metrics import accuracy_score accuracy_score(y_testSet, y_predictSet)
9	Model optimization and application	—is→	Predicting new data with the trained model; Optimizing the model or selecting other algorithms

In Machine Learning, the original dataset is usually split into three independent subsets:
- The training set is a subset to train a model.
- The test set is a subset to test the trained model after training.
- The validation set is a subset to validate model performance during training, especially to tune the hyperparameters and make model selection.

Notes

5.2.1 Business understanding

Business understanding is the first phase of a data science project process.

Notes

In this chapter, we provide a case project with the Scikit-learn.

The dataset used in this case is obtained from Wisconsin Breast Cancer Database (https://archive.ics.uci.edu/ml/datasets/breast+cancer+wisconsin+(diagnostic)).

The dataset involves the columns(attributes) such as ID number, Diagnosis (M = malignant, B = benign) and 10 real-valued features are calculated for each cell nucleus. They are:

1) radius (mean of distances from the center to points on the perimeter)
2) texture (standard deviation of gray-scale values)
3) perimeter
4) area
5) smoothness (local variation in radius lengths)
6) compactness (perimeter^2 / area - 1.0)
7) concavity (severity of concave portions of the contour)
8) concave points (number of concave portions of the contour)
9) symmetry
10) fractal dimension ("coastline approximation" - 1)

The main objective of this case project is to understand the application of machine learning in data science.

Firstly, we split the training set and test set from the dataset – "bc_data.csv".

Secondly, a k-Nearest-Neighbors (KNN) model is trained on the training set.

Then, we use the trained model to predict the diagnosis on the test set.

Finally, the prediction results of KNN are compared against the diagnostic results of bc_data.csv to measure the accuracy of the KNN classifier.

Tips

5.2.2 Data loading

In[1]

```python
# Using os.getcwd() method to get current working directory

import pandas as pd
import numpy as np
import os
os.chdir(r'C:\Users\soloman')

print(os.getcwd())
```

Out[1]   C:\Users\soloman\clm

Tips

Here, 'C:\Users\soloman\clm' is the working directory on the author's computer.

In[2]

```
# to load data from the current working directory into Panda's DataFrame

bc_data = pd.read_csv('bc_data.csv', header=0)
bc_data.head()
```

Out[2]

	id	diagnosis	radius_ mean	...	concave_ points_worst	symmetry_ worst	fractal_ dimension_ worst
0	842302	M	17.99	...	0.2654	0.4601	0.11890
1	842517	M	20.57	...	0.1860	0.2750	0.08902
2	84300903	M	19.69	...	0.2430	0.3613	0.08758
3	84348301	M	11.42	...	0.2575	0.6638	0.17300
4	84358402	M	20.29	...	0.1625	0.2364	0.07678

5 rows × 32 columns

Tips

The original data file, 'bc_data.csv', can be found in the learning resources associated with this textbook.

Tips

The *bc_data.head()* method returns the first 5 rows. For further details, please refer to [4.4 DataFrame].

5.2.3 Data understanding

In[3]

```
# to get the shape of the bc_data DataFrame

print(bc_data.shape)
```

Out[3]   (569, 32)

Tips

For further details, please refer to [4.4 DataFrame].

In[4] | # to get the column names(properties) of the bc_data DataFrame
print(bc_data.columns)

Out[4] Index(['id', 'diagnosis', 'radius_mean', 'texture_mean', 'perimeter_mean',   'area_mean', 'smoothness_mean', 'compactness_mean', 'concavity_mean', 'concave points_mean', 'symmetry_mean', 'fractal_dimension_mean', 'radius_se', 'texture_se', 'perimeter_se', 'area_se', 'smoothness_se', 'compactness_se', 'concavity_se', 'concave points_se', 'symmetry_se', 'fractal_dimension_se', 'radius_worst', 'texture_worst', 'perimeter_ worst', 'area_worst', 'smoothness_worst', 'compactness_worst', 'concavity_worst', 'concave_points_worst', 'symmetry_worst', 'fractal_dimension_worst'], dtype='object')

Tips

For further details, please refer to [4.4 DataFrame].

In[5] | ## to generate descriptive statistics for the bc_data DataFrame
print(bc_data.describe())

Out[5]

	id	radius_ mean	texture_ mean	perimeter_ mean	area_mean\
count	5.690000e+02	569.000000	569.000000	569.000000	569.000000
mean	3.037183e+07	14.127292	19.289649	91.969033	654.889104
std	1.250206e+08	3.524049	4.301036	24.298981	351.914129
min	8.670000e+03	6.981000	9.710000	43.790000	143.500000
25%	8.692180e+05	11.700000	16.170000	75.170000	420.300000
50%	9.060240e+05	13.370000	18.840000	86.240000	551.100000
75%	8.813129e+06	15.780000	21.800000	104.100000	782.700000
max	9.113205e+08	28.110000	39.280000	188.500000	2501.000000

	smoothness_ mean	compactness_ mean	concavity_ mean	concave points_ mean\
count	569.000000	569.000000	569.000000	569.000000
mean	0.096360	0.104341	0.088799	0.048919
std	0.014064	0.052813	0.079720	0.038803
min	0.052630	0.019380	0.000000	0.000000
25%	0.086370	0.064920	0.029560	0.020310
50%	0.095870	0.092630	0.061540	0.033500
75%	0.105300	0.130400	0.130700	0.074000
max	0.163400	0.345400	0.426800	0.201200

	symmetry_mean		radius_worst	texture_worst \
count	569.000000	...	569.000000	569.000000
mean	0.181162	...	16.269190	25.677223
std	0.027414	...	4.833242	6.146258
min	0.106000	...	7.930000	12.020000
25%	0.161900	...	13.010000	21.080000
50%	0.179200	...	14.970000	25.410000
75%	0.195700	...	18.790000	29.720000
max	0.304000	...	36.040000	49.540000

	perimeter_worst	area_worst	smoothness_worst	compactness_worst\
count	569.000000	569.000000	569.000000	569.000000
mean	107.261213	880.583128	0.132369	0.254265
std	33.602542	569.356993	0.022832	0.157336
min	50.410000	185.200000	0.071170	0.027290
25%	84.110000	515.300000	0.116600	0.147200
50%	97.660000	686.500000	0.131300	0.211900
75%	125.400000	1084.000000	0.146000	0.339100
max	251.200000	4254.000000	0.222600	1.058000

	concavity_worst	concave_points_worst	symmetry_worst\
count	569.000000	569.000000	569.000000
mean	0.272188	0.114606	0.290076
std	0.208624	0.065732	0.061867
min	0.000000	0.000000	0.156500
25%	0.114500	0.064930	0.250400
50%	0.226700	0.099930	0.282200
75%	0.382900	0.161400	0.317900
max	1.252000	0.291000	0.663800

	fractal_dimension_worst
count	569.000000
mean	0.083946
std	0.018061
min	0.055040
25%	0.071460
50%	0.080040
75%	0.092080
max	0.207500

[8 rows x 31 columns]

Tips   For further details, please refer to [4.4 DataFrame].

5.2.4 Data wrangling

Notes

Data wrangling is one of the crucial phases in data science projects. In this case, it refers to the process of defining the feature matrix and target vector, as well as splitting the dataset into the training set and test set.

In[6]
```
# to remove the id column from the bc_data DataFrame
data = bc_data.drop(['id'], axis=1)
print(data.head())
```

Out[6]

	diagnosis	radius_mean	texture_mean	perimeter_mean	area_mean\
0	M	17.99	10.38	122.80	1001.0
1	M	20.57	17.77	132.90	1326.0
2	M	19.69	21.25	130.00	1203.0
3	M	11.42	20.38	77.58	386.1
4	M	20.29	14.34	135.10	1297.0

	smoothness_mean	compactness_mean	concavity_mean	concave points_mean\
0	0.11840	0.27760	0.3001	0.14710
1	0.08474	0.07864	0.0869	0.07017
2	0.10960	0.15990	0.1974	0.12790
3	0.14250	0.28390	0.2414	0.10520
4	0.10030	0.13280	0.1980	0.10430

	symmetry_mean	...	radius_worst	texture_worst\
0	0.2419	...	25.38	17.33
1	0.1812	...	24.99	23.41
2	0.2069	...	23.57	25.53
3	0.2597	...	14.91	26.50
4	0.1809	...	22.54	16.67

	perimeter_worst	area_worst	smoothness_worst	compactness_worst\
0	184.60	2019.0	0.1622	0.6656
1	158.80	1956.0	0.1238	0.1866
2	152.50	1709.0	0.1444	0.4245
3	98.87	567.7	0.2098	0.8663
4	152.20	1575.0	0.1374	0.2050

	concavity_worst	concave_points_worst	symmetry_worst\
0	0.7119	0.2654	0.4601
1	0.2416	0.1860	0.2750
2	0.4504	0.2430	0.3613
3	0.6869	0.2575	0.6638
4	0.4000	0.1625	0.2364

	fractal_dimension_worst
0	0.11890
1	0.08902
2	0.08758
3	0.17300
4	0.07678

[5 rows x 31 columns]

Tips

Here, the ID column is not an independent variable, so we will remove it from the data DataFrame and create a new feature matrix named X_data.

In[7]
```
X_data = data.drop(['diagnosis'], axis=1)
X_data.head()
```

Out[7]

	radius_ mean	texture_ mean	...	concave_points_ worst	symmetry_ worst	fractal_ dimension_ worst
0	17.99	10.38	...	0.2654	0.4601	0.11890
1	20.57	17.77	...	0.1860	0.2750	0.08902
2	19.69	21.25	...	0.2430	0.3613	0.08758
3	11.42	20.38	...	0.2575	0.6638	0.17300
4	20.29	14.34	...	0.1625	0.2364	0.07678

5 rows × 30 columns

Notes

Here,
   Axis=0 will act on all the ROWS in each COLUMN;
   Axis=1 will act on all the COLUMNS in each ROW;

In[8]
```
# to create the target vetor
y_data = np.ravel(data[['diagnosis']])
y_data[0:6]
```

Out[8]   array(['M', 'M', 'M', 'M', 'M', 'M'], dtype=object)

Tips

np.ravel() function converts a two-dimensional array into a one-dimensional array and returns a contiguous flattened array.

Notes

In data science projects, the *np.ravel()* function can be used to define target vectors(arrays).

In[9]
```
# to split the original data into training subsets and test subsets

from sklearn.model_selection import train_test_split
X_trainingSet, X_testSet, y_trainingSet, y_testSet = train_test_split(X_data, y_data, random_state=1)
```

Tips

The *sklearn.model_selection .train_test_split()* function is used to split arrays or matrices into random train and test subsets.

Here, X_trainingSet is the feature matrix and y_trainingSet is the target vector of training set. Besides, X_testSet is the feature matrix and y_testSet is the target vector of test set.

Tips

In[10] | # to show(extract) the shape of the feature matrix in training set

print(X_trainingSet.shape)

Out[10] (426, 30)

In[11] | # to show(extract) the shape of the feature matrix in testing set

print(X_testSet.shape)

Out[11] (143, 30)

5.2.5 Model selection and hyperparameter tuning

In[12] | # to import KNeighborsClassifier for training the k-nearest neighbors model

from sklearn.neighbors import KNeighborsClassifier

The first step is to select an appropriate algorithm. In this case we select KNN, so KNeighborsClassifier is imported.

Tips

In[13] | # to describe the algorithm and set its hyperparemters

myModel = KNeighborsClassifier(algorithm='kd_tree')

The second step is to describe the machine learning algorithm and set the hyperparameter——algorithm='kd_tree'.
The KNN classifier implement different algorithms (BallTree, KDTree or Brute Force) to calculate the nearest neighbors.

Tips

5.2.6 Model training

In[14] | # to train a model on the training set

myModel.fit(X_trainingSet, y_trainingSet)

Out[14] KNeighborsClassifier(algorithm='kd_tree')

Here,
    X_trainingSet is the feature matrix in the training set.
    y_trainingSet is the target vector of the training set.

Tips

5.2.7 Predicting with a trained model

Notes

The trained model can be utilized to predict the labels for the test set.

In[15] # to predict the target vector for the test set

y_predictSet = myModel.predict(X_testSet)

Tips

Here, X_testSet is the feature matrix(independent variables) of test set.

In[16] # to print the predicted labels

print(y_predictSet)

Out[16] ['M' 'M' 'B' 'M' 'M' 'M' 'M' 'M' 'B' 'B' 'B' 'M' 'M' 'B' 'B' 'B' 'B' 'B'
     'B' 'M' 'B' 'B' 'M' 'B' 'M' 'B' 'B' 'M' 'M' 'M' 'M' 'B' 'M' 'B' 'B' 'B'
     'M' 'B' 'B' 'B' 'B' 'B' 'B' 'B' 'B' 'M' 'B' 'B' 'B' 'M' 'M' 'M' 'B' 'B'
     'B' 'B' 'B' 'M' 'B' 'B' 'B' 'M' 'B' 'M' 'B' 'B' 'B' 'M' 'B' 'B' 'B' 'B'
     'M' 'M' 'B' 'M' 'B' 'B' 'B' 'M' 'B' 'M' 'B' 'M' 'B' 'B' 'M' 'B' 'M' 'B'
     'B' 'M' 'B' 'B' 'M' 'M' 'B' 'B' 'B' 'B' 'B' 'B' 'B' 'B' 'B' 'B' 'B' 'B'
     'M' 'M' 'B' 'B' 'B' 'B' 'M' 'M' 'B' 'B' 'B' 'B' 'B' 'M' 'M' 'B' 'B' 'M'
     'M' 'M' 'M' 'M' 'B' 'B' 'B' 'M' 'B' 'M' 'M' 'M' 'B' 'B' 'M' 'M' 'B']

In[17] # to print the labels in the test set and compare against the predicted labels

print(y_testSet)

Out[17] ['B' 'M' 'B' 'M' 'M' 'M' 'M' 'M' 'B' 'B' 'B' 'M' 'M' 'B' 'B' 'B' 'B' 'B'
     'B' 'M' 'B' 'B' 'M' 'B' 'M' 'B' 'B' 'M' 'M' 'M' 'M' 'B' 'M' 'M' 'B' 'B'
     'M' 'B' 'M' 'B' 'B' 'B' 'B' 'B' 'B' 'M' 'B' 'B' 'B' 'M' 'M' 'M' 'B' 'B'
     'B' 'B' 'B' 'M' 'B' 'B' 'B' 'M' 'B' 'B' 'B' 'B' 'B' 'M' 'B' 'B' 'B' 'B'
     'M' 'M' 'B' 'M' 'M' 'M' 'B' 'M' 'B' 'M' 'B' 'M' 'B' 'B' 'M' 'B' 'M' 'B'
     'B' 'M' 'B' 'B' 'M' 'M' 'B' 'B' 'B' 'B' 'B' 'B' 'B' 'B' 'B' 'B' 'B' 'B'
     'M' 'M' 'M' 'B' 'B' 'B' 'M' 'M' 'B' 'B' 'B' 'B' 'B' 'M' 'M' 'B' 'B' 'M'
     'M' 'B' 'M' 'M' 'B' 'B' 'B' 'M' 'B' 'M' 'M' 'B' 'B' 'B' 'M' 'M' 'B']

5.2.8 Model evaluation

Notes

The *accuracy_score( )* function is called to calculate the performance of classification based upon Confusion Matrix.

In[18]

```
# to calculate the accuracy score of the trained model

from sklearn.metrics import accuracy_score
print(accuracy_score(y_testSet, y_predictSet))
```

Out[18]   0.9370629370629371

Here,
   y_testSet refers to the test set;
   y_ predictSet refers to the predicted values.

Tips

5.2.9 Model optimization and application

We use elbow method to select the optimal number of clusters for KNN clustering.

Notes

In[19]

```
# to create a for loop that trains various KNN models with different k values

from sklearn.neighbors import KNeighborsClassifier
NumberOfNeighbors = range(1,23)
KNNs = [KNeighborsClassifier(n_neighbors=i) for i in NumberOfNeighbors]
scores = [KNNs[i].fit(X_trainingSet, y_trainingSet).score(X_testSet,y_testSet) for i
in range(len(KNNs))]

scores
```

Out[19]   [0.9230769230769231,
           0.9020979020979021,
           0.9230769230769231,
           0.9440559440559441,
           0.9370629370629371,
           0.9230769230769231,
           0.9300699300699301,
           0.9230769230769231,
           0.9230769230769231,
           0.9230769230769231,
           0.9230769230769231,
           0.9230769230769231,
           0.9230769230769231,
           0.9230769230769231,
           0.9230769230769231,
           0.916083916083916,
           0.916083916083916,
           0.916083916083916,
           0.916083916083916,
           0.916083916083916,
           0.916083916083916,
           0.9090909090909091]

Tips

Measuring the accuracy scores of the KNN model for values of k ranging from 1 to 23, and storing them in a list named "scores".

In[20]

```python
# to visualize the accuracy scores of the KNN models with k=1 to 23

import matplotlib.pyplot as plt
%matplotlib inline
plt.plot(NumberOfNeighbors,scores)
plt.rcParams['font.family'] = 'simHei'
plt.xlabel('k value')
plt.ylabel('score')
plt.title('Elbow Curve')
plt.xticks(NumberOfNeighbors)
plt.show()
```

Out[20]

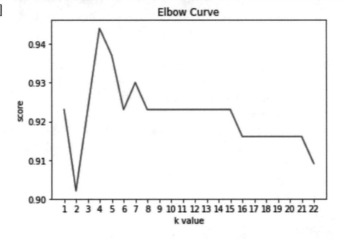

Tips

We can see that the optimal number of clusters(k) is 4.

In[21]

```python
# to retrain KNN model with the best K value(k=4) and calculate its accuracy score

from sklearn.neighbors import KNeighborsClassifier
myModel = KNeighborsClassifier(algorithm='kd_tree',n_neighbors=4)
myModel.fit(X_trainingSet, y_trainingSet)
y_predictSet = myModel.predict(X_testSet)
from sklearn.metrics import accuracy_score
print(accuracy_score(y_testSet, y_predictSet))
```

Out[21]   0.9440559440559441

Tips

The accuracy score is increased to 0.9440559440559441.

Notes

The *metrics.plot_roc_curve()* function is used to plot receiver operating characteristic (ROC) curve.

In[22]
```
# to plot the ROC curve

import matplotlib.pyplot as plt
from sklearn import  metrics
metrics.plot_roc_curve(myModel,X_testSet, y_testSet)
plt.show()
```

Out[22]

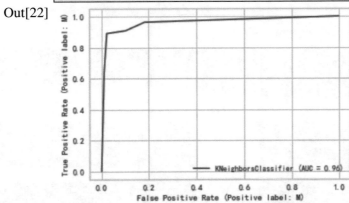

Tips

For further details, please refer to the official website —— https://scikit-learn.org/stable/modules/generated/sklearn.metrics.plot_roc_curve.html.

5.3 Natural language understanding with NLTK

Q&A

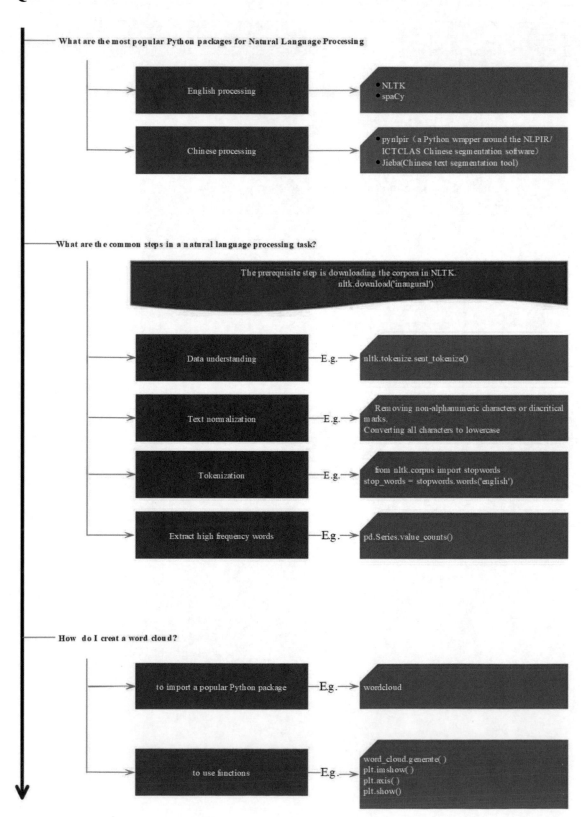

What are the most popular Python packages for Natural Language Processing

English processing → • NLTK
• spaCy

Chinese processing → • pynlpir（a Python wrapper around the NLPIR/ICTCLAS Chinese segmentation software）
• Jieba(Chinese text segmentation tool)

What are the common steps in a natural language processing task?

The prerequisite step is downloading the corpora in NLTK.
nltk.download('inaugural')

Data understanding —E.g.→ nltk.tokenize.sent_tokenize()

Text normalization —E.g.→ Removing non-alphanumeric characters or diacritical marks.
Converting all characters to lowercase

Tokenization —E.g.→ from nltk.corpus import stopwords
stop_words = stopwords.words('english')

Extract high frequency words —E.g.→ pd.Series.value_counts()

How do I creat a word cloud?

to import a popular Python package —E.g.→ wordcloud

to use functions —E.g.→ word_cloud.generate( )
plt.imshow( )
plt.axis( )
plt.show()

5.3.1 Business understanding

Natural Language Tool Kit (NLTK) and spaCy are two of the most popular English Natural Language Processing (NLP) tools available in Python.

In this chapter, we will use NLTK (Natural Language Toolkit) to analyze the inaugural speeches of the US presidents from 1789 to 2017 and compare the first speeches of four presidents: Clinton, Bush, Obama, and Trump. The data consists of multiple inaugural speeches collected from the inaugural corpus of NLTK.

5.3.2 Data loading

The official website of the NLTK package is https://www.nltk.org/, we recommend readers to access the official website for further details.

In[1]
```python
# to import the packages needed for this project

import numpy as np
import pandas as pd
import re
import matplotlib.pyplot as plt
%matplotlib inline
import nltk
```

In[2]
```python
# to download the NLTK corpus "inaugural"
nltk.download('inaugural')
```

If the output is "True", it means that the download has been completed. If the download speed is slow or the download fails, an alternative option is to directly download that package on GitHub (https://github.com/nltk/nltk_data), and put it in the path of file "nltk_data".

In[3]
```python
# to check the file IDs in the "inaugural" dataset

from nltk.corpus import inaugural
print(inaugural.fileids())
```

Out[3] ['1789-Washington.txt', '1793-Washington.txt', '1797-Adams.txt', '1801-Jefferson. txt', '1805-Jefferson.txt', '1809-Madison.txt', '1813-Madison.txt', '1817-Monroe. txt', '1821-Monroe.txt', '1825-Adams.txt', '1829-Jackson.txt', '1833-Jackson. txt', '1837-VanBuren.txt', '1841-Harrison.txt', '1845-Polk.txt', '1849-Taylor. txt', '1853-Pierce.txt', '1857-Buchanan.txt', '1861-Lincoln.txt', '1865-Lincoln. txt', '1869-Grant.txt', '1873-Grant.txt', '1877-Hayes.txt', '1881-Garfield.txt', '1885-Cleveland.txt', '1889-Harrison.txt', '1893-Cleveland.txt', '1897-McKinley. txt', '1901-McKinley.txt', '1905-Roosevelt.txt', '1909-Taft.txt', '1913-Wilson. txt', '1917-Wilson.txt', '1921-Harding.txt', '1925-Coolidge.txt', '1929-Hoover.txt', '1933-Roosevelt.txt', '1937-Roosevelt.txt', '1941-Roosevelt.txt', '1945-Roosevelt.txt', '1949-Truman.txt', '1953-Eisenhower.txt', '1957-Eisenhower.txt', '1961-Kennedy.txt', '1965-Johnson.txt', '1969-Nixon.txt', '1973-Nixon.txt', '1977-Carter.txt', '1981-Reagan. txt', '1985-Reagan.txt', '1989-Bush.txt', '1993-Clinton.txt', '1997-Clinton.txt', '2001-Bush.txt', '2005-Bush.txt', '2009-Obama.txt', '2013-Obama.txt', '2017-Trump.txt']

Tips

After the corpus is downloaded successfully, we import the package directly without executing nltk.download().

In[4]
```
#to count the file IDs in the "inaugural" dataset

len(inaugural.fileids())
```

Out[4] 58

Tips

It is evident that there are 58 documents in the inaugural corpus. We first analyze all the documents, and then select a few presidential inaugural speeches for in-depth comparative analysis.

5.3.3 Data understanding

Notes

First, We create an empty DataFrame (df_inaugural) with four columns of "year", "president name", "president", and "speech text".

In[5]
```
# to create a list and define 4 column names
cols = ['year','president name','president', 'speech text']

#to create an empty DataFrame with the column names
df_inaugural = pd.DataFrame(columns=cols)
df_inaugural
```

Out[5]

year	president name	president	speech text

Notes

We fill in the DataFrame with the speech year, president name, combination of time and name, speech text.

In[6]
```
for i in inaugural.fileids():
    year = i[0:4]
    name = re.findall(r'\-(.*)\.',i)[0]
    president = year+name
    text = inaugural.raw(i)
            df_inaugural    =    df_inaugural.append({'year':year,'president
name':name,'president':president,'speech text':text}, ignore_index=True)

df_inaugural.head()
```

Out[6]

	year	president name	president	speech text
0	1789	Washington	1789Washington	Fellow-Citizens of the Senate and of the House...
1	1793	Washington	1793Washington	Fellow citizens, I am again called upon by the...
2	1797	Adams	1797Adams	When it was first perceived, in early times, t...
3	1801	Jefferson	1801Jefferson	Friends and Fellow Citizens:\n\nCalled upon to...
4	1805	Jefferson	1805Jefferson	Proceeding, fellow citizens, to that qualifica...

Tips

The first column is used to render the first four digits of the file name, i.e. speech year. The second column indicates the president's name which are extracted from the characters between the symbol "-" and the symbol "." with the regular expression method.
The third column is used to render the combination of time and name.
The forth column refers to president's speech text.

Notes

To fill in a DataFrame with speech year, president name, combination of time and name, and speech text, you can use the DataFrame.apply() method. This method allows you to apply a function to each row or column of the DataFrame.

In[7]

```
df_inaugural['"America" count'] = df_inaugural['speech text'].apply(lambda x: x.count('America'))
df_inaugural['"we" count'] = df_inaugural['speech text'].apply(lambda x: x.count('we' or 'We'))
df_inaugural['"you" count'] = df_inaugural['speech text'].apply(lambda x: x.count('you' or 'You'))

df_inaugural.head()
```

Out[7]

	year	president name	president	speech text	"America" count	"we" count	"you" count
0	1789	Washington	1789 Washington	Fellow-Citizens of the Senate and of the House...	2	10	13
1	1793	Washington	1793 Washington	Fellow citizens, I am again called upon by the...	1	0	1
2	1797	Adams	1797 Adams	When it was first perceived, in early times, t...	8	23	1
3	1801	Jefferson	1801 Jefferson	Friends and Fellow Citizens:\n\nCalled upon to...	0	18	14
4	1805	Jefferson	1805 Jefferson	Proceeding, fellow citizens, to that qualifica...	1	22	8

Tips

"America", "we", and "you" were selected as keywords, and the value of frequencies these three words appeared in the speech text are returned.

In[8]

```
# to plot the frequency of those words

fig = plt.figure(figsize=(16,5))
plt.xticks(size = 8, rotation = 60)

plt.plot(df_inaugural['president'],df_inaugural['"America" count'],c='r',label='"America" count')
plt.plot(df_inaugural['president'],df_inaugural['"we" count'],c='g',label='"we" count')
plt.plot(df_inaugural['president'],df_inaugural['"you" count'],c='y',label='"you" count')

plt.legend()
plt.title("The number of times the three words 'America', 'we', and 'you' appear in the presidents' inaugural speeches")

plt.show()
```

Out[8]

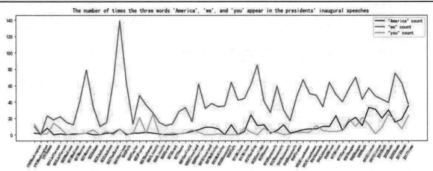

Tips

The word "we" appeared most frequently, and "we" is the most common word in Van Buren's speech in 1837. The word "America" was used frequently by Trump in 2017.

Notes

We count the number of words in each speech by splitting words with spaces.

In[9]

```
df_inaugural['word count'] = df_inaugural['speech text'].apply(lambda x: len(str(x).split(" ")))
df_inaugural.head()
```

Out[9]

	year	president name	president	speech text	"America" count	"we" count	"you" count	word count
0	1789	Washington	1789Washington	Fellow-Citizens of the Senate and of the House...	2	10	13	1426
1	1793	Washington	1793Washington	Fellow citizens, I am again called upon by the...	1	0	1	135
2	1797	Adams	1797Adams	When it was first perceived, in early times, t...	8	23	1	2306
3	1801	Jefferson	1801Jefferson	Friends and Fellow Citizens:\n\nCalled upon to...	0	18	14	1725
4	1805	Jefferson	1805Jefferson	Proceeding, fellow citizens, to that qualifica...	1	22	8	2153

Notes

We also plot a bar chart of the total number of words in each speech text.

In[10]
```
fig = plt.figure(figsize=(16,5))
plt.xticks(np.arange(len(df_inaugural['president'])), df_inaugural['president'],size = 8,
rotation = 60)
plt.bar(np.arange(len(df_inaugural['word count'])),df_inaugural['word count'], color='blue',
alpha=0.5)
plt.title("The number of words in the presidents' inaugural speeches")
```

Out[10]   Text(0.5, 1.0, "The number of words in the presidents' inaugural speeches")

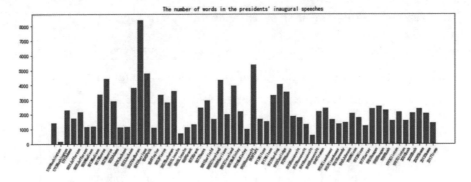

Notes

The *sent_tokenize()* function in the NLTK.tokenize package can be used to split a text to sentences.

In[11]
```
from nltk.tokenize import sent_tokenize
df_inaugural['sentence count'] = df_inaugural['speech text'].apply(lambda x: len(sent_
tokenize(x)))
df_inaugural.head()
```

Out[11]

	year	president name	president	speech text	"America" count	"we" count	"you" count	word count	sentence count
0	1789	Washington	1789 Washington	Fellow-Citizens of the Senate and of the House...	2	10	13	1426	23
1	1793	Washington	1793 Washington	Fellow citizens, I am again called upon by the...	1	0	1	135	4
2	1797	Adams	1797 Adams	When it was first perceived, in early times, t...	8	23	1	2306	37
3	1801	Jefferson	1801 Jefferson	Friends and Fellow Citizens:\n\nCalled upon to...	0	18	14	1725	41
4	1805	Jefferson	1805 Jefferson	Proceeding, fellow citizens, to that qualifica...	1	22	8	2153	45

In[12]
```
fig = plt.figure(figsize=(16,5))
plt.xticks(np.arange(len(df_inaugural['president'])), df_inaugural['president'],size = 8,
rotation = 60)
plt.bar(np.arange(len(df_inaugural['sentence count'])),df_inaugural['sentence count'],
color='purple', alpha=0.5)
plt.title("The number of sentences in the presidents' inaugural speeches")
```

Out[12]   Text(0.5, 1.0, "The number of sentences in the presidents' inaugural speeches")

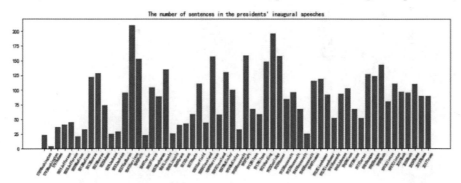

Tips | It can be seen that Van Buren's speech text had a relatively high number of words and sentences in 1837, while Washington's speech had a relatively low number in 1793.

Notes | Next, we choose the speeches of Trump, Obama, Bush and Clinton for analysis. Since there are some presidents who are re-elected, we choose the speeches of their first inauguration ——"2017-Trump.txt", "2009-Obama.txt", "2001-Bush.txt", "1993-Clinton.txt".

In[13]
```
president_speech = df_inaugural[df_inaugural['year'].isin(['2017','2009','2001','1993'])]
president_speech = president_speech.reset_index(drop=True)
president_speech
```

Out[13]

	year	president name	president	speech text	"America" count	"we" count	"you" count	word count	sentence count
0	1993	Clinton	1993Clinton	My fellow citizens, today we celebrate the mys...	33	57	12	1583	81
1	2001	Bush	2001Bush	President Clinton, distinguished guests and my...	20	43	9	1580	97
2	2009	Obama	2009Obama	My fellow citizens:\n\nI stand here today humb...	15	75	18	2383	110
3	2017	Trump	2017Trump	Chief Justice Roberts, President Carter, Presi...	35	37	23	1425	90

5.3.4 Text normalization

In[14]
```
president_speech['speech text'] = president_speech['speech text'].apply(lambda x: " ".join(x.lower() for x in x.split()))
president_speech['speech text']
```

Out[14]
```
0    my fellow citizens, today we celebrate the mys...
1    president clinton, distinguished guests and my...
2    my fellow citizens: i stand here today humbled...
3    chief justice roberts, president carter, presi...
Name: speech text, dtype: object
```

Tips | Converting all characters to lowercase.

```
In[15]  president_speech['speech text'] = president_speech['speech text'].str.replace('[^\
        w\s]','')
        president_speech['speech text']
```

Out[15] 0   my fellow citizens today we celebrate the myst...
1   president clinton distinguished guests and my ...
2   my fellow citizens i stand here today humbled ...
3   chief justice roberts president carter preside...
Name: speech text, dtype: object

Removing all special characters except space from a string.

Tips

Regular Expression is used. It is a sequence of characters that forms a search pattern. In the above code, "\w" returns a match where the string contains any word characters (characters from a to Z, digits from 0-9, and the underscore _ character); "\s" returns a match where the string contains a white space character.

Tips

5.3.5 Tokenization

One of the major forms of tokenization is to filter out stopwords.

Notes

Stopwords are words that are extremely common in human language but carry minimal meaning since they represent highly frequent words such as "the", "to"," "of," and "to."

Notes

```
In[16]  from nltk.corpus import stopwords
        stop_words = stopwords.words('english')
        president_speech['speech text'] = president_speech['speech text'].apply(lambda x:
        " ".join(x for x in x.split() if x not in stop_words))
        president_speech['speech text']
```

Out[16] 0   fellow citizens today celebrate mystery americ...
1   president clinton distinguished guests fellow ...
2   fellow citizens stand today humbled task us gr...
3   chief justice roberts president carter preside...
Name: speech text, dtype: object

NLTK includes a list of 40 stop words, including: "a", "an", "the", "of", "in", etc.

Tips

In[17]
```
add_stopwords = ['us','i','in','shall']
stop_words.extend(add_stopwords)
stop_words=set(stop_words)
president_speech['speech text'] = president_speech['speech text'].apply(lambda x: " ".
join(x for x in x.split() if x not in stop_words))
president_speech['speech text']
```

Out[17] 0   fellow citizens today celebrate mystery americ...
          1   president clinton distinguished guests fellow ...
          2   fellow citizens stand today humbled task grate...
          3   chief justice roberts president carter preside...
Name: speech text, dtype: object

There are still some useless words (such as "us") after filtering out stopwords. So we add custom stopwords and then remove them from speech texts.

The custom stopwords are "us", "i", "in", "shall".

5.3.6 Extracting high frequency words

We recorded the frequency of word occurrences in each of the four presidents' speeches. The 5 words with the highest frequency are extracted as high frequency words.

In[18]
```
speech_1993Clinton = president_speech['speech text'][0]
freq_words_1993Clinton = pd.Series(speech_1993Clinton.split()).value_counts()[:5]

speech_2001Bush = president_speech['speech text'][1]
freq_words_2001Bush = pd.Series(speech_2001Bush.split()).value_counts()[:5]

speech_2009Obama = president_speech['speech text'][2]
freq_words_2009Obama = pd.Series(speech_2009Obama.split()).value_counts()[:5]

speech_2017Trump = president_speech['speech text'][3]
freq_words_2017Trump = pd.Series(speech_2017Trump.split()).value_counts()[:5]
```

The *pd.Series().value_counts()* function returns a series containing counts of unique values.

In[19]   freq_words_2017Trump

Out[19]   america   19
          american   11
          people   10
          country   9
          one   8
          dtype: int64

The high frequency words in Trump's speech are "america", "american", "people", "country", "one". The word "america" appears 19 times in his speech.

Tips

In[20]
```
plt.figure(figsize=(16,16))

fig,ax = plt.subplots(2, 2, figsize=(10,6))
plt.subplots_adjust(wspace=1.0, hspace=0.3)

ax[0][0].barh(freq_words_1993Clinton.index, freq_words_1993Clinton, color='red',
alpha=0.3)
ax[0][0].set_title("High-frequency words in Clinton's inaugural speech in 1993")

ax[0][1].barh(freq_words_2001Bush.index, freq_words_2001Bush, color='green',
alpha=0.3)
ax[0][1].set_title("High-frequency words in Bush's inaugural speech in 2001")

ax[1][0].barh(freq_words_2009Obama.index, freq_words_2009Obama, color='yellow',
alpha=0.3)
ax[1][0].set_title("High-frequency words in Obama's inaugural speech in 2009")

ax[1][1].barh(freq_words_2017Trump.index, freq_words_2017Trump, color='teal',
alpha=0.3)
ax[1][1].set_title("High-frequency words in Trump's inaugural speech in 2017")

plt.show()
```

Out[20]   <Figure size 1152x1152 with 0 Axes>

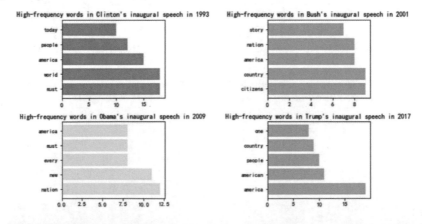

The horizontal bar charts of high frequency words are drawn with matplotlib.

Tips

Tips

The *plt.subplots(2, 2)* method stacks subplots in two directions.

5.3.7 Generating word clouds

Notes

Finally, we import the wordcloud package to generate word clouds for the speeches of the four presidents, respectively.

In[21]

```
# to generate the word cloud of Clinton's inaugural speech in 1993

from wordcloud import WordCloud
word_cloud = WordCloud(font_path='calibri.ttf',
            background_color='white',
            stopwords=stop_words)
word_cloud.generate(speech_1993Clinton)
plt.subplots(figsize=(8,5))
plt.imshow(word_cloud)
plt.axis('off')
plt.title("Word cloud of Clinton's inaugural speech in 1993")
```

Out[21]   Text(0.5, 1.0, "Word cloud of Clinton's inaugural speech in 1993")

In[22]

```
# to generate the word cloud of Bush's inaugural speech in 2001

word_cloud.generate(speech_2001Bush)
plt.subplots(figsize=(8,5))
plt.imshow(word_cloud)
plt.axis('off')
plt.title("Word cloud of Bush's inaugural speech in 2001")
```

Out[22]   Text(0.5, 1.0, "Word cloud of Bush's inaugural speech in 2001")

In[23]

```
# to generate the word cloud of Obama's inaugural speech in 2009

word_cloud.generate(speech_2009Obama)
plt.subplots(figsize=(8,5))
plt.imshow(word_cloud)
plt.axis('off')
plt.title("Word cloud of Obama's inaugural speech in 2009")
```

Out[23]   Text(0.5, 1.0, "Word cloud of Obama's inaugural speech in 2009")

In[24]

```
# to generate the word cloud of Trump's inaugural speech in 2017

word_cloud.generate(speech_2017Trump)
plt.subplots(figsize=(8,5))
plt.imshow(word_cloud)
plt.axis('off')
plt.title("Word cloud of Trump's inaugural speech in 2017")
```

Out[24]   Text(0.5, 1.0, "Word cloud of Trump's inaugural speech in 2017")

5.4 Image processing with OpenCV

Q&A

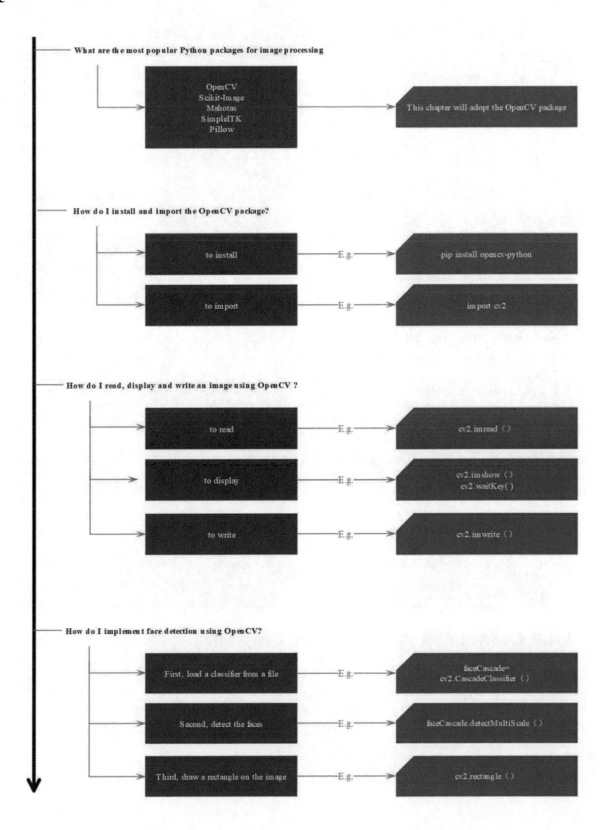

5.4.1 Installing and importing opencv-python package

Notes

The command to download opencv-python package is "pip install opencv-python".

Notes

Here, the module import name name(cv2) differs from the package name(opencv-python). cv2 (old interface in old OpenCV versions was named as cv) is the name that OpenCV developers chose when they created the binding generators.

In[1] | # to import the opencv package
       |
       | import cv2

Tips

OpenCV (Open Source Computer Vision Library) is an open-source library that includes several hundreds of computer vision algorithms. In this chapter, we use the haarcascades algorithm, which is a machine learning-based object detection algorithm, for face detection.

5.4.2 Loading image from file

Notes

To load the image file "test.jpg" into the image object named "image," you can use the *imread()* method from the "opencv-python" package.

In[2] | # to load(read) the mage file from the current working directory
       |
       | image = cv2.imread("test.jpg")

Tips

The image file "test.jpg" is available in the learning resources for this textbook.

5.4.3 Converting a RGB image into Grayscale

Notes

In OpenCV-Python, it is necessary to convert an RGB image into grayscale before using the *faceCascade.detectMultiScale()* function, as it expects grayscale inputs.

Notes

To display the converted grayscale image object "gray" in OpenCV-Python, we can use the *imshow()* function and the *waitKey()* function from the *cv2* module.

In[3]

```
# to convert an image from colour to grayscale

gray = cv2.cvtColor(image,cv2.COLOR_BGR2GRAY)

# to show the grayscale
cv2.imshow("Showing gray image", gray)
cv2.waitKey(0)
```

Out[3]   -1

Tips

The *cv2.imshow()* method is used to display an image in a window. Its argument "Showing gray image" returns a string representing the name of the window in which image to be displayed. Its argument *gray* refers to the image that is to be displayed.

Tips

The *waitkey()* function allows users to display a window for given milliseconds or until any key is pressed.
Here, the waitkey(0) means that it will display the window infinitely until users actually press any key.

5.4.4 Detecting faces

In[4]

```
# to load the haarcascade frontalface classifier

faceCascade=cv2.CascadeClassifier(cv2.data.haarcascades + "haarcascade_frontalface_
default.xml")

# to show the value of cv2.data.haarcascades
cv2.data.haarcascades
```

Out[4]   'C:\\ProgramData\\Anaconda3\\lib\\site-packages\\cv2\\data\\'

Tips

A Haar-Cascade Classifier is a machine learning classifier that works with Haar-like features. Haar-like features are digital image features widely used in object recognition. For further detail, please refer to the paper "Viola, P., & Jones, M. (2001, December). Rapid object detection using a boosted cascade of simple features. In Proceedings of the 2001 IEEE computer society conference on computer vision and pattern recognition. CVPR 2001 (Vol. 1, pp. I-I). Ieee."

Tips

A range of Haar cascade XML files are provided in OpenCV, each of which holds the Haar features for different objects. In this data science project, we employ a pre-defined Haar cascade XML file (haarcascade_frontalface_default.xml) in order to detect frontal faces in an image. You can access the list of Haar cascade XML files from this link: https://github.com/opencv/opencv/tree/master/data/haarcascades.

Notes

In OpenCV-Python, we can use the *CascadeClassifier.detectMultiScale()* function to detect faces in an image. This function takes an image as input and returns a list of rectangles representing the detected faces.

In[5]
```
faces=faceCascade.detectMultiScale(gray
                    ,scaleFactor=1.1
                    ,minNeighbors=5
                    ,minSize=(30,30))
```
Out[5]   'C:\\ProgramData\\Anaconda3\\lib\\site-packages\\cv2\\data\\'

Tips

In the *CascadeClassifier.detectMultiScale()* function:
1. The scaleFactor is an argument that specifies how much the image size is reduced at each image scale.
2. The minNeighbors is an argument that specifies how many neighbors each candidate rectangle should have to retain it.
3. The minSize is an argument that determines the minimum size of the object you want to detect.

Notes

In OpenCV-Python, we can use the *cv2.rectangle()* function to draw a rectangle on the image for each detected face.

In[6]
```
# to draw a rectangle on the image for each detected face

for (x,y,w,h) in faces:
        cv2.rectangle(image,(x,y),(x+w,y+h),(0,255,0),2)
```

Tips

In the *cv2.rectangle(image,(x,y),(x+w,y+h),(0,255,0),2)* function:

(x,y) is the argument that determines the starting coordinates of the rectangle.

(x+w,y+h) is the argument that determines the ending coordinates of the rectangle.

(0,255,0) refers to the color of the border line of the rectangle to be drawn. For example, (0,0,255) corresponds to the color red.

2 determines the thickness of the rectangle's border line in pixels

5.4.5 Showing images

Notes

We call the *cv2.imshow()* function to display the image with the detected face and the added rectangle border.

In[5]
```
# to show the image

cv2.imshow("Window Name", image)
cv2.waitKey(0)
```

Out[5]   -1

5.4.6 Writing images

Notes

To write an image with rectangles according to the specified format in the current working directory using OpenCV-Python, you can use the *cv2.imwrite()* function.

In[6]
```
# to write the image

cv2.imwrite("test.png",image)
```

Out[6]   True

Exercises

[1]   Select the appropriate option to complete the following code.

```
import statsmodels.api as sm
#Set the super parameter of intercept
( )
X_add_const
Model = sm.OLS(y, X_add_const)
```

A. X_add_const=sm.add_constant(X)
B. X=sm.add_constant(X)
C. X_add_const=sm.add(X)

[2]   Which of the following founction will be used to execute the variance of array data when using Python for statistical analysis?

A. data.mean()
B. data.median()
C. data.var()
D. data.std()

[3]   Which of the following is false of data consolidation?

A. Two tables can be stacked horizontally or vertically with the *concat* method.
B. Two tables can be stacked horizontally or vertically with the *append* method.
C. When the argument axis in the *concat* function is 0, it indicates vertical operation, and when axis is 1, it indicates horizontal operation.
D. The argument join in the *concat* function indicates whether other indexes in the axial direction are merged by intersection or union.

[4]   Which of the following statements about the characteristics of Min-max normalization is false?

A. The overall distribution of data will not change with Min-max normalization.
B. When the data is equal to the minimum value, the data will become 1 with Min-max normalization.
C. If the range of data is too large, the difference between the normalized data will be very small.
D. If a value in the dataset is too large, the normalized value will be close to zero with Min-max normalization.

[5]   Select the appropriate code to reduce the dimension of the column quantity.

```
import pandas as pd
import numpy as np
import os
data = pd.read_csv('data.csv', header=0
sort_data = _____(data[['quantity']])
```

A. pd.ravel
B. np.ravel
C. os.ravel

[6]   Which of the following is false of the regression algorithm?

A. Linear regression is applicable to the case where there is a linear relationship between the dependent variable and the independent variable.
B. Logistic regression is generally applicable to the case where the dependent variable has two values: 1 and 0 (yes or no).
C. Ridge regression is applicable to the case of multicollinearity between independent variables.
D. Principal component regression is applicable to the case where there is no collinearity between independent variables.

[7] **According to the generation mode of individual learners, ensemble learning can be roughly divided into two categories. One is a parallelization method that can be generated simultaneously without strong dependency between individual learners. The representative of this method is ( )**
    A. boosting
    B. bagging
    C. decision tree
    D. reboot

[8] **Which of the following algorithms has no corresponding API in sklearn?**
    A. Support vector machine
    B. K nearest neighbor classification
    C. Gauss naive Bayes
    D. Bayes

[9] **Which of the following is not an evaluation indicator of the classification model?**
    A. Accuracy rate
    B. Recall rate
    C. Mean square error
    D. ROC curve

10. **Which of the following is flase of the arguments in the *train_ test_ Is* function?**
    A. *Test size* represents the size of the test set.
    B. *Train size* represents the size of the training set.
    C. *Random state* represents random seed number, which by default is 1.
    D. *shuffle* represents whether to sample with or without replacement.

[11] **Which of the following is not a method of the sklearn converter?**
    A. fit
    B. transform
    C. fit transform
    D. transform fit

[12] **Which of the following is a package for Chinese natural language processing in Python?**
    A. NTLK
    B. spaCy
    C. Jieba

[13] **Which of the following function can be used to customize vocabulary?**
    A. pynlpir.AddUserWord()
    B. nlpir.AddUserWord()
    C. pynlpir.get_key_words()
    D. pynlpir.nlpir.AddUserWord()

[14] **What are the features of text corpus?**
    A. Word count in text
    B. Vector annotation of words
    C. Part of speech tag
    D. Basic dependency grammar
    E. All of the above

[15] **Which of the following indicator can be used to calculate the distance between two word vectors?**
    A. Lemmatization
    B. Euclidean distance
    C. N-grams

[16] Which of the following is false of the lifting algorithm?

    A. Each step of boosting algorithm will create a weak prediction model. Finally, all weak prediction models will be accumulated and summarized to obtain a total model.

    B. The generation of each weak prediction model will depend on the gradient decline of the loss function.

    C. GDBT and AdaBoost are both methods in boosting learning.

    D. AdaBoost can only use the decision tree (CART) as the weak classifier, and the loss function used by GDBT is still the least squares loss function.

[17] Which of the following is false of face recognition?

    A. Face recognition is a technology that can recognize or verify the identity of the subject in the image or video.

    B. Face recognition has become one of the most studied topics in the field of computer vision and biometrics.

    C. Faces in-the-wild have a high degree of variability.

    D. Face recognition is inherently invasive, which means that it is the most natural and intuitive biometric method.

[18] Which of the following is not a face recognition application?

    A. Face unlock

    B. Safety protection

    C. Retinal recognition

    D. Signature identification

[19] Which of the following is not an application of face recognition technology?

    A. Automatically capture and scan records when people or vehicles enter and leave the community, eliminating manual records and saving time and effort.

    B. Quickly extract the focus of attention in user comments, directly reflect the subjective feelings of brands or products, facilitate market, operation, products and other relevant personnel to collect market information, and adjust or optimize products and strategies.

    C. AI scanning and capturing instruments are used for face recognition and license plate recognition, and the images captured through the network of recognition instruments are clustered and analyzed by peers.

    D. The identification technology is used to classify and identify the resident population and floating population in the community, and early warning the action track of suspicious persons in advance.

[20] Which of the following statements about face recognition is true?

    A. The four features of face recognition include geometric features, model-based features, statistics-based features and neural network-based features.

    B. The three main technologies of face recognition include face detection technology based on features, face detection technology based on template matching and face detection technology based on statistics.

    C. Face recognition is mainly based on human facial image features. How to recognize the facial changes caused by posture has become one of the difficulties of this technology.

    D. All of the above

Appendix I Best Python Resources for Data Scientists

1 Websites

[1]. python official website: https://www.python.org
[2]. Python packages index: https://pypi.org/project/pip/
[3]. Free Interactive Python Tutorial: LearnPython.org
[4]. Learn R, Python & Data Science Online: https://www.datacamp.com/
[5]. The pydata community for developers and users of open source data tools https://pydata.org/
[6]. pystatsmodels: https://groups.google.com/forum/#!forum/pystatsmodels
[7]. Python cheat sheet: https://ehmatthes.github.io/pcc/cheatsheets/README.html
[8]. PEP 8: The Style Guide for Python Code: https://www.python.org/dev/peps/pep-0008/
[9]. Kaggle Machine Learning and Data Science Community: https://www.kaggle.com
[10]. Python Weekly: https://www.pythonweekly.com/
[11]. The GitHub open source community: https://github.com/open-source
[12]. Stack Overflow: https://stackoverflow.com/

2. Books

[1]. VanderPlas, J. (2016). Python data science handbook: Essential tools for working with data. O'Reilly Media, Inc.
[2]. McKinney, W. (2012). Python for data analysis: Data wrangling with Pandas, NumPy, and IPython.O'Reilly Media, Inc.
[3]. Kirk, M. (2017). Thoughtful machine learning with Python: a test-driven approach.O'Reilly Media, Inc.
[4]. Ramalho, L. (2015). Fluent Python: Clear, concise, and effective programming.O'Reilly Media, Inc.
[5]. Chambers, B., & Zaharia, M. (2018). Spark: The definitive guide: Big data processing made simple.O'Reilly Media, Inc.
[6]. Grus J. Data science from scratch: first principles with python[M]. O'Reilly Media, 2019.
[7]. Lutz, M. (2013). Learning python: Powerful object-oriented programming.O'Reilly Media, Inc.
[8]. Matthes, E. (2019). Python crash course: A hands-on, project-based introduction to programming. No Starch Press.

3. Python Packages

[1]. Data Wrangling: Pandas,Numpy,Scipy
[2]. Data Visualization: Matplotlib,Seaborn,Bokeh,Basemap,Plotly,NetworkX
[3]. Machin Learning: SciKit-Learn, PyTorch, TensorFlow, Theano,Keras
[4]. Statistical analysis: Statsmodels
[5]. Natural Language Processing: Natural Language Toolkit (NLTK), Gensim CoreNLP,spaCy,TextBlob, PyNLPl
[6]. Web Scraping :Scrapy,Beautiful Soup, Requests,Urllib
[7]. Image Processing:OpenCV,Scikit-Image, Mahotas,SimplelTK,Pillow

Appendix II Answers to Chapter Exercises

Chapter I   Python and Data Science

1.B	2.A	3.B	4.B	5.D
6.C	7.D	8.B	9.D	10.C

Chapter II   Basic Python Programming for Data Science

1.C	2.B	3.B	4.D	5.A
6.D	7.D	8.B	9.C	10.C
11.A	12.C	13.C	14.D	15.B
16.C	17.C	18.B	19.C	20.D

Chapter III   Advanced Python Programming for Data Science

1.A	2.C	3.D	4.C	5.B
6.D	7.C	8.D	9.B	10.A
11.D	12.C	13.C	14.D	15.A
16.B	17.C	18.A	19.A	20.C

Chapter IV   Data wrangling with Python

1.C	2.B	3.C	4.A	5.B
6.B	7.B	8.D	9.B	10.B
11.C	12.A	13.B	14.C	15.B
16.B	17.D	18.C	19.D	20.D

Chapter V   Data analysis with Python

1.A	2.C	3.B	4.B	5.B
6.D	7.B	8.D	9.C	10.C
11.D	12.C	13.D	14.E	15.B
16.D	17.D	18.D	19.B	20.D